PEOPLE
OF THE
TROPICAL
RAIN FOREST

This book was produced in conjunction with the exhibition
Tropical Rainforest: A Disappearing Treasure, organized by
the Smithsonian Institution Traveling Exhibition Service.

PEOPLE OF THE TROPICAL RAIN FOREST

Edited by
JULIE SLOAN DENSLOW
and
CHRISTINE PADOCH

UNIVERSITY OF CALIFORNIA PRESS
BERKELEY LOS ANGELES LONDON
in association with
SMITHSONIAN INSTITUTION TRAVELING EXHIBITION SERVICE
WASHINGTON, D.C.

University of California Press
Berkeley and Los Angeles, California

University of California Press, Ltd.
London, England

Library of Congress Cataloging-in-Publication Data

People of the tropical rain forest.

    Bibliography: p.
    Includes index.
    1. Human ecology—Tropics. 2. Ethnology—Tropics.
3. Rain forests. 4. Tropics—Social conditions.
5. Tropics—Economic conditions. I. Denslow, Julie
Sloan. II. Padoch, Christine.
GF54.5.P46 1988   304.2'0915'2   87–30173
ISBN: 0–520–06295–7 (cloth)
ISBN: 0–520–06351–1 (paper)
Alkaline paper

Printed in Japan

2 3 4 5 6 7 8 9

PAGE 2–3: A meander of the Ramu River twists through mature tropical rain forest near Madang in Papua New Guinea.

PAGE 6–7: The Transamazon Highway of Brazil stretches over 5,400 kilometers from east to west.

PAGE 11: This computer-generated map of Costa Rica documents the decline of intact forest coverage between 1940 and 1977. The NASA computer images are based on interpretations of aerial and satellite photographs done by Costa Rican scientists. Despite a high deforestation rate, Costa Rica has safeguarded over 10 percent of its land area in forest preserves.

PAGE 14–15: This cluster of houses is situated along a tributary of the Amazon River at the edge of the forest in Brazil.

CONTENTS

FOREST CHANGE
1940-1977

▪ 1940 FOREST
▪ 1977 FOREST
— ROADS
— RAILROADS

NASA/NSTL/ERL

FOREWORD

The Smithsonian Institution has long been involved in the study of tropical biology. Even before the formal establishment of the Smithsonian's Tropical Research Institute in 1923, individual scientists pursued systematic and taxonomic studies surrounded by the rich diversity of tropical forests and delved into the cultures, both past and present, of those who lived there.

It is probable that researchers in the eighteenth and early nineteenth century went about their studies unconcerned that the rain forest would ever be threatened. Man's foray into complex technologies was only beginning, and its implications were not well understood. Later many became aware of the twin pressures of population and development nibbling away at the edges of a scientific paradise.

Now, however, we are all alert to the constantly diminishing forests of our world. I will not quote the depressing facts and figures regarding the daily, monthly, and yearly loss of acreage; these are contained elsewhere in this volume and in others. But the fact remains that the planet is losing, in ever-increasing amounts, a precious heritage of diversity, both biological and cultural, that can never be replaced. The forces at play in this drama are human ones and they are complex. Economic, political, and social factors come together in myriad ways to exert pressures on a fragile, but extremely valuable, ecosystem. Governments struggle with these issues with no clear agenda, on a schedule that does not necessarily guarantee answers in time.

Central to the tropical forest issue are people—those who have lived there traditionally, those who see the uninhabited territory as the sole hope of land ownership they have never experienced, and those in the cities who make the decisions regarding its resources. This volume looks at all the people who are involved.

Science does not hold the answers to balancing these needs, but it does offer some tools with which to make the decisions. The Smithsonian supports tropical studies in the hope that the forest world in which they are practiced will continue to exist, not only for the practical benefits it can extend to all of us but because its survival may be a harbinger of our own.

ROBERT McC. ADAMS
Secretary, Smithsonian Institution

PREFACE

book about the tropical rain forest is above all else a book about diversity. The tropical rain forest is many species of plants and animals in many forests on many soils. Its immense variety humbles any visitor who first sees it, any scientist who presumes to know it, and any writer who attempts to describe it.

The people of the tropical rain forests of the world, while all one species with similar needs, capabilities, and tolerances, are also an enormously varied lot. They differ in the effects their presence has on the forest and in the ways the forest affects them. The few remaining Amazonian, Bornean, or African natives who walk softly through the forest and receive from it all their life's necessities and return to it all they have produced are a vanishing minority among today's rain-forest peoples. Many more forest folk participate in markets—local, national, or international. They fell large trees with chainsaws; they plant crops that originated on the other side of the globe; their dreams reflect the lives of people who never saw a rain forest; and they worship gods who only walked in deserts. Nevertheless, they too are people of the rain forest; they make a living from its resources and what they do determines its fate.

There are yet other people of the rain forest. These are people who may rarely see a rain-forest tree, but whose decision in a boardroom may fell a thousand acres, may replace two hundred species of forest trees with neat rows of a single exotic pine, or may move a thousand forest dwellers to make room for a dam.

Such people of the rain forest also differ greatly one from another: in their understanding of what they are using or destroying or replacing and in what they trade for that forest.

As difficult as it may be to formulate generalizations about rain-forest environments and peoples, it is even more difficult to say how rain forests should be managed and by whom. No people have ever lived in the forest without affecting and changing it, however subtly. In our times, as many of us are first learning of its natural marvels, we are being warned that the seemingly limitless expanse of jungle is fast disappearing. The accelerating rate of forest clearing endangers not only uncounted biological species but also a wealth of human cultures. As we seek to understand the causes of this destruction, we want to know who among those people of the rain forest are the villains and who are the victims.

Pointing the finger of guilt is, however, frequently not a simple task. The forest is falling under the heavy hand of development in ways that are complex and seemingly contradictory. Smallholders, whose techniques of mobile, slash-and-burn agriculture are wonderfully adapted to fragile rain-forest soils, are, by their very numbers, major agents of forest clearing. Large-scale commercial plantations, which have so often been doomed to failure in the New World tropics, have helped bring Peninsular Malaysia into the ranks of middle-income nations. The geographical distance of developed countries belies their involvement in changes in the tropics. Through lending policies, the activities of multinational organizations, and the tremendous purchasing power of manufacturing economies, First World countries influence the fates of forests and forest people in the Third World.

This book offers no solutions to the "rain forest problem." We have instead asked our contributors to explore the diverse ways in which people use the forest and forest lands. We hope that, as a result, the book helps to separate some of the falsehoods from some of the truths.

Following an introduction to the ecology of tropical rain forests by Julie Denslow, Francis E. Putz and N. Michele Holbrook graphically illustrate the changing and rarely realistic image of the tropics in Western art and literature since the early ages of exploration. Subsequent chapters are organized according to the ways in which people and forest interact and include examples from the tropical rain-forest cultures of South and Central America, Africa, and Asia. Single issues, examples, or viewpoints are highlighted in special insets that follow some chapters. Betty J. Meggers and Karl L. Hutterer interpret the scant artifacts available to archaeologists to sketch a picture of life in the rain forests of the Amazon basin and tropical Asia before the arrival of Europeans. Their pictures do not differ radically from the practices of some modern tribal cultures described in ensuing essays on Amazonian peoples by Robert L. Carneiro; the Kayapó by Darrell Posey; the Lacandon Maya by James D. Nations; and the Pygmies of the Congo basin by David S. Wilkie, but contrast with the larger, socially complex villages of the Hmong and Lua' of Thailand described by Peter Kunstadter. The Hmong and Lua' are active participants in regional, national, and sometimes international markets. Like traditional tribal cultures, more recent arrivals to the rain forest depend on swidden, or slash-and-burn, agriculture for staple crops of rice, corn, or manioc and on the forest and rivers for game and fish. Villagers like the caboclos and ribereños of the Amazon floodplain, described by Christine Padoch, trace strong ties to a tribal heritage but engage in active trade for cash and manufactured goods within a larger market economy. The migrants discussed by Emilio F. Moran and Gloria Davis, in contrast, are generally recent arrivals, encouraged by the Brazilian or Indonesian governments to settle "empty" areas and to provide relief for long-settled, overcrowded regions. Spontaneous migrants like the Bugis, described by Andrew P. Vayda, move to take advantage of better economic opportunities.

Forest tribal cultures and smallholders alike see their resources and ways of life threatened under the pressures of development and the increasing incursions of outsiders. Kenneth I. Taylor discusses the difficulties of establishing the legal rights of Indian tribes in the Amazon basin countries, and Miguel Pinedo-Vasquez describes the efforts of one campesino group to establish control over their means of livelihood. Jayl Langub and a tribal leader describe the inroads being made onto Penan lands by logging companies in Borneo.

The widespread impact of such business ventures as logging, plantation forestry, mining, and cattle ranching are traced in chapters on the Amazon basin by Marianne Schmink, the Grande Carajás mining operation in Brazil by Roger D. Stone, tropical Asia by Malcolm Gillis, and India and Peninsular Malaysia by Peter S. Ashton. The prospects of these ventures have fluctuated widely over their history, ending in grandiose failure at some times and places and proving a major force for national development in others. The authors explore the consequences of government policies and economic realities on the future of large stands of tropical rain forest in these countries. The last chapters draw on many years of observing development in the tropics to present the authors' perspectives on the future for the rain forest and rain-forest peoples. Setijati Sastrapradja discusses the prospects for conservation in Indonesia. Harold C. Brookfield draws together these diverse strands of thought to discuss the consequences of the new great age of clearance of the tropical Asian rain forest.

We are grateful to our authors for their thoughtful, stimulating essays. Each brings to the discussion the weight of many years' first-hand experience in the field and internationally recognized expertise on the issues. While all their statements are solidly grounded in fact, the reader will notice differences in interpretation and in opinion. These authors do not all agree on some of the issues presented. The discrepancies reveal not a shortcoming in knowledge on the part of any one of them, but rather that the truth about what is happening in the tropics and where solutions might be sought is not monolithic. Had we the opportunity to invite more colleagues to contribute, we would surely have found even more diversity.

We are indebted to the many reviewers who read and commented on the articles. Because of their special task they must remain anonymous; they too are, however, each great experts in their fields and have added much to this book. We also wish to acknowledge the advice of many colleagues who suggested authors and reviewers, as well as sources of photographs and other illustrations, and the friends old and new who dug through slide collections and entrusted their photographic treasures to us and the postal service: M. Balick, D. E. Brosius, J. Browder, D. Campbell, D. Daly, A. Echols, J. Ewel, J. Foxx, C. Gracie, S. B. Hecht, A. Henderson, M. Hiraoka, S. Hormuth, H. H. Iltis, A. Joyce, S. King, Lee Ying Fah and the Forest Department of Sabah, M. Leighton, A. Long, L. A. McIntyre, G. T. Prance, F. E. Putz, K. Redford, A. Rokach, and H. Soedjito. We would also like to thank the curators and editors at the Smithsonian Institution Traveling Exhibition Service, M. Cappelletti and A. Stevens; the University of California Press, S. Warren, D. Feinberg, and B. A. Kevles; and Perpetua Press, L. B. O'Connor and D. Levy, for their vision, support, and professional contributions, which made production of this volume a rewarding experience. A special word of gratitude is also due to the Smithsonian Institution for its generous financial support.

From first planning discussions to final proofreading, our families and our friends at the New York Botanical Garden and Tulane University have remained steadfastly enthusiastic and patient. For this we are especially grateful.

JULIE SLOAN DENSLOW
Tulane University
New Orleans, Louisiana

CHRISTINE PADOCH
New York Botanical Garden
Bronx, New York

ACKNOWLEDGMENTS

This book accompanies a major exhibition developed by the Smithsonian Institution Traveling Exhibition Service (SITES), entitled TROPICAL RAINFOREST: A DISAPPEARING TREASURE. Without the funding for that exhibition and the support of the Smithsonian Institution at all stages of the project, this book would not have been possible.

I would like to thank the talented and unflagging editors of this volume, Julie Denslow and Christine Padoch, as well as the following people and organizations: Robert McCormick Adams, Secretary of the Smithsonian Institution, because all true institutional support starts at the top; Assistant Secretaries David Challinor and Tom Freudenheim for their support of funding through the Smithsonian's Special Exhibition Fund; Peggy Loar, former director of SITES, for her early enthusiasm without which the project would not have gone forward; John Reinhardt and Gretchen Ellsworth for early and continued championing of the exhibition; Ed Bastian for his wonderful ideas during the initial stages; Judith Gradwohl, curator of the exhibition, whose research, writing, and unwavering commitment turned an idea into an exhibition with the help of a fine design firm, Miles Fridberg-Molinaroli, Inc.; the World Wildlife Fund, which has contributed research and photographs as well as developed the curriculum guide that accompanies the exhibition; the John D. and Catherine T. MacArthur Foundation for belief in this project and support of that belief with major funding; the George Gund Foundation for its generous grant; the James Smithson Society for the much-needed planning grant to get it all started; the exhibition project team whose good humor and hard work helped make it all a reality: Karen Johnson, Elliott Gimble, Monica Valley, George Angehr, Eric Carlson, Lisa Hartgens, Susan Hormuth, and Maria del Carmen Cosu; Andrea Stevens, SITES' Publications Director, for her work on this volume; the University of California Press for its vision and sure hand in the production of this book; and lastly, the exhibition Advisory Committee whose wisdom and suggestions about content of both the exhibition and book have guided us from the very beginning: Tom Lovejoy, Assistant Secretary for External Affairs, Smithsonian; Peter Raven, Director, Missouri Botanical Garden; Peter Ashton, Director, Arnold Arboretum, Harvard; Michael Robinson, Director, National Zoological Park; Ira Rubinoff, Director, and James Karr, Assistant Director, Smithsonian Tropical Research Institute; Stanwyn Shetler, Assistant Director, National Museum of Natural History; Terry Irwin, Curator, Department of Entomology, National Museum of Natural History; Betty Meggers, Research Associate, Department of Anthropology, Smithsonian Institution; Roger Stone, Senior Research Fellow, World Wildlife Fund; William Burley, World Resources Institute; Julie S. Denslow, Department of Biology, Tulane University; and Christine Padoch, Institute of Economic Botany, New York Botanical Garden.

MARTHA CAPPELLETTI
Senior Project Director
SITES

THE CONTRIBUTORS

PETER S. ASHTON, Arnold Professor of Botany at Harvard University and Director of its Arnold Arboretum, has thirty years' research experience in the forests of tropical Asia where his interests have been in the Philippine mahogany family, Dipterocarpaceae, and in rain-forest dynamics.

HAROLD C. BROOKFIELD is Professor of Human Geography in the Research School of Pacific Studies of the Australian National University. He has conducted field research in human ecology and development in Fiji, Papua New Guinea, the Caribbean, and most recently in Southeast Asia, especially Malaysia and Indonesia. He has written or edited eight books and many articles.

ROBERT L. CARNEIRO is Curator of South American Ethnology at the American Museum of Natural History, where he has worked since 1957. He has carried out field research among the Kuikuru of central Brazil, the Amahuaca of eastern Peru, and the Yanomami of southern Venezuela.

GLORIA DAVIS received her Ph.D. in anthropology from Stanford University in 1975. In preparation for her thesis, she spent two years living with Indonesian transmigrants in Central Sulawesi. She joined the World Bank as an anthropologist in 1978 and is now Chief of the Asia Region Unit for Environment and Social Affairs.

JULIE S. DENSLOW is a tropical forest ecologist on the faculty of Tulane University and Director of its Mesoamerican Ecology Institute. She studies natural regeneration processes in the lowland rain forests of Central and South America. She is currently serving as President of the Association for Tropical Biology.

MALCOLM GILLIS is Professor of Public Policy and of Economics at Duke University, where he also serves as Dean of the Graduate School and Vice-Provost for Academic Affairs. He has worked in many tropical countries in Asia, Africa, and Latin America. Much of his more recent research on tropical forest issues is contained in the forthcoming book, *Public Policy and the Misuse of Forest Resources,* edited by Roberto Repetto and Malcolm Gillis, to be published by Cambridge University Press.

N. MICHELE HOLBROOK received her B.A. from Harvard University and currently is a graduate student at the University of Florida. Her research concerns biomechanics and the physiological ecology of plants.

KARL L. HUTTERER is Professor of Anthropology and Curator of the Division of the Orient at the Museum of Anthropology, University of Michigan. He specializes in the prehistory and ethnology of Southeast Asia, with special emphasis on the human ecology of tropical environments.

PETER KUNSTADTER is affiliated with the Program in Medical Anthropology and the Institute for Health Policy Studies of the University of California at San Francisco. Since 1963 he has been conducting research in Southeast Asia, principally northern Thailand, on upland agriculture, population, and health.

JAYL LANGUB holds the post of Principal Assistant Secretary in the State Planning Unit of Sarawak, Malaysia. A Sarawak native, he visited many Penan communities as a Sarawak Administrative Officer in the far interior Belaga District from 1971 to 1974. His current position with the State Planning Unit allows him to visit Penan groups occasionally.

BETTY J. MEGGERS, a Research Associate in the Department of Anthropology of the Smithsonian Institution in Washington, D.C., has conducted archaeological investigations in Amazonia since 1948. For the last ten years she has been coordinating archaeological research in Amazonia with the field research done by Brazilian archaeologists. She has published numerous books and articles on cultural adaptation and prehistory, including *Amazonia: Man and Culture in a Counterfeit Paradise* (Harlan Davidson, 1971).

EMILIO F. MORAN is Professor of Anthropology and Environmental Affairs at Indiana University, Bloomington. He was elected a Fellow of the American Association for the advancement of Science in 1985. He is the author of *Human Adaptability* (Westview, 1982) and *Developing the Amazon* (Indiana University Press, 1981).

JAMES D. NATIONS is Director of Research for the Center for Human Ecology, a conservation research group based in Austin, Texas.

CHRISTINE PADOCH is an Associate Scientist with the Institute of Economic Botany of the New York Botanical Garden. An ecological anthropologist, she has done research on traditional resource management in Sarawak, Malaysia, and East Kalimantan, Indonesia. Her most recent research focused on farming practices and marketing networks in the lowland Peruvian Amazon.

MIGUEL PINEDO-VASQUEZ holds a degree in forestry from the Universidad Nacional de la Amazonía Peruana in Iquitos, Peru. He is a native of the Peruvian Amazon where he has worked for many years with tribal and ribereño groups. He is currently an advisor to the Federación Campesina de Maynas, the Comité de Productores de Arroz de Maynas, and the Comité de Productores de Yute de Maynas.

DARRELL ADDISON POSEY is currently the Coordinator of the Núcleo de Etnobiologia (Nucleus of Ethnobiology) at the Museu Paraense Emílio Goeldi, Belém, Pará (Brazil). During the past five years he has coordinated the Kayapó Project, a multidisciplinary ethnobiological project to study the knowledge of the Kayapó about the natural resources of Amazonia.

FRANCIS E. PUTZ is Associate Professor of Botany at the University of Florida. He conducts research on plant community ecology, physiology, and tropical silviculture.

SETIJATI SASTRAPRADJA is a botanist and Director of the Centre for Research in Biotechnology of Indonesia. From 1973 through 1986 she was Director of the National Biological Institute of Indonesia. She has published extensively on botany, environmental education, and plant genetic resource conservation. She is a member of the National Research Council of Indonesia and has served as a member of the International Board for Plant Genetic Resources and as chairman of the Southeast Asian Programme on Plant Genetic Resources.

MARIANNE SCHMINK is Associate Professor of Latin American Studies and Anthropology and since 1980 Executive Director of the Amazon Research and Training Program, Center for Latin American Studies, University of Florida. Since 1976 she has carried out research on migration and settlement changes in Brazilian Amazonia and has published several articles on colonization, migration, and small-scale mining. With Dr. Charles H. Wood, she co-edited *Frontier Expansion in Amazonia* (Univ. of Florida Press, 1984).

ROGER D. STONE, Armand G. Erpf Conservation Fellow at the World Wildlife Fund-U.S., is the author of *Dreams of Amazonia* (Viking/Penguin, 1985). A former foreign correspondent for *Time*, banker, and an executive of several non-profit organizations, he is the author of many articles on conservation/development issues.

KENNETH I. TAYLOR is the Executive Director of Survival International (USA). An anthropologist, he has done fieldwork with indigenous peoples in northwest Greenland (Umanaq Bay), Alaska (Kodiak Island), and among the Sanuma and Yanoam subgroups of the Yanomami Indians in Brazilian Amazonia. He is currently working on several cases in Latin America and the U.S. government's plans for relocation of Hopi and Navajo Indians of Big Mountain, Arizona.

ANDREW P. VAYDA is Professor of Anthropology and Ecology at Rutgers University. Formerly Professor of Anthropology at Columbia University, he has also taught at the University of Indonesia and has directed human ecology projects in Indonesia and Papua New Guinea. He has published more than seventy articles and several books. He founded the journal, *Human Ecology*, and was its editor for five years.

DAVID S. WILKIE is Research Assistant Professor in the Department of Anthropology, University of Utah, at Salt Lake City. Between 1981 and 1983 he lived in the Ituri forest of Zaire studying the impact of shifting cultivation on Pygmy hunting practices and on the diversity and abundance of exploited fauna. He is now using satellite images to validate a simulation model of shifting cultivation.

PEOPLE
OF THE
TROPICAL
RAIN FOREST

I

THE TROPICAL
RAIN-FOREST
SETTING

JULIE SLOAN DENSLOW

Around the world, the tropical rain forests are being cut at a staggering rate. One estimate (Myers 1980) puts the loss rate at ten million hectares (twenty-seven million acres) a year or 1.2 percent of the approximately sixteen hundred million hectares (four billion acres) remaining. Another (Lanly 1982) suggests that deforestation is occurring at a much lower rate, or around 7.5 million hectares (18.5 million acres) a year. All define tropical rain forest and deforestation differently, and all depend on data from often remote forests in Third World countries with inadequate facilities or labor to monitor the fates of their forests. Reliable figures for rates of deforestation are understandably difficult to obtain and have generated much discussion.

There is little disagreement, however, on the importance of such deforestation. It has been linked to changes in global climatic patterns and rising sea levels, to the economic and political instability that accompany declining living standards of the rural poor, to the tragic loss of cultural diversity as rain-forest peoples and their lands come under pressure of national development goals, and to the extinction of species that will dwarf the great natural extinctions of geologic history.

The immediate causes and rates of deforestation vary among regions. Clearing for cattle pasture is a major source of forest loss in the Amazon basin and Central America but is not a significant contributor in Africa and tropical Asia. In the Amazon basin clearing for pasture and, indirectly, land speculation is affecting primarily the southern, western, and eastern edges with relatively little impact in the vast, remote central region. The overall rate of deforestation in the Amazon basin is therefore relatively low (0.33 percent a year).

In Central America, however, the forest is more accessible and more vulnerable; it is being cleared at the staggering rate of 3.2 percent a year, primarily for pasture to supply low-grade beef to the U.S. fast-food industry. The rain forests of Asia are being intensively exploited by logging companies for timber and by shifting cultivators who follow logging roads into the newly accessible forest. Deforestation in western Africa primarily is due to timbering and slash-and-burn (swidden) agriculture, but inaccessibility has protected the rain forest of the Congo basin.

Forty percent of the original extent of the world's tropical forests have been destroyed, although in some areas deforestation is even further advanced. Current statistics project that outside of reserves, rain forest will be completely gone from Peninsular Malaysia by the early 1990s and from Central America by the year 2000. They have disappeared now from Haiti, on the island Columbus once described to Ferdinand and Isabella:

◁ An emergent canopy tree, *Dipteryx panamensis* (Leguminosae), rises in full bloom over the forest of the Smithsonian Tropical Research Institute, Barro Colorado Island, Panama.

BOTTOM LEFT: Freshly cut Lua' swidden fields drying in preparation for burning in Pa Pae, Thailand.

A rainstorm sweeps over the Rio Solimoes, as the Amazon is known in Brazil above Manaus.

BOTTOM RIGHT: Oxides of iron give the bright red color typical of many tropical soils like those exposed in this new road near Roraima, Brazil.

World map showing the distribution of tropical rain forest.

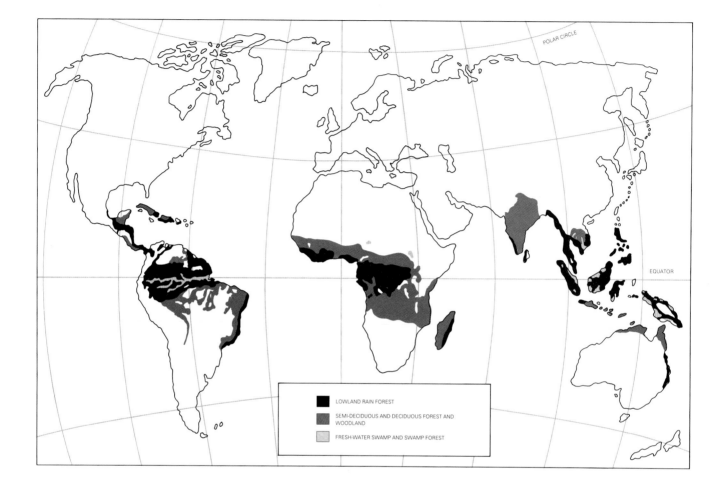

POLAR CIRCLE

EQUATOR

LOWLAND RAIN FOREST

SEMI-DECIDUOUS AND DECIDUOUS FOREST AND
WOODLAND

FRESH-WATER SWAMP AND SWAMP FOREST

Its lands are high; there are in it very many sierras and very lofty mountains. . . . All are most beautiful, of a thousand shapes; all are accessible and filled with trees of a thousand kinds and tall, so that they seem to touch the sky. I am told that they never lose their foliage, and this I can believe, for I saw them as green and lovely as they are in Spain in May, and some of them were flowering, some bearing fruit, and some at another stage, according to their nature.

We seem to be watching a reenactment of the opening of the great eastern deciduous forest of North America during the eighteenth and nineteenth centuries. Settlement of North America extended pasture and farmland at rates comparable to those now occurring in many parts of the tropical lowlands. Like the present-day tropics much of the clearing was carried out by loggers and homesteaders.

Moreover, the impact of such massive forest destruction in North America does not seem to have been permanent. We can trace few species extinctions to habitat loss in those early years (although several were lost to hunting pressure). Today much of that land has returned to young forest. Economically marginal farms on stoney forest soils of New England were abandoned as the deep prairie soils to the west were brought into production. In America north of the Rio Grande today there is more land in forest than when the pilgrims landed.

Is it alarmist then that we decry the disappearance of the tropical rain forest? Is the tropical forest so very different from the North American deciduous forest? Can't its productivity be channeled for the human good? Isn't the exuberance of its growth evidence of an innate resilience to human disturbance? The answers to these questions lie in an understanding not only of the things that set the tropical rain forest apart from its temperate counterparts but also in an understanding of the role of human activities in its survival.

The rain forest and the people who make their living from it are inextricably interwoven. Not only do the activities of hunter-gatherers, small farmers, plantation owners, and loggers have strikingly different consequences for the survival of the forest, the health of the forest likewise affects their own well being. In the succeeding chapters the lives, histories, and futures of these people of the rain forest are described—how they use forest resources, how they manipulate the forest and forest soils, and the prospects for their future in the forest.

From country to country and from people to people, the resources of the forest are used and managed for different purposes and to different advantages. Plantations of rubber trees and oil palms have helped move Malaysia into the ranks of developed nations, where elsewhere plantations have met chronic insect and disease problems. Smallholders in Brazil, Zaire, and Thailand farm a wide diversity of crops on rain-forest soils in such different ways that shifting cultivation almost defies definition.

There remain, however, important biological similarities among rain-forest ecosystems that constrain and influence those who would exploit its resources. Of all the many facets of the tropical rain forest perhaps the most difficult to grasp and the most threatened by deforestation is the diversity of its species. With only 6 percent of the world's land area the tropical moist forests are thought to house almost half its species. Although Costa Rica is smaller than West Virginia, it supports more than 12,000 species of vascular plants, 150 species of reptiles and amphibians, 237 species of mammals, 850 species of birds, and 543 species of butterflies in 3 families alone. That is more species of birds than in the United States and Canada combined. Madagascar has more than 2,000 tree species in comparison with only about 400 in all of temperate North America. Peninsular Malaysia has 7,900 plant species compared to Great Britain with 1,430 in twice the area. The Amazon and its tributaries hold more than 2,000 species of fish. E. O. Wilson counted 43 species in 26 genera of ants in a single tree in Peru's Tambopata Reserve, "about equal to the entire ant fauna of the British Isles."

It is not surprising therefore that large numbers of species are threatened as rain-forest habitats are altered or destroyed, but tropical species are especially vulnerable for other reasons as well. In contrast to their temperate counterparts, tropical species are often highly localized in their distributions. Islands, mountaintops, valleys, drainage systems, watersheds, and local pockets of high rainfall are characterized by high numbers of endemic species: plants and animals occurring nowhere else. For example, almost half the 708 bird species in Papua New Guinea are endemic. In part this is because very few species are common and most are rare. In addition many tropical species do not spread very easily. Many tropical trees have large seeds that are not carried far from the parent tree, and some bird species of the rain-forest understory will not fly across open fields or large rivers. Consequently, the populations of these species tend to be highly localized.

Scientists believe that other distributions reflect the locations of old rain-forest refugia, islands of rain forest that persisted in a surrounding sea of savanna ten to twenty thousand years ago. During the Pleistocene periods of glaciation in north temperate zones, rainfall decreased in the tropics. In Africa and South America the extent of the rain forest shrank to small pockets with high rainfall. With the return of high rains during interglacial periods (such as today), the rain forest expanded, but the locations of the old refugia are still evident in the modern distributions of some species.

At Manaus, Brazil, the muddy waters of the Rio Solimoes meet the clear, black waters of the Rio Negro. The waters of the Rio Negro are made black by dissolved tannins from vegetation growing on the nutrient-poor soils of the river basin.

The Lua' of Pa Pae, Thailand, set fire to their swidden ▷ fields in a carefully controlled pattern to ensure a hot, complete burn without endangering surrounding fields.

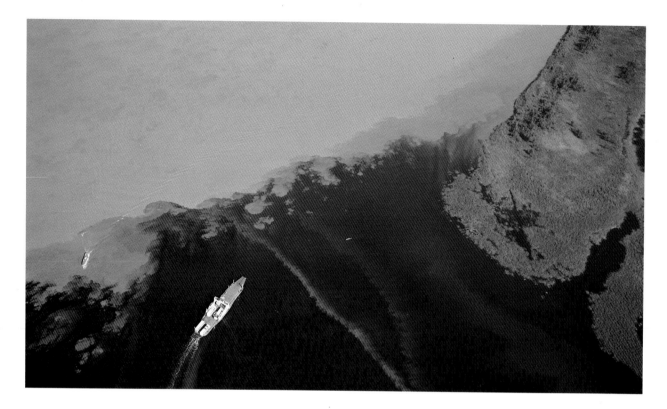

Still other distributions are evidence of habitat specialization in heterogeneous tropical landscapes that can vary between the constant warm, moist conditions of tropical-lowland rain forest and the daily freezing temperatures of alpine tundra within a few miles. Other species, including many insects, are restricted by the distribution of their food species. Whatever the cause, large proportions of endemic species and species with restricted ranges are especially vulnerable to extinction when the forest is cleared or degraded.

Biological diversity is the true wealth of the tropical forest, but a wealth we are too slowly beginning to appreciate. Many crops that feed the world came from the tropics, and the tropics still house their wild and domestic relations: corn, potatoes, manioc, sweet potatoes, and tomatoes originated in Latin America and rice, bananas, coconut, and yams in tropical Asia. To these should be added important industrial crops such as sugarcane, tobacco, oil palm, coffee, jute, rubber, and cacao. Forty percent of the food-crop production of North America is dependent on crops that originated in Latin America, although not all from rain-forest habitats. The magnitude of our dependence on the genetic diversity of the tropics was highlighted by the corn blight that in 1970 spread to national epidemic proportions in our genetically uniform fields and again eight years later when a previously unknown species of perennial corn was discovered near a Mexican cornfield. Genes from that species are being used

to protect the U.S. hybrid-corn crop from fungus, and there is hope that a perennial variety with commercial potential may soon be developed.

As the world's agricultural productivity grows to feed an expanding population, it becomes increasingly dependent on the genetic resources of the wild relatives and local varieties of these internationally important crops. In the evolutionary race between crops and pests, crop varieties do not remain long in production. As yields decline in the face of new onslaughts of pests and diseases or other strains appear with improved yields or performance characteristics, varieties are replaced. Sugarcane varieties in Hawaii may last ten to twelve years, while cotton varieties in California are typically replaced after only three or four years. Modern agricultural methods, which rely on homogeneous fields of single improved crop varieties, are susceptible to equally successful invasions of "improved" pest varieties. Two years after the planting in Indonesia, Vietnam, and the Philippines of a rice variety, IR26, resistant to the brown plant hopper, a new race of brown plant hopper appeared. IR36, with resistance to the new biotype, was introduced to replace IR26. A few years later a new race of plant hopper appeared in Sumatra and the southern Philippines; plant breeders at the International Rice Research Institute were ready with IR56 and IR60. New sources of germ plasm are continually sought by plant hunters even as their natural habitats, the tropical forests and the diverse swid-

den fields of small-scale tropical farmers, disappear.

Out of the rain forests have also come drugs that changed the course of civilization: quinine from the bark of the cinchona tree is used in the treatment and prevention of malaria; steroids from a Mexican yam were central to the development and early wide dissemination of birth-control pills; curare from a woody vine is used as a muscle relaxant during surgery; vincristine and vinblastine from the Madagascar periwinkle are true miracle drugs for the treatment of childhood leukemia. Tragically the expense of putting new drugs into production and risks of dependence on wild plants have discouraged commercial drug companies from investing in plant exploration. In the United States today most such exploration for potential medicinal plants is in the hands of a few large herbaria such as the New York Botanical Garden.

The rain forests lie between the tropics of Cancer and Capricorn, which are the northern- and southernmost limits to the track of the sun. In fact, the word *tropics* derives from the Greek *tropos,* "a turning." Between these latitudes, the sun is directly overhead twice a year and all year long its rays strike the ground almost perpendicularly rather than obliquely as in higher latitudes. There are major areas of these complex forests in the Amazon basin of South America, Congo basin of Africa, and islands of Sumatra, Borneo, and New Guinea. Although only about 6 percent of the land area, the tropical moist forests account for more than 17 percent of the world's productive land (the deserts and the tundra being discounted). Their high annual productivity accounts for a substantial portion of the total biological activity on earth—32 percent of the living matter produced on land each year. Pound for pound, tropical trees are no more productive than temperate ones during the middle of the growing season; year-round growing conditions, however, mean that annual productivity of tropical rain forests is among the highest on earth.

This high influx of solar energy has several important consequences. First and most obviously, the tropics are constantly warm. Near the equator the temperature varies more in a day (five to seven degrees centigrade) than the monthly average temperature varies in a year (less than one degree centigrade). There is no cold month, and where rainfall is abundant, no season of dormancy for plants and animals. Biological activity continues year round. Three crop rotations a year (five, if plantings overlap) can be obtained under such conditions.

Much of temperate North American weather is a product of frontal air masses that move east in response to prevailing westerly winds. Local weather reflects the relative strengths of the cold, dry arctic air masses and warm, moist air masses from the Gulf of Mexico. Much tropical weather, in contrast, is generated lo-

cally. Warm air, rising over land heated by the overhead sun, is heavy with moisture transpired from the forest below and evaporated from adjacent warm tropical oceans. As the rising air cools it drops its moisture load as rain, often in late afternoon storms. Brazilian meteorologists estimate that more than half the water falling as rain in the Amazon basin is recycled from the adjacent forest—evaporated and transpired from the large mass of foliage. As a consequence, extensive deforestation has been implicated in changes in local rainfall patterns.

Rain forests also lie at the heart of the earth's heat pump. The warm air generated in the tropics is carried poleward, distributing tropical warmth to the higher latitudes. Any large-scale destruction of this forest would seem to precipitate global changes in climate, although the effects of tropical deforestation on global weather patterns are still highly speculative.

Equally speculative are the effects of deforestation on the global carbon-dioxide balance. Increases in atmospheric carbon dioxide are closely linked to global warming trends and rising sea levels. Scientists estimate that the amount of carbon in the biomass of the world's forests exceeds that in the atmosphere by at least three times. Oxidation of organic matter in vegetation and underlying soils could thus potentially alter the concentration of carbon dioxide in the atmosphere. Some researchers suggest that atmospheric carbon input from the clearing of tropical forests is second only to that from the burning of fossil fuels. Although reliable estimates of the actual amounts of carbon dioxide released by the conversion of tropical forest to agriculture are scarce, the potential for major climatic consequences of widespread deforestation remains.

Rain-forest environments are almost constantly warm and wet. It is a mistake, however, to think that the tropics are without seasons. Tropical seasons follow the rains, and the rains follow the sun, bringing generally two rainy and two dry seasons a year. Some ecologists restrict the designation of tropical rain forests to those forests receiving at least sixty inches of rain evenly distributed throughout the year. Dry seasons, of course, are relative. In general the driest month receives at least five inches of rain, although exceptions exist. Many forests receive more than 160 inches a year, and some like Chocó Province, inland from Colombia's Pacific Coast, are inundated with 236 inches.

Farther north or south of the equator, total rainfall decreases and its distribution becomes more seasonal. The two dry and two wet seasons merge into a single dry season and a single rainy season. Under the increasingly long and severe dry season, the height and complexity of the forest decreases. A large proportion of the trees lose their leaves during the dry season, and many animals become dormant or migrate to such moister areas as the gallery forests along water courses. The more salubrious climates of tropical seasonal environments have brought the tropical dry forests under pressures of development and deforestation for a longer time than the rain forests. Few preserves of tropical dry forest exist, and around the world they are heavily exploited for timber, charcoal, pasture, and crop land. In the drier climates fire is also an important force in forest clearing and in maintenance of grasslands. With further decreases in rainfall, trees become more widely spaced or restricted to river banks. Grasses become established in the intervening spaces, and forests give way to savanna and grassland.

In the rain forest much of the rain falls in torrential downpours. Single storms of more than thirty-seven millimeters (one and one-half inches) an hour are common, and two hundred millimeters (eight inches) falling in a day are not unusual; yet under the forest canopy it is unusual to see .water standing after such a rain, except on trails or other areas where soils have become compacted. Even in hilly areas landslides are relatively uncommon, except where the slopes have lost their forest cover. Deeply weathered soils, interlaced by channels of decomposed roots and by the tunnels of earthworms and other soil creatures, absorb even the heaviest rains.

In the constant warm, humid conditions of the forest floor, fallen leaves and twigs and other organic matter rapidly disappear. Such nutrients as nitrogen, phosphorus, potassium, and calcium are released as the leaves decompose to be taken up again by the mass of fine roots and fungi that explore the surface layers of the forest floor.

Tropical red and yellow earths are nutrient poor because they have been washed by tropical rains for eons. Nutrients are washed out of the living foliage and fallen leaves. Mineral-bearing sands and silts are weathered out of the upper layers of soil. Many of these soils were in place 180 million years ago when the southern continents that today bear the tropical forests began to drift into their current positions. Spared from continental glaciers and mountain building that renewed the mineral soils of the northern latitudes and higher altitudes, much of the land under today's rain forest has long been undisturbed. With the exception of the expansion of savanna during the temperate ice ages (beginning about 100 thousand years ago), much of that land has been under wet tropical forest for most of that time. Two hundred million years of warm, heavy rain has washed and weathered tropical soils so deeply that nutrient-bearing bedrocks are now far below the reach of roots (more than seventy meters in some areas).

The agricultural qualities of tropical soils, like their temperate counterparts, vary widely. Most (about 60 percent) are nutrient-poor red and yellow earths. About 7 percent of tropical soils are extremely poor sandy soils of old river terraces or highly weathered uplands. These soils have very little agricultural potential and support a stunted vegetation. In the Amazon basin, where river meanders have traveled frequently and widely across the ancient floodplain, extremely poor soils are intermixed with pockets of more fertile soils.

Another 15 percent of tropical soils includes a wide range of relatively fertile soils with more promising agricultural potential. These soils are often found on volcanic parent material where they support high population densities and intensive agriculture as on the islands of Java and Sumatra. Often, however, rich soils are intermixed with very poor soils as in parts of the Amazon basin. The failure of newly arrived settlers and government officials to distinguish the promising from the disastrous soils has been a major detriment to the success of Brazil's resettlement schemes. Farmers with long experience in the region can distinguish soils by the composition and characteristics of the forests they support; the success rates of these old Amazon hands in new land-colonization schemes has been predictably higher than that of new arrivals.

About 8 percent of tropical soils is subject to frequent flooding. Their fertility depends on the quality of the silt sediment deposited annually by the flood waters. The Mekong delta and Amazon floodplain are fertile with good agricultural potential, if cropping systems can take into account the high flood risk. In contrast the seasonally flooded *igapo* forests of Rio Negro in Venezuela are on extremely infertile soils; the Rio Negro itself drains a basin largely composed of nutrient-poor white sand soils.

With the exception of notably rich soils, most old tropical soils are poor agricultural risks for a multitude of reasons, all associated with their great age. Most are poor in such nutrients as phosphorus (the only new sources of which are soil minerals and bedrock), potassium (which is only very weakly held in the soil matrix), calcium, and magnesium. Bacteria, often associated with roots of plants in the legume family, convert nitrogen from the atmosphere to ammonium, which other microbes convert to nitrates that can be taken up by plant roots. Nitrogen is thus replenished by the living vegetation, but the rapid decay of organic matter means that nitrogen is quickly depleted when the forest is cleared. Millennia of weathering have left behind the oxides of iron and aluminum, which give warm-climate soils their red and yellow colors and make tropical soils extremely acidic, with high concentrations of aluminum that are toxic to many crops.

Much of the phosphorus in tropical soils is firmly bound to the clays of the highly weathered soils. Phosphates thus do not reach roots in the dilute soup the flows down through the soil column. Roots must seek

Corn cobs from a single field near Toluca, Mexico, show the tremendous genetic diversity present within local races of corn.

it out, and the floors of some tropical forests are carpeted by a thick mat of fine roots at the soil surface. Phosphorus uptake is also facilitated by their association with symbiotic fungi (called mycorrhizae), which grow closely associated with root cells. The fine network of the fungus more quickly and thoroughly penetrates the soil and freshly fallen litter than do plant roots. Through these mycorrhizae, plants are able to obtain sufficient phosphate for growth in otherwise nutrient-poor soils.

Under an intact forest nutrients released by decaying litter are thus likely to be quickly reabsorbed into the living vegetation. Very little is lost into the groundwater, but at the same time little is stored in the soil itself. Tropical soils under many rain forests are thus deceptively poor. The lush vegetation suggested to early settlers that these were regions of great untapped potential that would yield abundant harvests under enlightened modern agricultural techniques. Repeated trials have shown, however, that these soils are very fragile and, unless carefully fertilized, apt to be productive for only a few short years.

Cleared of vegetation the soil is exposed to the full force of the tropical sun and rain. With the root and fungus network no longer in place to capture nutrients released from decaying vegetation, leaching and erosion deplete the soil of its few nutrients. If the trunks and branches are burned, as they are in most forms of swidden agriculture, nutrients in the litter are

converted to ash fertilizer for the crops. The ash also lowers the high acidity of soil, improving the availability of phosphorus. The first crops are improved under this scheme, but as the ash is quickly depleted and the remaining trunks and branches decay, soil fertility returns to its original poor state. Experiments in Amazonian Peru show that some crops develop nitrogen and potassium deficiencies in the first eight months, phosphorus and magnesium deficiencies within two years, and deficiencies in micronutrients such as calcium, zinc, and manganese within the next several years. Yields decline sufficiently from weed invasion and decreased soil fertility that small farmers generally abandon their fields after only two years. Pastures last a bit longer, but similar factors generally force their abandonment within ten years.

The use of perennial crops solves many of these problems. The canopies of such crops as coffee, teak, oil palm, cacao, and bananas protect the soils from the impact of rain and dessication of the sun. Litter is often allowed to decay in place or is burned to provide more ash fertilizer. Planting of many tropical crops requires only minimal disturbance of the soil surface; manioc is planted and replanted by inserting a short section of stem in the ground. Yams and plantains are handled similarly. Weeding is accomplished by machete and rarely by tillage of the soil.

Most swidden fields are a mélange of crops of different species, sizes, and growth forms. The mix-

Newly planted corn emerges among the charred logs of a swidden field near Leticia, Colombia.

tures of crop species may prevent population outbreaks of insect pests that might otherwise explode on monocultures of single species. Devastating pest loads are a more serious threat to crops in the tropics than in temperate climates where freezing temperatures annually reduce pest populations. In the absence of chemical controls, tropical farmers rotate crops, intermix species and varieties, and abandon their fields for a long fallow period in an effort to minimize losses. They also mimic many aspects of the natural succession in an old field. Such annual crops as upland (dry) rice and corn are planted at the same time as such longer-lived species as beans, manioc, squash, and yams. Economically important timber species or favored fruit trees may be allowed to stand or are planted in with the short-lived crops. By the time the early crops are harvested, the later species are beginning to spread their crowns over the soil. In this way a plot of land is in continuous production and rarely laid bare to the elements. Even after the growth of weeds and declining soil fertility significantly diminish yields, farmers may return to their old fields to harvest fruits of palms and other trees planted when the field was first opened.

Fields are allowed to lie fallow for varying numbers of years depending on soil characteristics, plant requirements, and local farming practices. In the western Amazon basin fourteen to twenty fallow years seem necessary to sufficiently improve soil fertility. In Peninsular Malaysia a shorter, bush fallow (in which the land is again cleared before trees become large) is common. Differences depend on the quality of the soil, crop requirements, and labor invested in weeding and soil management. Reestablishment of the forest during this period improves the structure and fertility of the soil and diminishes the weed and insect populations. After the fallow period the forest may again be cleared and burned and the land farmed for a year or two in a diverse mixture of tropical root, grain, and fruit crops.

These cropping schemes vary. A single family may have several different fields in various stages of production, and the composition and management of successive fields also differ depending on a family's requirements for crops, the production from other fields, and vicissitudes of local markets. The nutrient requirements of crops importantly influence their management. Corn and upland (dry) rice require relatively high-nutrient availability; they are planted on the best soils or following long fallow periods or soon after the slash has been burned. Manioc is tolerant of very poor soils and will reliably produce tubers for several years following forest clearing. These variations have at least one important characteristic in common: high population densities cannot be supported on slash-and-burn systems that rely on a long forest fallow to renew the soil.

Swidden agriculture is ecologically sound and functional over a large part of the tropics, wherever population density is low. Where forests are extensive and cash and transportation scarce, it is an economically viable method of ensuring subsistence and even producing something for market. Increasing populations and reduced access to forest, however, dangerously reduce the fallow period in many parts of the tropics.

Moreover, national policies, loan programs, and tax incentives often encourage the clearing of large parcels of land. In Amazonia and Central America cattle ranchers and land speculators consolidate the land of smallholders, delaying the return of the forest for the temporary establishment of pasture. Marginal and inadequate soils are often cleared of their forests in large-scale Indonesian and Amazonian resettlement schemes, and under the stimulus of government tax incentives and their own indebtedness, settlers may clear more land than they are able to manage adequately.

Where large areas are cleared or the soil is continuously disturbed (as under pasture), the reestablishment of forest is much delayed. The seeds of most tree species, except fast growing, weedy species, are large, short lived, and poorly dispersed; they are thus unlikely to reach slash-and-burn fields or pasture unless seed trees are close by. Mycorrhizal fungi, which can only survive in association with living roots, also decline in large clearings; seedlings of many forest trees are unable to grow in the absence of their phosphorus-gathering mycorrhizae. Those seedlings that do get started are often those of aggressive tropical grasses and other weeds that strangle crops and tree seedlings. The intense tropical sun and soil compaction, like nutrient depletion, also impede the establishment of young seedlings because their roots are not able to penetrate deeply enough to reach a reliable water supply during the dry season. Great expanses of rain-forest lands, originally cleared for slash-and-burn plots and then converted to pasture, have been severely degraded into scrubland, unusable for either cattle or agriculture and unable to support a potentially productive forest. The forest has been, in effect, mined for a few short years of productivity.

The impact of heavy tropical rains, cattle, and machinery compact the soils, collapsing the fine earthworm tunnels and old root channels. Rainwater is no longer absorbed into the soil but runs over the surface carrying topsoils, silts, and clays into the streams and rivers. Fluctuations in water levels of major rivers become increasingly chaotic; at low water, rivers become unnavigable and floods are higher and more destructive. On slopes, landslides expose the poor subsoils and destroy villages, roads, and bridges. The silt from unprotected watersheds fills reservoirs quickly so that the life expectancy of dams in tropical forests is drastically shortened. In many cases the electricity generated during the brief life of the reservoir falls far short of paying for the construction of the dam.

There is good reason to mourn the loss of the tropical rain forest. The great diversity of its plant and animal life make the tropical rain forest a resource of special value to humankind, unmatched by any other ecosystem on earth. For all our well-meaning attempts to preserve this diversity in zoos, botanical gardens, seed banks, and germ-plasm preserves, our greatest efforts can only safeguard for a limited time a miniscule number of species and varieties. This diversity and the fragility of most tropical soils make the rain forests especially vulnerable under the heavy hand of large-scale development, endangering both the wealth of the forest and productivity of the land on which it stands. Even more vulnerable is the accumulated knowledge of forest ecology and resources among rain-forest peoples. We will not preserve what we do not know and understand. Our best hope is in the reasoned development of some rain-forest land and resources for the sustained benefit of its people, in the preservation of other forests with all the intricacies of their structure and interactions intact, and in the conservation of the cultural heritage of the people who live close to the forest.

I am very grateful for the support and encouragement of Donald E. Stone, Executive Director of the Organization for Tropical Studies, and John F. Reed, Vice President for Education at the New York Botanical Garden.

2

TROPICAL
RAIN-FOREST
IMAGES

FRANCIS E. PUTZ
AND
N. MICHELE HOLBROOK

Under the trees . . . the number of lovely parasites everywhere illustrated the kindly influence of light and air. Even where the trees were largest the sunshine penetrated, subdued by the foliage to exquisite greenish-golden tints, filling the wide lower spaces with tender half lights, and faint blue-and-grey shadows. . . . How far above me seemed that leafy cloudland into which I gazed!

W. H. Hudson, *Green Mansions,* 1904

And in the midst [of the giant trees] the merciless creepers clung to the big trunks in cable-like coils, leaped from tree to tree, hung in thorny festoons from the lower boughs, and, sending slender tendrils on high to seek out the smallest branches, carried death to their victims in an exulting riot of silent destruction.

Joseph Conrad, *Almayer's Folly,* 1895

More than any other geographical province or landscape, tropical lands fascinate the artists who portray them. The idea of a winterless land filled with fantastic and unknown plants and animals evokes a landscape and rhetoric of superlatives and excesses. Powerful and often conflicting images typify portrayals of tropical rain forest. Well-known works such as W. H. Hudson's novel *Green Mansions,* Henri Rousseau's painting *The Dream* (1910), and John Huston's film *The African Queen* (1951) are evidence of the fascination with tropical nature. These works in turn represent the visual and emotional cords that bind European culture to the equatorial zone.

Say the word *jungle* and one conjures up a vision of riotous impenetrable vegetation, drenched with steam and mist, teeming with wondrous, unfamiliar, and perhaps dangerous beasts. Say the word *jungle* again and the view shifts to an idyllic setting of palm trees and jewellike flowers in which the gentle inhabitants live in harmony with their surroundings. A third time and now the tropical forests form the backdrop for scenes of adventure, conquest, and discovery. The visual and literary arts give substance to these images; paintings, novels, comic strips, and films are the primary avenue of contact between the torrid regions and the safe confines of the Western mind.

It is important to emphasize that the social and political climate in which most Europeans have entered the tropics has been one of exploration and exploitation. During the five hundred or so years in which Westerners have ventured into the equatorial zone, their primary role has been laying claim to and exploiting the resources of the region. Viewing themselves in the context of conquerors, colonists, and custodians, their perception of the tropical environment, including native peoples, has been colored by the arrogance associated with their assumed superiority. These attitudes in turn work to establish and maintain a sense of distance and unfamiliarity between Western and tropical ways. Artists are not exempt from prevailing views; the social, religious, and economic rationale for the northern presence in the tropics forms an underlying theme in many artistic portrayals of the equatorial region.

Since the advent of printing, northern peoples have had an insatiable appetite for jungle tales. *The Travels* of Marco Polo, which introduced fourteenth-

Jan Breughel, *The Garden of Eden with the Temptation and Fall of Adam and Eve,* ca. 1600. Museum of Fine Arts, Seville.

century Europe to many of the wondrous plants and products of tropical Asia, was one of the first books to be available for general readership; Juan Diego de Valdez's tale "The Lost City of Zinj" fascinated seventeenth-century Portuguese readers with accounts of tail-bearing men having carnal knowledge of native women in the tropical forests of Africa. Thousands of Americans in the mid-nineteenth century lined up to pay twenty-five cents to see Frederic E. Church's tropical landscape *The Heart of the Andes* (1859), making it the most viewed American painting of its day. In our own century we have had appetite sufficient to consume more than one thousand jungle novels and hundreds of jungle movies. Even though nearly all these books probably would be excluded from a compendium of great literature and some of the films represent all-time cinematic lows, it is certain that they inspire and are in turn inspired by the jungle's powerful image.

Reference to "tropical regions" has exotic and wonderful connotations, but the "torrid zone" (from the Latin *torrere,* to roast, also, to be highly passionate, ardent, zealous) captures a more vivid image. Many tropical biologists object to calling the tropical rain forest "jungle" because both the popular image and etymological roots of the word *jungle* suggest a misconception. The word is derived from the Hindustani word *djanghael* or *jangal,* meaning wasteland or uncultivated ground. With the imposition of British colonialism the use of the word became generalized from the land itself to the vegetation occupying such untended areas. Although the original application of this term was to dry, scrubby thickets, *jangal* soon came to refer to any wild, luxuriant tropical environment. British colonial officers, when transferred from regions of *djanghael* to other parts of the empire, brought this exotic term with them, while such popular nineteenth-century accounts of discovery and exploration

Thomas Cole, *Expulsion from the Garden of Eden,* 1827–28. Museum of Fine Arts, Boston.

as David Livingstone's *Narrative of an Expedition to the Zambesi* introduced the term to temperate-zone readers. Rudyard Kipling's *The Jungle Books* (1894–95) forever linked the word *jungle* with the exotic inhabitants of the tropical forest.

The mystique of a region so vastly different and more diverse than the temperate zone fascinates artist and audience alike. In the minds of distant artists the concept of the unknown jungle is subject to continual change. Exotic tropical landscapes, more than familiar scenery, act as free vessels in which the social, political, and religioscientific concerns of the day can book passage. Even as an artistic matrix, however, the tropical environs are never quite passive. Artists who venture into the equatorial zone bear the mark of a direct experience with the jungle. The portrayal of tropical nature in Western art, literature, and film has created enduring images of the tropical rain forest as the original paradise, source and progenitor of evil, an arena

for adventure and discovery, a region of vast wealth, and as a treasurehold of biological diversity.

The Garden of Eden: A Tropical Vision

> Time writes no wrinkle on thine azure brow,
> Such as creation's dawn beheld, thou rollest now!
> J. E. Warren, "The Romance of the Tropics,"
> *Knickerbocker Magazine* (June 1849).

The idea of a lost golden age in which peace, harmony, and immortality prevailed is a myth shared by many cultures. Characterized by perpetual spring and an absence of fear or need, lands of primal innocence are removed in space and time and thus unattainable without divine intervention. The tropics provided a ready source of inspiration for paradise. Homer's Elysian Plains, a land "where life is easiest for men," is also without snow or great storms, while Virgil transformed Arcadia from what had been a rough and rural land of rustic, familiar folk to a landscape of luxuriant vegetation and perpetual spring. The Cardinal Pierre d'Ailly, whose book Columbus was to use as a major reference in planning his voyage, reported the existence of a race of people at the equator who never die except when they become bored with their happy existence and throw themselves into the sea.

With the onset of the Age of Exploration and the reality of global travel, paradise became transformed from something distant in time to something perhaps distant only in space. That early expeditions believed in the possibility of discovering paradise on earth has been well documented. Christopher Columbus wrote Queen Isabella that he had indeed discovered the Garden of Eden in the West Indies. Other explorers and settlers shared this impression; the first European children born on the island of Madeira were aptly named Adam and Eve. Lush tropical vegetation harmonized with earlier notions of the golden age. Furthermore the tropics were by far the largest portion of the world unknown to Europeans at that time and thus provided the most probable location for the lost Garden of Eden. Sir Walter Raleigh devoted the entire first book of his *History of the World* (1614) to questions regarding paradise. Drawing on his travels in the tropical regions of Spanish America, he wrote,

> That if there be any place upon the earth of that nature, beauty, and delight that Paradise had, the same must be found within . . . the Tropicks . . . so many sorts of delicate fruits, ever bearing and at all time beautified with blossom and fruit both green and ripe, as it may of all other parts be best compared to the Paradise of Eden.

Later in the seventeenth century John Milton described in *Paradise Lost* a land of eternal spring, where "Blossoms and Fruits at once of golden hue / Appeared," where "palmy hillock" and "Flowers worthy of Paradise" make up a "Nature boon / Poured forth profuse on Hill and Dale and Plain." Depictions of Eden, such as that by Jan Breughel, bring together tropical and temperate nature in a peaceful and lush rendering of the golden age, while others such as Henri Rousseau's fabulous jungle scenes and *Expulsion from the Garden of Eden* by the nineteenth-century American painter Thomas Cole are wholly tropical. Many artists, probably influenced by the biblical phrase "the tree of life, which bear twelve manner of fruits, and yielded her fruit every month" (Revelation 22:2), captured the idea of an eternal spring by painting both flowers and fruit on the same tree. Eden was pictured as a tropical paradise not only because it is lush and peaceful but because it is also perceived to be unchanging and seasonless. In depicting a tropical Eden these artists represented not just spring, fruitfulness, and abundance but an eternal spring, unfailing fruitfulness,

and endless abundance. If paradise has been lost to humankind, its timeless aspect suggests it remains to be regained.

Artistic views of the inhabitants of the equatorial regions shared in this association of Edenic innocence. J. H. Bernardin de Saint-Pierre's *Paul et Virginie,* a late eighteenth-century romantic novel set on a lush tropical island, draws the parallel between the two children and their Edenic counterparts. In Herman Melville's 1846 novel *Typee* the natives exist in a state of original grace; their life on the idyllic islands of the Marquesas is reminiscent of the Garden of Eden.

> The penalty of the Fall presses very lightly upon the valley of Typee. . . . I scarcely saw any piece of work performed there which caused the sweat to stand upon a single brow. As for digging and delving for a livelihood, the thing is altogether unknown. Nature has planted the breadfruit and the banana, and in her own good time she brings them to maturity, when the idle savage stretches forth his hand and satisfies his appetite.

The jungle is also the land of dreams, a place where dreamlike realities hold sway. The painter Rousseau wrote of his experiences in the tropical greenhouse at the Jardin des Plantes in Paris (the closest that he ever came to the real jungle) that "when I enter these hothouses and see these strange plants from exotic countries I feel as if I have stepped into a dream." His painting *The Dream* depicts a young woman reclining on a settee amidst a tropical setting. She dreams of the forest and becomes transported among its lush vegetation.

Not satisfied with visits to botanical gardens and hothouses, many nineteenth-century American painters such as Frederic E. Church, Martin Johnson Heade, and George Catlin traveled to the tropics to capture its fascination firsthand. When Church's first large tropical landscape, *The Heart of the Andes,* was exhibited in 1859, it was an immediate success. Flanked by black velvet curtains, surrounded by potted tropical plants, and lit by gaslights, this painting was more than just another canvas. Spectators were advised to bring opera glasses, schoolchildren were given instruction in front of it, and interpretive pamphlets were written to guide the viewer through its many marvels. There in exquisite detail and clarity, tropical nature is displayed in all its diversity and harmony. Theodore Winthrop, in his 1859 pamphlet, wrote:

> No one calls for quinine after seeing his pictures, or has nightmares filled with caymans and vampires. . . . Llamas may feed there undisturbed by anacondas. No serpent hugs; no scorpion nips; never a mosquito hums over all this fair realm. Perpetual spring reigns. . . . Life here may be a sweet idyl.

Church's contemporary, Martin Johnson Heade, cast tropical images with a dreamy, shadowy presence.

Although best known for his illustrations of tropical hummingbirds, his landscapes retain the possibility of unlimited potential and thus create an image of the tropics without destroying a vision. They partake of the romance of the tropics as well as its Edenic associations. In his *South American River* (1868), for example, it is not the overwhelming fullness of tropical nature but the mystery of the unknown that dominates. Substituting shadow for clarity and atmosphere for detail, such vaporous and dreamy portrayals of tropical rain forests present a seductive and persistent image, one reflecting the myths and dreams of the age.

Nineteenth-century painters such as Paul Gauguin and John La Farge left the Industrial Revolution behind in search of tropical natives whose lives lay closer to what they believed was the original innocence of the human spirit. The romantic works of this tradition present an idyllic, peaceful setting and capture the essence of Eden in their portrayal of a life free from toil, struggle, or care.

While twentieth-century artistic depictions of rain-forest peoples are decidedly less romantic, the perception that the tropical rain forest can absorb and absolve the evils of modern civilization remains. A familiar theme in literature and folklore is that of a lost child accepted and sheltered by the jungle and raised in an original state of innocence. These children develop into wild but morally superior beings who, in turn, frequently become the saviors of the true natives of the forest. Mowgli, of Kipling's *The Jungle Books,* is an early example of this pattern, followed by Rima in W. H. Hudson's *Green Mansions,* and Tarzan in Edgar Rice Burroughs's *Tarzan of the Apes* (1914). The same story line is followed in such movies as *The Blue Lagoon* (1980), *Sheena, Queen of the Jungle* (1984), and *The Emerald Forest* (1985). So manifest and compelling was the concept of a soul of tropical innocence that in London's Hyde Park a bird sanctuary and statue were dedicated to Rima, the heroine in *Green Mansions.*

The Jungle as the Source of Evil

> "It is just as it was in Paradise," said our pilot, an old Indian of the Missions. . . . But in carefully observing the manners of animals among themselves, we see that they mutually avoid and fear each other. The golden age has ceased; and in this Paradise of the American forests, as well as everywhere else, sad and long experience has taught all beings that benignity is seldom found in alliance with strength.
>
> > Alexander von Humboldt, *Personal Narrative of Travels to the Equinoctial Regions of the New Continent, during the Years 1799–1804* (1807–33)

A negative image of the tropics existed even before actual and sustained contact had been made with the equatorial region. Thomas Aquinas, following Aris-

totle, supposed the equator to be uninhabitable due to its proximity to the sun. Sir Thomas More located *Utopia* (1516) in the New World but placed it in the south temperate zone, believing the equatorial belt to contain only "great and wyde desertes and wyldernessess . . . intollerable heate . . . wyld beastes and serpentes." Nineteenth-century explorer H. M. Stanley, whose enormously popular book *Through the Dark Continent* (1878) influenced many later novelists, found the tropical rain forest to be a "region of horrors," a place where it was difficult to "accustom myself to its gloom and its pallid solitude. I could find no comfort for the inner man nor solace for the spirit." Even the seasonless and timeless character of the tropics could be perceived in a foreboding manner. Herman Melville, in "The Encantadas" (published in *The Piazza Tales,* 1856), writes of the "special curse" of these equatorial islands, "that which exhalts them in desolation . . . is that to them change never comes; neither the change of seasons nor of sorrows."

The overwhelming complexity and disorder of the natural vegetation and landforms is evidence to some of the darker side of tropical nature. In *The Emperor of the Amazon* (1977), Marcio Souza writes,

> Someone in Belém once told me that you become mute in the face of the Amazonian setting. Not so . . .you become humiliated, by the blinding intuition of absolute prehistory. An experience which made me feel profoundly uneasy. As a son of the sea of Cádiz, I had

Frederic E. Church, *The Heart of the Andes,* 1859.
Metropolitan Museum of Art, New York.

FRANCIS E. PUTZ AND N. MICHELE HOLBROOK

already known the crushing power of nature. But the sea is classical-implacable perhaps, but without obfuscation. The jungle is reticent, Muslim: no tides, no waves, no sun on the back of emeralds and foam.

Recent works, such as *Jewelled Jungle* (1958) by American painter Mark Tobey and *The Jungle* by Cuban painter Wilfredo Lam (1943), give visual form to this image of the jungle as labyrinthine and chaotic.

The inability to comprehend the tropical rain forest causes some people a sense of alienation and places the jungle outside the realm of human reason. The jungle landscape provides fertile ground for the deepest suspicions of the nature of man. Another contemporary South American writer, Gabriel García Márquez, confirms this is his book *One Hundred Years of Solitude* (1967):

> Then, for more than ten days, they did not see the sun again. The ground became soft and damp, like volcanic ash, and the vegetation was thicker and thicker, and the cries of the birds and the uproar of the monkeys became more and more remote, and the world became eternally sad. The men on the expedition felt overwhelmed by their most ancient memories in that paradise of dampness and silence, going back to before original sin, as their boots sank into pools of steaming oil and their machetes destroyed bloody lilies and golden salamanders.

Along with its incomprehensibility, the irresistible, seductive nature of the jungle is an important theme in twentieth-century Western portrayals. While natives appear to move easily through the jungle with little resistance, northerners are thwarted at every step. Antithetical to the realm of reason and order to the outsider the jungle seems to emit a force that acts to reclaim and destroy any structure that is foolishly placed within its grasp. For Western explorers this often means that direct return is impossible as their freshly cut trails "close up with a new vegetation that seemed to grow right before their eyes" (*One Hundred Years of Solitude*). For residents in tropical lands it signifies that constant vigilance is needed to preserve one's shelter lest one return to find it "literally burst apart by the force of the plants that had grown into it, pushing up the roof, cracking the walls, turning to dead leaves, rot, what once had been the materials of which a home was made" (A. Carpentier, *The Lost Steps,* 1956). Kipling's tale "Letting in the Jungle," which appears as part of *The Jungle Books,* treats directly this primal urge to reclaim and destroy the structures of human civilization. Whole villages have little hope against this onslaught, which leaves only the "roaring jungle in full blast on the spot that had been under plough not six months before." The story culminates in a paean of the jungle against the lives and structures of the villagers.

> I have untied against you the club-footed vines,
> I have sent in the jungle to swamp out your lives.
> The trees—the trees are on you!

Humphrey Bogart drags the boat through the swamp in a scene from *The African Queen,* 1952 (John Huston).

The house-beams shall fall,
And the *karela,* the bitter *karela,*
Shall cover you all!

The jungle is equally destructive of human willpower and resolve. Dreams, madness, and a regression to infantile behaviors constitute the "logic" of the jungle. In both Vladimir Nabokov's "Tierra Incognita" (1931) and Ernest Hemingway's "The Snows of Kilimanjaro" (1935) tropical illness leads to fever-crazed madness that renders the protagonists unable to avert their inevitable demise. Outside the domain of human will, the jungle is beyond the reach of Christianity and prayer as Peter Matthiessen notes in *At Play in the Fields of the Lord* (1965):

> In the dark tunnels of the rain forest the dim light was greenish. Strange shapes caught at his feet, and creepers scraped him; putrescent smells choked his nostrils with the density of sprayed liquid. He fell to his knees on the rank ground and began to pray, but instantly jumped up again. He had wandered into a cathedral of Satan where all prayer was abomination, a place without a sky, a stench of death, vast somber naves and clerestories, the lost cries of savage birds—he whooped and called, but no voice answered.

The most potent metaphor, however, is the association of the jungle with the unconscious mind. Envisioned as a powerful, uncharted, and untamed region beyond the control of will or order, twentieth-century views of the unconscious form nearly a point for point correspondence with earlier fantasies of the jungle. Lack of order, intense fertility, and nearly overwhelming power are characteristics of both the jungle and the inner mind. Each is also a place where dreams, madness, and infantile behaviors reign.

The idea of a journey is central in novels and movies that explore this relationship between the jungle and the mind. A journey deeper and deeper into the irresistible, yet unforgiving tropical forest parallels a journey into the mind's hidden depths. Joseph Conrad draws on this in *The Heart of Darkness* (1902).

> It was like a weary pilgrimage amongst hints for nightmares. . . . Going up that river was like travelling back to the earliest beginnings of the world, when vegetation rioted on the earth and the big trees were kings. . . . I tried to break the spell—the heavy, mute spell of the wilderness—that seemed to draw him to its pitiless breast by the awakening of forgotten and brutal instincts, by the memory of gratified and monstrous passions.

The darkness of Conrad's forest, its wild and savage character, is made all the more terrifying by the "dim suspicion of there being a meaning in it which you— you so remote from the night of first ages—could comprehend." Civilization, culture, religion, and will stand opposed to this dark and subliminal side, reinforcing the idea of the jungle as something to be overcome, subdued, exterminated.

Henri Rousseau, *The Dream,* 1910. Museum of Modern
Art, New York.

Bottom: Charles Christian Nahl, *Incident on the Chagres
River,* 1867. Bancroft Library, University of California,
Berkeley, CA.

FRANCIS E. PUTZ AND N. MICHELE HOLBROOK

John La Farge, *Afterglow, Tautira River, Tahiti,* 1891.
National Gallery of Art, Washington, D.C.

Jungles Filled with Danger and Adventure

Far-off and poorly known tropical lands have long inspired curiosity and aroused the imagination. Three thousand years ago travelers returning from the torrid zone fascinated Egyptian courtiers with tales of monkeys and tiny humans in much the same way as accounts of new species and complicated interactions among species fascinate people today. Predominant in later visions of life in tropical rain forests is the concept of violent struggle; nowhere is nature portrayed as being more "red in tooth and claw" (as Tennyson wrote). Such jungle safari stories as R. M. Ballantyne's *The Gorilla Hunters* (1862), M. Reid's *The Tiger Hunter* (1875), and Richard Connell's *The Most Dangerous* *Game* (1924) have greatly influenced the popular image of tropical rain forests. Hungry lions, wounded buffalos, poisonous snakes, and rampaging bull elephants are everywhere abundant on the pages and celluloid of tropical fiction. Peculiar to this fiction is the image of danger from above; big cats, snakes, and snipers add a vertical dimension to fear. Professor Challanger and his associates in Sir Arthur Conan Doyle's *Lost World* (1912) even had to deal with both man-eating plants and huge dinosaurs presumed extinct for more than one hundred million years. The overall impression is that to survive in the jungle one must be agile, heavily armed, and constantly aware of the nearest climbable tree.

Some of the creatures taken from the rain forest might better have been left where they were. Larger-than-life jungle creatures and modern civilization often have trouble coming to terms with one another. The best-known example is King Kong (from *King Kong,* 1933). Typical of many of his jungle brethren, Kong was a gentle sort, an admirer of beauty, and morally superior to many of his human captors. His brutish inclinations only emerged when confronted with civilization. Kong was better off in the jungle that spawned him, and certainly only the jungle could contain him.

The most enduring figure in jungle adventure is Tarzan, the King of the Jungle. Born of English nobility and raised by giant anthropoid apes, this scantily clad denizen of the jungle left his own indelible impression of tropical rain forests on readers and moviegoers. Tarzan's creator, Edgar Rice Burroughs, based his rather sketchy descriptions of tropical rain forests on Stanley's *In Darkest Africa* (1890). In reading the twenty-four novels in the Tarzan series (translated into more than thirty languages) few descriptions of the forests are encountered. Burroughs left much to the reader's imagination. In the first book of the series, *Tarzan of the Apes* (1912), only two pages of the long novel contain any description of the jungle at all. Apparently even early in the twentieth century the public had enough of an image of the tropical rain forest that a sentence like "From a great mass of impenetrable foliage a few yards away emerged Tarzan of the Apes" was enough to conjure up a fabulously exotic setting, a landscape suitable for a hero like Tarzan. In 1918, six years after the creation of Tarzan, the first of an estimated one hundred movies featuring the King of the Jungle was released. Filmed primarily in Louisiana, the first *Tarzan of the Apes* capitalized on the presence of palms, Spanish moss, and large grapevines to create the fantastic landscape that the jungle required.

For Tarzan the jungle is home. Although he faces threats almost every day, Tarzan is part of the system: he hunts and is hunted. As in Kipling's *The Jungle Books,* however, evil enters the tropical rain forest in the form of other humans. The jungle itself is envisioned as only a setting for danger not as a source of treachery and corruption.

> Men were indeed more foolish and more cruel than the beasts of the jungle! How fortunate was he [Tarzan] who lived in the peace and security of the great forest!

In line with the prevailing views of Western superiority, Burroughs portrays natives in his books as evil, stupid, or both, while the Europeans who enter the forest do so under duress, to escape capture by the law, or to steal something. The forest generally thwarts these evildoers, allowing Tarzan to rid his home once again of human corruption.

Jungle quest and jungle escape stories invariably include a scene in which the protagonist fights, chops,

swings, or crawls through a miserable tangle just before the treasure is discovered or the captor eluded. Although in real life the understory of most tropical rain forests is sufficiently open to allow normal foot travel, the adventurers that people the pages and films of the tropics are invariably separated from their goal by impenetrable masses of spiny, snake-ridden tangles of vegetable matter. One scene that has left a particularly vivid impression of the extreme difficulties of travel in the tropics is Humphrey Bogart pulling the *African Queen* through the leech-infested swamps of central Africa, almost a relief after the swarms of insects biting with such ferocity that Rose Sayers (Katharine Hepburn) is driven to temporary hysteria.

The true dangers and difficulties of passage through tropical rain forests were brought to public attention during the 1800s by those who chose a trans-isthmian passage on their way to the California gold fields. Diseases such as yellow fever and malaria struck down many as did other dangers of travel. The Chagres River, which formed an integral part of the Panamanian passage, inspired the following poem by J. S. Gilbert (1905):

> Beyond the Chagres River
>   'Tis said—the story's old—
> Are paths that lead to mountains
>   Of purest virgin gold;
> But 'tis my firm conviction,
>   Whatever tales they tell,

> That beyond the Chagres River
>   All paths lead straight to hell!

In spite of the difficulties, several of those successful in the gold fields later commissioned artists to capture their memories of the tropical passage.

The reputation of Central America as a hellhole of organic corruption was sealed by those who built railroads through the forests and worked on the Panama Canal. In *Cabbages and Kings* (1904), a rather humorous account of the lives of jungle railroad workers, O. Henry captures a widely held image of the tropical rain forest.

> T'was a sort of camp in a damp gorge full of wildness and melancholies. . . . The trees was all sky-scrapers; the underbrush was full of needles and pins; . . . ye stood knee-deep in the rotten water and grabbled roots . . . surrounded by a ragin' forest full of disreputable beasts . . . waiting to devour ye. The sun strikes hard, and melts the marrow in your bones. Ye get similar to the lettuce-eaters the poetry books speaks about. . . . 'Tis a land, as the poet says, "Where it always seems to be after dinner."

Powerful images of tropical rain forests are also derived from the hundreds of jungle war novels and films. Involvement in jungle wars has resulted in a vivid and distinctly unfavorable impression of tropical rain forests in the minds of temperate-zone soldiers, readers, and moviegoers. The ever-present

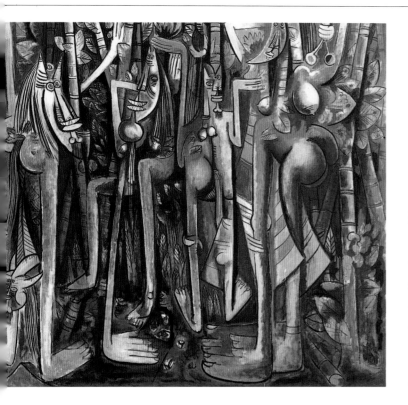

threat of ambush, the heat, and almost inevitable diseases and internal disorders might very well diminish a soldier's love of the forest. In Tim O'Brien's novel of the Vietnam War, *Going after Cacciato* (1975) the author succinctly summarizes much of what is to be loathed and feared in the jungle.

> It was jungle. Growth and decay sweating green, the smell of chlorophyll, jungle sounds and jungle depth. . . . Itching jungle, lost jungle. A botanist's madhouse.

Tropical vegetation for the Western soldier impedes progress and further hides an enemy that somehow seems naturally camouflaged. Exposing the enemy seems to necessitate destroying the forest, which is the cloak and shield of the enemy. The forces of modern technology are overwhelmed by the jungle's onslaught as Norman Mailer points out in *The Naked and the Dead* (1948).

> It seemed impossible to maintain any sort of order . . . the jungle offered far more resistance than the Japanese. . . . In the heart of the forest the trees grew almost a hundred yards high, their lowest limbs sprouting out two hundred feet from the ground. . . . Beneath them . . . a choked assortment of vines . . . wild banana trees . . . brush and shrubs squeezed against each other, raised their burdened leaves to the doubtful light that filtered through, sucking for air and food like snakes at the bottom of a pit. . . . Every-

thing was damp and rife and hot as though the jungle were an immense collection of oily rags growing hotter and hotter under the dark stifling vaults of a huge warehouse. Heat licked at everything, and the foliage, responding, grew to prodigious sizes. . . . No army could live or move in it.

In modern times the jungles of giant trees and grasping creepers have given way to those of tall buildings and crowded streets. The urban or concrete jungle carries with it much the same associations of competition and struggle. In Upton Sinclair's turn-of-the-century novel, *The Jungle,* the depiction of a Chicago meat-packing factory and heartless demise of even the best intentioned brings to mind the image of the jungle as a region of brutality and fear.

The Riches of the Tropics

Eldorado—the golden one! How many stories have been told, pages written, and reels of film shot about the pursuit of the elusive hidden wealth of South America? This theme is treated with varying degrees of respect in such modern films as *Indiana Jones and the Temple of Doom* (1984), *Aguirre: The Wrath of God* (1972), and *Romancing the Stone* (1984). To satisfy audiences' cravings for adventure searches for Eldorado are often combined with ones for the fountain of youth and encounters with tribes of fierce but provocative Amazons. Quests, however, generally entail great hardships, and searchers for Eldorado are depicted as suffering their share. The image of the hardships of the quester was captured by Werner Herzog's *Aguirre;* crazed by lust for gold and exhausted by heat, insects, hunger, hostile natives, and mutinous troops, Aguirre sits staring out at his nemesis, the jungle.

The "dark continent" is also depicted as a source of hidden wealth in the form of elephant graveyards and the treasures of the Lost Tribe of Israel. It was a greed for ivory that lured Conrad's Mr. Kurtz and others into the "heart of darkness." Novels and films of tropical adventures all too frequently envision the strong, intelligent, and generally light-skinned northerner sweeping in to "discover" or "rescue" the treasure, presumed to be of little use in such "uncivilized" country. Such exploits, however, are generally fraught with danger and travail as the jungle provides little welcome to outsiders. In H. Rider Haggard's action-packed Victorian novel *King Solomon's Mines* (1885), fierce, cannibalistic natives and ancient curses plague the hero Allan Quatermain. That this story has been committed to film no fewer than five times attests to the power of the tale.

Of all the true and fictionalized accounts of wealth to be gained in the tropics, the story of the rubber boom in South America perhaps brings fact closest to surpassing fiction. Rubber barons actually did light cigars with hundred dollar bills on the steps of the opulent opera house in Manaus. Like most fortunes, however, the wealth of the rubber barons was accumulated at the expense of tremendous human suffering. Apparently the rubber barons took to heart the fifteenth-century Portuguese proverb "Beyond the equator, everything is permitted." Vast wealth stimulated vast excesses and wild schemes. The idea of dragging a steamboat over a mountain, as in Herzog's movie *Fitzcarraldo* (1982), may not have seemed that preposterous to people who were sending their soiled linen from Brazil to France for proper laundering.

In addition to tales of gold, jewels, fountains of youth, and new species, visitors to tropical rain forests often told, and still tell, of the great agricultural potential of the lands where winter never comes. The implication is that a sturdy and preferably Protestant farmer could get wealthy planting crops and exploiting the apparently fertile soil. This unfortunate fallacy is based on the assumptions that northern farmers and farming methods are far superior to tropical ways and that the luxuriance of the natural tropical vegetation suggests unlimited fertility. For example, in 1853 A. R. Wallace wrote the following in *A Narrative of Travels on the Amazon and Rio Negro*:

> When I consider the excessively small amount of labour required in this country, to convert the virgin forest into green meadows and fertile plantations, I almost long to come over with half-a-dozen friends, disposed to work, and enjoy the country; and show the inhabitants how soon an earthly paradise might be created.

What many people failed to realize and continue to ignore is that exuberant growth is possible only if the natural community and nutrient cycles are left intact.

The story of the Yankee farmer going to the tropics to exploit the agricultural potential is common in real life and in literature and film. The plantation of a steel-willed entrepreneur falls prey to the ravenous appetites of a huge, rampaging swarm of ants in C. Stephenson's "Leiningen versus the Ants" (1938). Even as terrified jaguars, tapirs, and kinkajous fled by his plantation Leiningen made his stand.

> Yes, Leiningen had always known how to grapple with life. Even here in this Brazilian wilderness, his brain had triumphed over every difficulty and danger it had so far encountered. First he had vanquished primal forces by cunning and organization, then he had enlisted the resources of modern science to increase miraculously the yield of his plantation. And now he was sure he would prove more than a match for the "irresistible" ants.

Despite modern science and organization, the denizens of the jungle, the irresistible ants, eventually have their way. A further dramatization of the myth of agricultural wealth occurs in Paul Theroux's *The Mosquito Coast* (1982). The attempt by a family of industrious farmers from Connecticut to transplant their temperate-zone way of life into the heart of the Honduran jungle fails miserably; the explosion of their ice factory (itself perhaps a symbol of the north and northern ways) marks the failure of their transplanted cultural system and heralds the onslaught of tropical nature.

The Allure of Diversity

In the eighteenth century hundreds of scientists and natural philosophers set off from Europe to explore the tropical unknown. Distinct from earlier adventurers, conquerors, and pirates, they had as their primary goals the discovery, documentation, and understanding of the diversity and abundance of tropical nature. The figure who best united these scientific concerns with the artistic world was Baron Alexander von Humboldt (1796–1859), explorer, poet, and natural philosopher par excellence. Following his explorations of South America, Humboldt tirelessly traveled among the courts and salons of Europe lecturing on the marvels of the tropics. He was the primary inspiration for European natural historians like Darwin and such artists as Church. Humboldt understood the role artists and particularly landscape painters could have in conveying these images and ideas to the public. He wrote in Volume 2 of *Cosmos* (1849):

> He who, with a keen appreciation of the beauties of nature manifested in mountains, rivers, and forest glades, has himself travelled over the torrid zone, and seen the luxuriance and diversity of vegetation . . . can alone feel what an inexhaustible treasure remains still unopened by the landscape painter.

Factual accounts of tremendous diversity of life-forms piqued the curiosity of biologists living in temperate lands where nature had long seemed somewhat subdued. Nearly every ship returning from equatorial lands brought proof of the existence of previously unanticipated biological diversity. The tropics came to be recognized as the place where discoveries were to be made and where adventure waited around every bend in the river. Naturalists' accounts and illustrations in popular publications gave the public the impression of the tropics as a land teeming with life. Phillip H. Gosse, who never visited the tropics personally, gave the following account of the tropical rain forest in his popular nineteenth-century book *Romance of Natural History* (1860–62).

> Solemn are those primeval labyrinths of giant trees, tangled with ten thousand creepers, and roofed with lofty arches of light foliage, diversified with masses of glorious blossom of all rich hues; . . . the gigantic scale of life strongly excited astonishment in these forests.

Fascination with tropical diversity did not, however, always ensure great accuracy in its portrayal. In the early eighteenth century, when the average person knew somewhat less of tropical biogeography than today, Johann David Wyss in *The Swiss Family Robinson* (1812–13) included hippos and ostriches from Africa, hummingbirds, iguanas, and capybaras from South America, and tigers from Asia all on one small island! This menagerie scurries about in the shade of rubber trees native to South America and talipot palms from southern Asia. Luckily the shipwrecked family found plenty to eat including strawberries, capers, pineapples, oranges, wild rice, manioc, sugarcane, bananas, chestnuts, and coconuts. Other famous biogeographical inaccuracies include the 1981 movie *Tarzania,* in which orangutans from Borneo and chimpanzees from Africa live together and the fabulous floating island of *The Story of Dr. Dolittle* (by Hugh Lofting, 1920).

Biological diversity is one of the true riches of the tropics that has long attracted and rewarded scientists. Many major developments in anthropology, ecology, and systematics are based on discoveries made in the tropics; much remains to be discovered. A common vision of tropical forests is that they are lands of biological marvels, sources of intellectual and sociological insights, and places where scientific reputations can be had for a song and some sweat. The media, including popular science publications and made-for-television documentaries, suggest that legions of missing links, hidden treasures, lost civilizations, new species, strange behaviors, and elaborate species interactions await the open-eyed scientist. The image of tropical naturalists as dedicated, near-sighted, monomaniacal eggheads whose obsession with the discovery and documentation of new species renders them oblivious to all else is captured in Nabokov's story, "Tierra Incognita":

> The unknown won out. We moved on. I was already shivering all over and deafened by quinine, but still went on collecting nameless plants, while Gregson, though fully realizing the danger of our situation, continued catching butterflies and Diptera as avidly as ever.

The nineteenth-century American painter John La Farge mourned the passing of the traditional Polynesian way of life in a letter home, which was published posthumously in *Reminiscences of the South Seas (*1912):

> There will soon come a day when even for those who care, it will be no more; when nowhere on earth will there be any living proof that . . . [it] . . . is not all the invention of the poet—the mere refuge of the artist in his disdain for the ugly in life.

This nostalgia and sense of intangible loss is awakened again today, nearly one hundred years later, as we contemplate the full-scale destruction of the tropical rain forest. This sense of sorrow reflects a cultural legacy that associates tropical nature with the beautiful and the primitive. Tropical rain forests derive value not only as strongholds of diversity but also as repositories of mystery and the romance of the unknown. In *Walden* (1854) H. D. Thoreau wrote,

> At the same time that we are earnest to explore and learn all things, we require that all things be mysterious and unexplorable, that land and sea be infinitely wild, unsurveyed and unfathomed by us because unfathomable.

As an image, jungles embody this charge. Recognition of our cultural debt may help in the campaign to prevent the destruction of the forests from whence such wondrous images have sprung.

3

THE PREHISTORY OF AMAZONIA

BETTY J. MEGGERS

The first Europeans to see Amazonia were astounded by the lush vegetation and good health of the indigenous population. The riverbanks, they wrote, were occupied by large settlements that were organized into provinces ruled by powerful chiefs. The French, Spanish, English, Dutch, and Portuguese competed for control of what they believed to be a region of great wealth, conscripting Indians to supplement their meager forces. Warfare, slavery, and epidemic soon eliminated most of the population along the Amazon but not the legends. As we search for resources to sustain burgeoning human needs, we look to "vacant" Amazonia and its still untapped wealth. If large self-sustaining towns existed in pre-Columbian times, how did they support themselves? Until the past decade we did not have sufficient archaeological information to address this question. Although many gaps remain to be filled, we now have some preliminary information with which to evaluate the reports of the early explorers.

The Environment

Tropical forest is the dominant vegetation over an area of some six million square kilometers (2.3 million square miles) east of the Andes, where elevation is below fifteen hundred meters (five thousand feet), relative humidity exceeds 80 percent, precipitation occurs during 130 or more days per year, and temperatures are warm the year round. These conditions prevail in most of the Amazon basin in Brazil and adjacent parts of Bolivia, Peru, Ecuador, Colombia, and Venezuela, as well as Guyana, Surinam, and French Guiana.

Although there is much local and regional diversity in soil, rainfall, flora, and fauna, the most important distinction from the standpoint of human exploitation is between the *varzea* and the *terra firme*. The varzea, comprising only about 2 percent of the area, consists of the floodplains of white-water rivers. These

rivers—actually a murky chocolate rather than white—derive their color from the suspended silt they carry down from the Andean highlands during the rainy season and deposit on islands and banks as water level drops. This annual renewal of fertility, like that of the Tigris-Euphrates and the Nile, makes the soil suitable for continuous intensive agriculture. Careful scheduling of planting so crops matured before inundation and coordinating labor to process and store plant and animal foods for use during the flood season permitted large and permanent settlements ruled by powerful chiefs to develop along the varzea after about A.D. 500.

The remaining 98 percent of Amazonia provides very different conditions. Guiana, an area that includes Guyana, French Guiana, Surinam, and adjoining parts of Brazil and Venezuela, is characterized by highly resistant bedrock. The Guiana and Brazilian uplands

◁ A village of Carajá Indians comes to life as dawn breaks over the Araguaia River, Brazil.

Like other many Amazonian Indian groups, the Yanomami live communally inside a large, palm-thatched hall or *shabono*. Here, women grate manioc tubers for use at a ceremonial occasion.

are among the most ancient terrestrial formations on the planet and have been reduced during millennia of erosion to extremely nutrient-poor soils. Rivers draining from them have been compared to distilled water, so free are they of sediment and soluble nutrients. The terra-firme vegetation efficiently recycles nutrients essential to plant growth. As soon as a leaf drops, it is attacked by decomposers and the nutrients released are taken up by symbiotic fungi in the roots. Agriculture disrupts this recycling: the negative consequences of loss of nutrients, exposure of the soil to sun and rain, and other modifications are manifested in rapidly declining harvests. The indigenous inhabitants of the terra firme adapted to this situation by living in small villages and moving to a different location every five to ten years when land suitable for cultivation within convenient distance was exhausted and hunting became unproductive. Depending on local factors, they could anticipate returning to a site after fifty or more years, the time required for the damage to be restored. In these small communities social organization was egalitarian and behavior was controlled by kinship obligations.

Problems of Reconstructing Prehistoric Adaptation

One reason we know so little about the origins of the two principal kinds of indigenous Amazonian societies is that little has survived. Because of the absence of

appropriate kinds of stone, almost everything was manufactured from wood, bone, tendon, plant fibers, seeds, feathers, and other perishable materials soon destroyed by the hot humid climate. Prior to the adoption of pottery, the principal direct evidence of humans is provided by paintings and engravings on rock surfaces, which occur on the periphery of the Amazonian lowlands.

Following the adoption of pottery, the archaeological situation improves. Although vessels are fragile, fragments are not only durable but also encode a variety of information. Distinctive decorative techniques and motifs serve as tracers of migration and diffusion. Changes in the proportions of pottery types can be used to establish relative chronologies. Comparing the locations of sites through time can tell us much about how people lived and how their societies were organized. Unfortunately, settlement sites were often on riverbanks where they are vulnerable to loss by erosion. When intact, they are often difficult to find unless a local resident has observed fragments of pottery while digging the foundation for a house, clearing a field, or following the trail of an animal. Earthworks occur in a few places, but even large ones may be obscured by vegetation. Cemeteries are undetectable unless the remains were placed in urns, which were interred or set on the surface in rock shelters or in isolated parts of the forest.

Three indirect sources of evidence provide addi-

The Amazon River basin showing the boundaries of the rain forest now and during the dry periods of the Pleistocene (approximately 22,000 to 13,000 years ago). Archaeological sites discussed in the text are noted on the map.

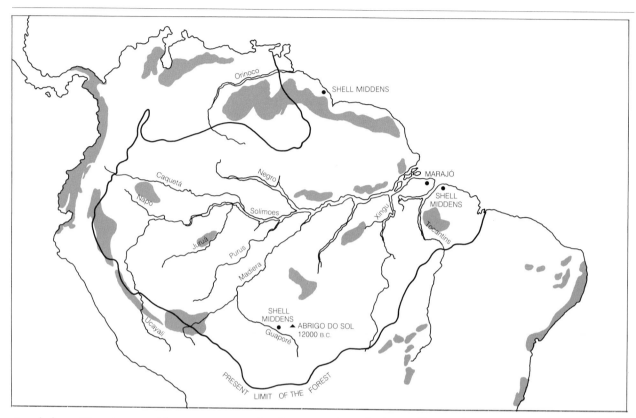

tional clues. Linguists are able to reconstruct the diversification of languages within families and to suggest dates of separation and geographic centers of dispersal, or homelands. They cannot, however, establish the locations of speakers between their departure and the time they were first reported. Ethnological data on subsistence and settlement behavior among surviving indigenous groups provide models for comparison with archaeological remains. Finally, archaeological evidence from the surrounding region where preservation is better can sometimes suggest what may have been happening in the Amazonian "black box," particularly during the millennia prior to the introduction of pottery. The evidence we use to reconstruct Amazonian prehistory is sparse and often inconclusive, but a few patterns are beginning to emerge.

The Earliest Human Occupation of the Lowlands

Compared to tropical Asia and Africa, tropical South America is a relatively recent habitat for our species. Existing evidence suggests that the first immigrants may have arrived via the isthmus of Panama only some fifteen thousand years ago; by contrast, the drama of human evolution took place in the Old World tropics during hundreds of thousands of years. Furthermore, adaptation to Amazonia occurred in relative isolation. Whereas the populations of Southeast Asia and tropical Africa received influences or inva-

sions during millennia from civilizations to the north, lowland South America appears to have been affected little if at all by the states and empires of the Andean highlands and Pacific coast. As a consequence the arrival of Europeans was a catastrophic event rather than another in a series of foreign encroachments.

Carbon-14 dates from reliable contexts indicate that by twelve thousand years ago humans were living east and south of Amazonia. Did these immigrants cross the lowlands or did they move down the Andes and eastward along the low ridges of the Brazilian upland? We may never find conclusive evidence, but there are reasons for believing that Amazonia was populated at the same time as the rest of the South American continent.

An important factor that leads to this conclusion is the character of the lowland environment during the Late Pleistocene-Early Holocene when the earliest migrants entered South America. Data from diverse sources (changes in pollen in lake sediments, biogeographic distributions of plants and animals, and patterns of land forms in the Amazon basin) all suggest that the climate of the lowlands was much drier at that time than it is today or than it was in the early Pleistocene. Under generally lower annual precipitation, the rain forest shrank. Although we don't know the exact extent of the reduction, it is likely that savannas and parklands were a much larger component of the late Pleistocene landscape than they were previously

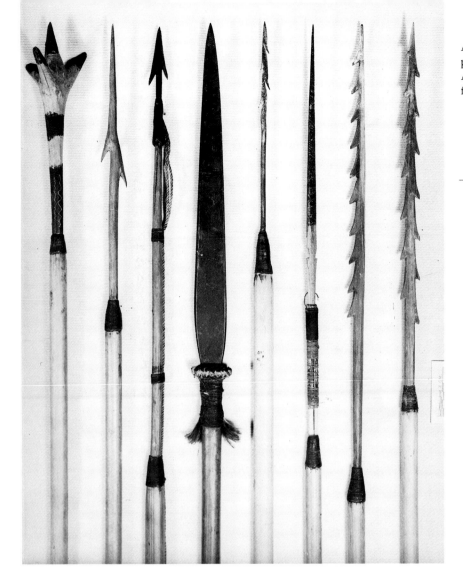

A variety of wooden spear points used by contemporary Amazonian groups to hunt different kinds of game and fish.

or are today. People accustomed to exploiting the plant and animal resources in grasslands and gallery forests to the north would thus have had the necessary skills to move across the central Amazon basin during the Late Pleistocene.

Nor would the absence of stone suitable for making tools have been a serious impediment. Early Indian groups in North America are known to have used bone rather than or in addition to stone for many purposes, and bone projectile points have been found in early sites east and south of Amazonia. The absence of stone points in Abrigo do Sol, a large rock shelter within the southern limit of the present forest occupied during the past twelve thousand years, also implies use of perishable substitutes.

Adaptation to the Rain Forest
Throughout the Americas the transition from the older Pleistocene era to the present Holocene was a time of drastic environmental change. In Amazonia the climate became wetter, allowing the rain forest to re-expand and replace more open formations. Small seasonal rivers developed into permanent watercourses. Animals associated with these habitats became more widely distributed. The alterations were probably sufficiently gradual that humans were unaware of their own adaptation to the new conditions. In the forests, however, they would have found hardwood trees that could be made into spear points effective for specific kinds of prey. Similarly, multiplication of varieties of vines, bamboos, and palms may have stimulated diversification of basketry, nets, snares, traps, and other kinds of artifacts useful for catching land and river fauna. Increasing familiarity with forest plants expanded the repertoire of foods and medicines, as well as poisons that increased the success of hunting and fishing.

Several kinds of archaeological remains dating from about six thousand years ago provide direct evidence of adaptation to different sets of resources. Large accumulations of shells on the coasts of Guyana and east of the mouth of the Amazon, as well as the swamps along the middle Guaporé River not far from Abrigo do Sol, show that human groups were seasonally using aquatic and terrestrial mollusks for food. The huge accumulations in the latter region consist of layers of crushed shell alternating with what must have been the floors of their homes. Postholes mark the locations of perishable shelters. The refuse contains a variety of tools made of bone and stone. Flattened baked-clay balls may have been used with bolas, a hunting device that was still being used on the pampas of Argentina when Europeans arrived.

A second and more widespread way of life is suggested by rock art on the surfaces of boulders and cliffs throughout northern South America. Although dates are not available, similarities of biomorphic and geometric elements to North American styles suggest that they may have been produced by the earliest

Modern Yanomami Indians hunt with arrows tipped in a poison derived from a forest vine.

immigrants. The occurrence of this style in South America north and south of the present limits of the tropical forest implies these populations were using a broad range of savanna and forest resources available throughout the lowlands at the end of the Pleistocene. Although the significance of the representations can never be ascertained, we think that some were intended to placate supernatural guardians of the animals and to insure an adequate supply of food.

Another style of rock painting occurs in the beds of streams in the forests of southern Guyana and eastern Colombia. These depictions of fish and devices interpreted as fishtraps are in locations invisible except during years of exceptionally low water, suggesting they were produced when the climate was drier than today. The only evidence of humans in central Amazonia around this time comes from the hunter-gatherers who camped on the same high banks later occupied by pottery-making groups.

It seems likely that the Amazonian staples, manioc and sweet potatoes, were domesticated during these millennia. Since wild forms occur throughout tropical America and the wet climate rapidly destroys organic remains, we may never know when and where they began to be cultivated. The appearance of sweet manioc about 1000 B.C. on the coast of Peru, where wild relatives of this crop do not occur, implies that domestication had been accomplished before that time. Manioc is an ideal staple for Amazonian terra-firme

populations because it flourishes in nutrient-poor soils, tolerates drought, has a high yield, and can be harvested throughout the year. It thus provides a reliable permanent source of carbohydrates in contrast to the seasonal availability of most wild plant foods.

These advantages are offset by the low concentration of essential nutrients, especially protein. The danger of overdependence on manioc is vividly illustrated by the prevalence of kwashiorkor, a protein deficiency syndrome, among tropical African populations that adopted this staple after the discovery of America. In Amazonia, by contrast, the transition to agriculture was apparently slow among terra-firme groups, who developed a combination of animal, wild plant, and cultivated foods that provided a balanced diet. This system dictated the size and nature of their groups. Since their only domesticated animal was the dog, which was not eaten, human communities had to hunt a good deal and therefore remained small, mobile, and dispersed. These restrictions made the kinds of sociopolitical and economic organization associated with states and empires both unsustainable and unnecessary.

The Origin and Spread of Pottery

The earliest pottery comes from sites on the large island of Marajó at the mouth of the Amazon, which date about 1400 B.C. Since pottery is too fragile and bulky to be compatible with the mobile existence of hunter-gatherers, its presence suggests that settled vil-

These elaborately decorated pottery vessels of the Marajoara culture are typical of the more complex level of development achieved by groups living along the *varzea* in pre-Columbian times. These two examples, one with an excised design, the other painted, were made on Marajó Island at the mouth of the Amazon between A.D. 400 and 1000.

lage life had been adopted by this time. Small village sites along streams in forest are comparable in area to the single communal dwellings used by many surviving indigenous groups. Pollen profiles reveal that the climate was wetter than today and that much of the land now occupied by savanna was forested. Agriculture may have been practiced, but wild plant and animal foods were probably prolific and may have been sufficient (along with fish and aquatic mammals) to sustain small settled communities. About 1000 B.C. the initial inhabitants of Marajó were assimilated by invaders who made different ceramics but were otherwise culturally similar. About 800 B.C. the forest began to give way to savanna and the island appears to have been abandoned by sedentary pottery-making groups.

During the last eight centuries B.C. populations in the many other parts of Amazonia also appear to have suffered hard times. Linguists date the long-range dispersals of the major South American language families to these centuries. Reconstructing what happened during these times is one of the most significant challenges facing archaeologists because after the beginning of the Christian Era, major changes again occur. Sites become numerous and pottery is more elaborate and diversified. This heterogeneity is a consequence of long- and short-range movements by groups of varying sizes and origins, who were exposed to different kinds of experiences and influences that they accepted, rejected, or modified in different ways. Pottery was certainly not the only cultural trait thus affected; it is simply the one that has survived.

Prehistoric Cultural Adaptation
Basic patterns of settlement and subsistence behavior similar to those on Marajó seem to have been established throughout the terra firme in the first century and their persistence among surviving Indian groups implies they reflect successful adaptations. Village sites often extend two hundred meters or more along the riverbanks. But careful examination shows that these represent multiple reoccupations of a site separated by periods of abandonment rather than large and permanent settlements. The varying combinations of large and small sites indicate that villages fissioned and fused in ways similar to what Amazonian groups do today. In general, the largest social unit seems to have been several extended families occupying one or more communal dwellings. Like similar communities today, they probably joined together for festivals, intermarried, and may have raided their neighbors. They seem to have moved within a territory whose boundaries remained relatively stable during several centuries. Men and women probably performed different tasks, but social and economic differences between members of these groups were small.

Sites reflecting a different way of life on the var-

In pre-Columbian times various groups interred their dead in urns. Some buried these urns, while others set them in isolated locations such as this rock outcrop on the Rupununi savanna in southern Guyana.

zea appear along the banks of the Amazon and its tributary, the Madeira, also during the first century. Although we still know little about how their inhabitants lived, there is some evidence suggesting that these sites represent larger and more stable settlements than existed on the terra firme. The elaborate decoration of pottery vessels and the burial of some individuals in anthropomorphic urns imply differences in social status similar to those reported by early Europeans.

Societies of this level of complexity require abundant, reliable, and concentrated subsistence resources. The first European explorers in the sixteenth century reported systematic exploitation of the resources of the varzea. Live turtles were kept in pens at the river edge; corn and other crops were grown on the fertile flood-plain soil; turtle eggs were collected and converted into oil in which manatee meat was preserved. Activities had to be coordinated with the rise and fall of the river, which required careful scheduling of the work force. Kinship obligations, sufficient to regulate the smaller, mobile terra-firme communities, were inadequate, so both social stratification and occupational specialization developed. An upper limit on population growth appears to have been set by the unpredictable oscillations of the river. When the water rose earlier and higher than normal, crops were destroyed. When it remained below normal, the floodplain did not receive its annual coating of silt. These uncertainties could not be countered by storing food, which

was feasible in drier climates. Existing archaeological evidence suggests that varzea communities reached their maximum level of complexity during the early centuries of the Christian Era, which was maintained without significant elaboration until European contact.

Increasing knowledge of the climate and biota of Amazonia is enhancing our ability to understand the adaptive aspects of these two general cultural configurations. Biologists have shown that plants may fail to flower when the rainy season is delayed. Animals dependent on nuts and fruits may starve or fail to reproduce. Fluctuations in the beginning and intensity of rainfall also have drastic effects on high and low water levels of the rivers and on the survival and reproduction of aquatic plants and animals. Humans are doubly jeopardized since they consume both plants and animals. In addition to these normal variations, evidence from pollen suggests there have been several periods of drought of different intensities and durations during the past five millennia, but the temporary local effects on the biota are still poorly known.

Adaptation to such uncertainties involved keeping the human population size and density at levels compatible with what the environment could support during lean years. Natural controls on population increase, such as malnutrition, were supplemented by a variety of cultural practices including food taboos, warfare, sorcery, blood revenge, and infanticide. On the terra firme, the requirement of abandoning a communal house on the death of the head offset any tendency to occupy a village long enough to cause long-term damage to the local environment. Garden clearings were sufficiently small to permit rapid regeneration of the forest and to minimize degradation of the soil. In addition, they created space suitable for secondary vegetation, increasing plant diversity and providing additional food sources for animals, which indirectly compensated to some extent for the effects of hunting. Recent studies of surviving terra-firme societies are revealing the subtlety and complexity of their integrations with the forest and the depth of their knowledge of its resources.

The functioning of the more complex varzea societies is obscured by the absence of surviving examples. The rich agricultural potential of the varzea was exploited by emphasis on corn, a crop of Mesoamerican origin that requires fertile soils. These populations also had access to terra-firme resources to supplement those of the floodplain. Although less vulnerable to fluctuations in local rainfall, they were confronted with unpredictable variations in the timing and intensity of flooding. Modern towns import food to supplement local resources, but pre-Columbian societies had no such option. In this context reports of practices that limited population increase on the terra firme—among them infanticide, blood revenge, and warfare—be-

These petroglyph designs found in Guyana are believed to have been drawn by some of the earliest immigrants to the region.

This modern village on the island of Marajó at the mouth of the Amazon floods seasonally with the rise and fall of the river.

come intelligible. It is unfortunate that so little information exists on prehistoric methods of exploiting varzea resources, since their application might permit more successful intensive use of the region today.

We can only speculate on the nature of relations between varzea groups and their terra-firme neighbors. Although early European accounts describe warfare, archaeological evidence suggests that adaptation to both habitats was too specialized to encourage territorial expansion in either direction. Even less is known about relations between terra-firme agriculturalists and hunter-gatherers. A recent study on the Rio Negro, a black-water river poor in fish, revealed that hunter-gatherers of the interior exchanged game for manioc grown by their more sedentary riverine neighbors. Such reciprocity in subsistence resources permitted larger populations in both kinds of habitats than could be sustained by local resources.

Some observers have interpreted the failure of Amazonian populations to develop the levels of cultural complexity attained in the adjacent Andean region as evidence of cultural stagnation. Even the superficial description given here of the constraints inherent in a habitat characterized by nutrient-deficient soils, dispersed plant and animal resources, and fluctuating seasonal rhythms makes it clear that stagnation is an inappropriate term. The skills and knowledge necessary to thrive under such conditions are truly remarkable. We should attempt to learn as much as we can from the native Amazonians before we drive the few survivors to extinction.

Many of the data on which this chapter is based were collected by Ondemar Dias, Eurico Miller, Bernardo Dougherty, Celso Perota, and Mario Simoes during fieldwork supported by the Neotropical Lowland Research Program of the Smithsonian Institution.

4

THE PREHISTORY
OF THE
ASIAN RAIN FORESTS

KARL L. HUTTERER

In May 1986 I spent a few days with the Penan, a group of hunter-gatherers who live in the interior forests of the island of Borneo. I had come to visit Pete Brosius, a graduate student at the University of Michigan, who had been living with the group for two years. Although far from being uncontacted, the Penan remain one of the most remote and traditional groups of forest people in the world. A two-hour ride by helicopter took me from the government capital Kuching (Sarawak, Malaysian part of Borneo) to the camp. The "heli" was supplied courtesy of the government power company, which is planning a monumental hydroelectric dam in the region. The way back took four days by foot, dugout canoe, logging trucks, motorized boats, and, finally, airplane.

The Penan are highly adapted to living in the forest: they hunt forest animals (particularly wild boar, *Sus barbatus*) and collect plants for their food; they use raw materials from the forest for clothing, shelter, and virtually all other material needs; and they weave fibers found in the forest into fine mats and baskets, which they sell to tribal groups farther downriver (who in turn often sell them for good profit in coastal towns). To me, an archaeologist, visiting the Penan was a fascinating experience. How long, I wondered, had people lived in the forest? Had they lived the same way for thousands of years? Indeed, was there a rain forest in Borneo thousands of years ago?

Plotting Prehistoric Forests

We often assume that tropical forests, "virgin jungles," have existed forever. The massiveness and majesty of rain-forest trees evoke an image of primeval origins, and botanists and geologists tell us that there is some basis for this impression. Many millions of years ago, the world was warmer than it is now, and tropical environments predominated over much of it. The history of humans and their immediate ancestors, however, extends back only two to three million years. This period falls mostly within the Pleistocene, a time span characterized by long-term climatic oscillations in which warm and cool cycles alternated, each lasting roughly one hundred thousand years.

Geologists and paleontologists have been able to reconstruct to a remarkable degree the effects these climatic fluctuations had on mid-latitude and northern environments. Much less is known about the impact of Pleistocene climatic oscillations on tropical environments. We do know that during the cool periods much of the global water reserve was bound up in massive glaciers that covered large portions of northern Eurasia and the North American continent. This drastically lowered the levels of the water reservoirs in the world's oceans, exposing large expanses of continental shelves that are now covered by water. In Southeast Asia, most of what now constitutes the larger islands of the region became linked to the Asian mainland through the exposure of what is known as the Sunda Shelf. The region's land area was effectively doubled.

Global fluctuations in temperature also affected the tropics. Some think the mean annual temperatures may at times have dropped by as much as five to seven degrees Centigrade (nine to thirteen degrees Fahrenheit), a serious drop but not in itself sufficient to wipe out tropical life. More important, the combined effect of changes in temperature and land area and the presence of vast glaciated regions to the north (and smaller ones to the south) must have had an impact on the patterns of prevailing winds and on the movement of rain-bringing tropical fronts. With these fluctuating patterns of rainfall, the humid rain forests of Southeast Asia probably contracted and expanded in area several times during the Pleistocene.

Unfortunately, we have very little specific and reliable information on this period. Since humans (*Homo sapiens*) and human predecessors (*Homo erectus*) have been present in Southeast Asia for a million years or more, it would naturally be of great value to know to what environments these early inhabitants had to adapt and to be able to study the long-range interactions of people with rain forests. We do know that during some periods of the Pleistocene large grazing and browsing animals (such as several species of stegodon and elephant) were present in parts of the region that have more recently been covered by rain forests, indicating that those areas may then have been open parklands or savannas. Paleontologists have also dug into the muddy bottoms of lakes and swamps where plant pollen can be preserved for many thousands of years. Most of the pollen sites studied are located in the highlands (one thousand meters/three thousand feet or more above sea level). The pollen from these sites shows that the vegetation in the highlands changed repeatedly under the influence of fluctuating climatic conditions. Unfortunately, we have so far very little evidence for the lowlands, where the typical rain forests are found.

The contemporary environments of Southeast Asia correspond very broadly to climatic and vegetational patterns found in other tropical regions of the world such as Africa and South America, allowing, of course, for specific local conditions caused primarily by the configuration of land masses. A significant factor affecting Southeast Asia is that the region is divided into a mainland portion and a large maritime portion dotted with thousands of large and small islands. Generally, humid tropical conditions without a significant dry season tend to prevail in a zone between about five degrees north and south of the equator. The large amount and relatively even distribution of rainfall fosters an evergreen moist tropical forest of enormous luxuriance, with hundreds of species of giant trees, dense canopies, and multitudes of climbing vines. Moving away from the equator in either direction, the length and severity of annual dry periods tend to increase; rainfall is concentrated mostly in the annual monsoon season. With these conditions, the forest declines in luxuriance, height, species diversity, and density and becomes more deciduous. This type of forest is often referred to as "monsoon forest." In general, the native vegetation of almost all of Southeast Asia consists of tropical forests of one sort or another.

Prehistoric Hunters and Collectors in the Forest

Southern and southeastern Asia have been settled for a million years or more, but we know little about the life of these earliest human ancestors. What we know derives from fossilized human teeth and fragments of skulls and arm and leg bones that were all found on the island of Java. This evidence is so limited that, when laid out, it occupies only the space of a single laboratory table.

Our knowledge of the period between 40,000 to 10,000 B.C. is somewhat better, due to the existence of sites scattered across Indonesia, the Philippines, Malaysia, and Vietnam. In these sites, mostly caves and rock shelters, stone tools have been found and even animal bones representing the remains of meals. We can deduce that these are remains of hunters and collectors, but little more. Since the sites are few and widely scattered, it remains difficult to reconstruct in detail the behavior and lifeways of their inhabitants. Indeed, given our hazy knowledge about the fluctuations of prehistoric environments in the region, we cannot even be sure whether any of the sites were, at the time of their occupation, actually located in the rain forest. This is an important question since anthropologists and ecologists are uncertain if it is possible to exist in the rain forest by hunting and collecting alone.

In 1974 Douglas Anderson, a professor of anthropology at Brown University, began excavations at Lang Rongrien, a rock shelter on the rocky but scenic western coast of south Thailand. Lang Rongrien is one of the few sites we know that was used starting around 40,000 B.C., but its use continued in one form or another until present times. Between 40,000 and 10,000 B.C., when sea levels were lower, the site would have been some distance inland. Around 10,000 B.C., when sea levels were rising and flooding what had been low-lying coastal regions, it became situated on the coast. Anderson noted a dramatic change in the stone tools used at the site from this time. While the

Pleistocene inhabitants of Lang Rongrien made a large variety of rather sophisticated flake tools (that is, implements fashioned from small stone chips), the people living there around ten thousand years ago relied heavily on sturdy, chipped river pebbles (pebble tools) as well as flakes for cutting and scraping implements. The change in technology coincides with a change from a cooler and drier to a wetter and hotter climate, probably entailing the establishment (or reestablishment) of rain forests in the area. Anderson thinks that there may have been a connection between the two events.

Similar pebble-tool assemblages had been found by French archaeologists in the province of Hoabinh in northern Vietnam more than fifty years ago and since then in much of mainland Southeast Asia, as well as on the islands of Sumatra and Luzon. Although the artifacts found in sites like these differ from region to region, there are persistent similarities as well, and their makers and users seem to have been very similar to each other in the ways in which they made their living. Many of the Hoabinhian sites are caves and rock shelters situated along streams and rivers in the hilly or mountainous interior. Remains of prehistoric meals, in the form of bits of animal bone and the like, indicate that these people hunted and collected an enormous variety of terrestrial and aquatic animals. Among them are rhinoceros, various sorts of cattle, wild pig, several kinds of deer, porcupines, monkeys and apes, tortoises, as well as freshwater and marine snails, bivalves, crustaceans, and fish. Less commonly found are elephants, squirrels, civet cats, rats, bats, hares, bears, tigers, dugongs (sea cows), and various reptiles. Obviously, remains of all these animals are not found in every site, but every site does have a remarkable number of species. In all, the animal bones reflect a hunting pattern that exploits a very broad range of animals found in the rain forest and along its fringes, a pattern that is shared by most contemporary hunting societies in Southeast Asia. This pattern is often described as a "broad spectrum" foraging pattern and is closely linked to the ecological diversity of the tropical forest. In this diversity, however, neither particular kinds of plants nor animals tend to occur in high concentrations in any given place, so the best strategy for collecting them is clearly one that can accommodate a very broad range of potential foods.

Some Hoabinhian sites located along the coasts of Vietnam, the Malay Peninsula, and Sumatra are not in caves but involve mounds of shellfish remains (known as "shell middens"). Many of these sites are very large, up to two hundred and more feet long, one hundred feet wide, and twenty feet thick. They consist mainly of the discarded remains of marine shellfish, ash, soil, and some bones of a variety of hunted forest game. These sites seem to represent a specialized exploitation of marine resources, perhaps by hunting bands who moved between forest and seashore according to seasonal conditions, a pattern that is common also among some contemporary hunters in Southeast Asia, such as the Agta of northeastern Luzon. It is apparent that all Hoabinhian peoples seem to have complemented the food they extracted from the forest with aquatic resources from rivers, streams, or the ocean.

Unfortunately, we do not at present know very much about plant foods collected by Hoabinhian peoples. Much of what we know comes from one site, Spirit Cave, in northern Thailand. The site was excavated in 1965 by Chester Gorman, then a doctoral student in anthropology at the University of Hawaii. The small cave was in occasional use as a camp between about 12,000 and 6,000 B.C. Through careful sieving of the dirt, Gorman found a remarkable number of plant remains, among them bits of nutshells and seed kernels from tree crops such as candlenut, canarium nut, butternut, terminalia nut, chestnut, and mango; materials or seeds deriving from bushes or bushlike plants such as bamboo, hackberry, and caster bean; vegetables such as bottle gourd, cucumber, water chestnut, broad bean, lotus, and bitter melon; and seeds of stimulants such as betel palm and betel plant. Spirit Cave is a small place and could have been used only by a family-size group. The vegetal foods collected by the group come from trees and shrubs still found today in the monsoon forests of the area and from "disturbances" (or openings) in the forest. The people of Spirit Cave exploited a broad spectrum of plant resources, which is consistent with their approach to hunting and with the ecology of tropical forests in general.

Since several of the seeds of fruits and vegetables found at Spirit Cave come from openings in the forest, Gorman and his teacher, Wilhelm Solheim, argued that these openings may have been small clearings or gardens and that the people of Spirit Cave were among the first people in the world to experiment with farming. This is an attractive idea since there is a question whether tropical forests actually produce enough edible plant food to sustain human communities. Unfortunately, it has so far not been possible to verify Gorman's suggestion—or to disprove it. Gorman made another interesting observation related to the nature of tropical forests: in many of the Hoabinhian sites, one finds grinding stones, very often stained red and associated with lumps of red ocher (hematite). Gorman suggested that the hematite was used in food processing to extract or neutralize poisonous compounds that are found in so many tropical plants. It all makes sense: many tropical forest peoples today eat poisonous plants after carefully preparing them; but, again, there is no firm proof.

Many sites occupied by prehistoric hunters and

◁ The Penan still make their living primarily from hunting and gathering in the rain forests of Borneo. Here a Penan man leaves on a hunting trip.

BELOW: A Penan woman begins to weave a mat of rattan, the fiber of a climbing palm.

CENTER: Penan blowgun darts are tipped with a poison and dried in front of a fire.

BOTTOM: Starch from the pith of the sago palm is extracted by washing it through a basket of rattan fiber. The sago palm is a major source of dietary starch for these non-farming people.

collectors after 10,000 B.C. are also found in the Southeast Asian islands. They differ from the mainland sites in that their tool assemblages rarely include pebble tools of the type found in great abundance in Hoabinhian sites. For the rest, however, if one accounts for specific differences in the environments in which they are located, the assemblages of animals and plants associated with them suggest a way of life remarkably similar to that represented by the Hoabinhian sites. In all, the archaeological picture presented is one of very small and highly mobile bands who hunt a wide variety of animals and collect a multitude of plants available in the forest or along its edges, that is, along the shores of rivers and lakes or the clearings created by tree fall.

Much of our information about the life of prehistoric peoples comes from their tools. They were used to extract food and other necessities from the environment, and they should therefore tell us something about the environment and how prehistoric peoples coped with it.

Pebble tools are common and important in Hoabinhian sites on the Southeast Asian mainland, while they are rare in island sites of the same period (ca. 10,000–5,000 B.C.). Does this reflect differences in the environments of mainland and island Southeast Asia at that period? Pebble tools were probably designed primarily for heavy-duty work such as chopping, while flake tools were meant for lighter tasks such as cutting and whittling. There are different types of pebble tools, with some types being more common in, say, Vietnam, others in Malaysia. It is likely that the varying preferences reflect technological adaptations to different environmental conditions, although we need to learn more about prehistoric environments before we can answer this question with certainty.

Several stone-tool technologies were used by post-Pleistocene hunters in the Southeast Asian islands. Many of these technologies are exceedingly simple in appearance, involving seemingly little more than smashing a rock and picking out from among the flakes and chips pieces that were suitable for a given task. I excavated such stone tools at Sohoton Cave in the Philippines in 1971. Tools like these were used over a long period of time, from ten thousand to five hundred years ago. Many similar finds have been reported from elsewhere in the islands, mostly from rain forest areas. Older generations of archaeologists sometimes thought that these tools reflected a simplicity of mind and lack of skill. We now think that these tools are highly functional within their ecological context. Rain forests are replete with such plant materials as hardwoods, bamboos, and rattans that furnish excellent raw materials for a wide variety of tools and implements. Microscopic analysis of traces of wear on the tool edges suggests that the prehistoric hunters

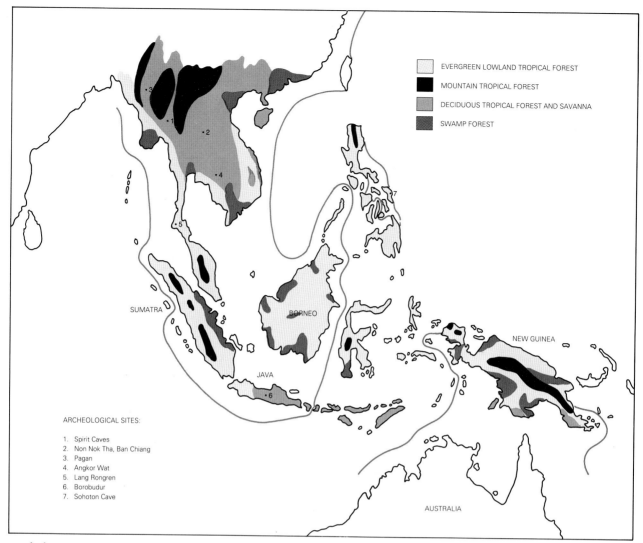

EVERGREEN LOWLAND TROPICAL FOREST

MOUNTAIN TROPICAL FOREST

DECIDUOUS TROPICAL FOREST AND SAVANNA

SWAMP FOREST

SUMATRA

BORNEO

NEW GUINEA

JAVA

ARCHEOLOGICAL SITES:

1. Spirit Caves
2. Non Nok Tha, Ban Chiang
3. Pagan
4. Angkor Wat
5. Lang Rongren
6. Borobudur
7. Sohoton Cave

AUSTRALIA

used the stone implements primarily to manufacture other tools made of woody materials. Probably these wooden tools were then used for hunting, trapping, and collecting. Unfortunately tools made from organic materials do not usually survive, and this interpretation remains largely speculative. Under tropical forest conditions using simple stone tools to make specialized wooden tools would have been a very economical way of putting together a technology that could allow effective hunting, trapping, and collecting of a very great variety of resources. Most tropical forest animals are highly specialized, being spatially distributed between forest floor and tree crowns and being active during different parts of the day or night. Many contemporary forest peoples in Southeast Asia follow similar strategies of maintaining diverse and highly specialized traps, arrows, nets, and baskets, all made of easily available materials, to hunt a broad range of animals and collect a broad range of plant resources occupying specialized niches in the forest.

Contemporary Hunters and Collectors

Southeast Asia is one of the few regions of the world where hunting and collecting peoples still exist. One can find them in the remaining tropical forests of the Philippines, Borneo, Sumatra, Malaysia, and Thailand. Do these societies carry on a tradition of hunting and foraging in tropical forests that has remained unaltered for many thousands of years? Can they be used as models for reconstructing the life ways of prehis-

toric, even Pleistocene-age, hunting societies? And why have they clung to hunting and collecting in the presence of apparently superior ways of making a living such as agriculture?

One thing stands out: virtually all contemporary hunting societies in Southeast Asia rely, to a greater or lesser extent, on economic exchanges with nearby agricultural societies. Most of the foragers clearly have the environmental knowledge and technological capabilities to survive in the forest in isolation, if necessary, but they choose not to do so. The Agta of Luzon, for instance, provide the neighboring Palanan farmers with wild meat and occasional field labor during periods of peak demand in exchange for rice, corn, and small amounts of cash to buy cloth and other goods offered in coastal markets. The Penan of Borneo make beautiful mats and baskets, which they trade for rice, cash, and manufactured goods. Other hunting groups collect resins, beeswax, rattan, and medicinal herbs, which they exchange again for agricultural starch staples and such industrial products as cloth, iron, beads, and, more recently, transistor radios.

Such interactions between foragers and farmers are pervasive throughout Southeast Asia (as well as Africa) but seem to be less common in Amazonia. They are often seen as symbiotic, that is, as providing important benefits to both parties. The rationale for these relationships can be seen in the rain-forest ecology. The common thread is the acquisition of carbohydrate staples by the hunters. This suggests that

Pebble tools of the Hoabinhian period of Vietnam.

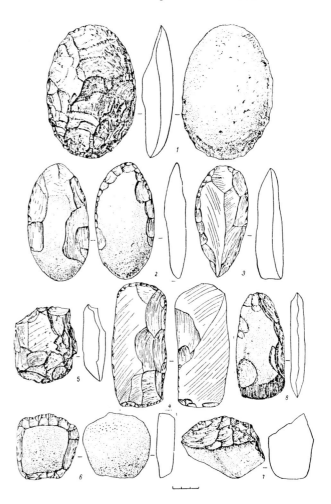

the limiting factor for maintaining and expanding human populations in Southeast Asian rain forests is the availability of starch foods. This is not to say that starchy foods are not available. On the contrary, they occur in a great variety of forms including roots (wild yams), fruits (bananas), palm pith (sago), cereals growing in disturbed areas (Job's tears), and so forth. These resources are, however, highly dispersed and, once harvested, reproduce only slowly. Collecting and preparing them often requires considerable effort.

It may be that enough starchy food simply does not exist in most rain forests to supply even small human groups on a reliable, long-term basis. In that case, prehistoric hunter-gatherers could not have lived in the deep forest but must have been more oriented toward its edges where they could collect food from several different habitats. The archaeological evidence is too fragmentary at present to prove this notion, but the fact that the Hoabinhians so consistently combined terrestrial food sources with aquatic foods supports it. According to this theory, occupation of interior forest areas would have become possible only after farmers, from whom complementary starch foods could be obtained, had established themselves along the forest edges. It is also possible that life in the deep forest has always been possible, but that, after farmers appeared on the scene, it was easier and more efficient to trade forest goods for farm products than to rely simply on collecting roots and seeds. In that case, the life of prehistoric forest peoples underwent a major change after they came in contact with farmers. A major challenge to archaeologists is to determine just how long hunting communities have lived in the interior rain forests of Southeast Asia and how they adapted to these environments over thousands of years.

There are no good comparative studies of the potential resources offered human foragers in Southeast Asian and Amazonian rain forests. Anthropologists have long debated whether the availability of animals (protein) in tropical South America is a major limiting factor for human populations living in the forest. Wild meat is one of the major products forest peoples in Southeast Asia provide to their agricultural trading partners; if there is a limiting set of resources, it would have to be starchy plants. It is possible that Southeast Asian and Amazonian rain forests differ in this regard.

Hunting communities are not the only ones that profit from the trade with farmers. The exchange is also to the advantage of farmers. Hunters provide cheap labor at crucial times in the agricultural cycle, and they provide raw materials that are essential in traditional Southeast Asian technology: for example, rattan has multiple uses in building and fastening, resins are used for caulking boats and for making torches. Farmers convert forest land into fields, but they must also rely on forest resources. In this dilemma between exploiting the forest for products and converting it to farmland, hunting communities are the ideal intermediaries. If this scenario is correct, it explains why hunter-gatherers still exist in the region today. The need for forest products by farmers opened an economic niche for specialized forest exploitation that some communities were willing to fill.

This adaptation to the forest is surely different from the life of Pleistocene-age foragers, but it has probably existed for several thousand years and has become an economic, technological, and social tradition of its own. It is only now seriously threatened by extinction. Logging, the drowning of vast watersheds to create hydroelectric dams, and the expansion of farmlands to feed growing populations is causing the destruction of huge areas that were once the habitat of foragers. When the Penan hitch a ride on a logging truck, they are quite aware that they are rolling down a road toward cultural and social extinction.

Prehistoric Farmers

It is naïve to think that small bands of hunters and collectors have no impact whatsoever on the forest environment. Terry Rambo, an anthropologist at the East-West Center in Honolulu, has studied a group of Semang foragers in Malaysia and found that they create considerable pollution, that they even cut young trees in order to get more easily at the fruit, and that they pluck plants from the forest to replant them in the

Wild boar provide the main source of animal protein and fat to the Penan of Borneo. A Penan hunter butchers a large pig.

clearings where they have set up camp. Pete Brosius has observed the Penan engaging in intensive management of sago palms, primarily by pruning them on a regular basis. Sago is one of the Penan's most important food sources and is, in fact, so productive that the Penan might well be able to supply themselves with sufficient starch without outside help. They may be an exception to the theory that availability of starch limits population size in rain forests.

Nevertheless, the impact of foragers on the forest is relatively insignificant because of their small numbers. By contrast, farmers have a much more severe impact, both because of their larger numbers and because farming is a far more drastic form of environmental interference. Even agriculture if it is to be successful, however, must be pursued in concert with given environmental conditions. There are two areas in which this relationship is most clearly expressed: in the set of plants and animals selected from the native environment for domestication and cultivation and in cultivation practices.

The diversity of tropical forests harbors a rich array of plants and animals that could potentially be domesticated. Indeed, every tropical region of the world has contributed important elements to the world's store of foods. Domesticated and cultivated foods deriving from the Asian tropics can tentatively be divided into two groups: those originating in the humid tropical zone and those originating in seasonal zones. Among staples of the first category are taro and banana, while crops in the second category include yam, a type of arrowroot, and sugar cane. Rice is the most important contemporary foodstuff originating in Asia. It feeds a large portion of the world's population, but the history of its domestication is still poorly known. Besides these staples, many other important domesticates derive from the Asian tropics. Among them are vegetables (eggplant, certain beans, and cucumbers), tree crops (coconut, breadfruit, citrus, mango), many important industrial raw materials (Manila hemp), and spices.

Three major sets of cultivation methods can be distinguished: swidden, permanent fields, and house gardens. Slash-and-burn (swidden) fields are small plots cleared from the forest, burned, and cultivated by hand for only a few years. By Western standards, swidden fields appear untidy, a jumble of diverse plants raised between the hulks of incompletely burned trees. To some degree, however, swidden fields mimic the complex ecology of the rain forest and, if cultivated only a few years, can be highly productive. Cultivation in permanent fields usually focuses on a single crop, traditionally rice or taro in irrigated plots, although secondary foods may be collected from permanent fields as well (rice fields, for instance, often provide snails and small fish). Draft animals are frequently used for soil preparation. Finally, house gardens are small but ecologically extremely complex plots in the

Temple ruins at Borobudur, Java, Indonesia, are the remnants of an early, highly developed trading empire.

vicinity of the home that furnish a variety of vegetables, fruits, and condiments. House gardens are always complementary to one or both of the other methods of cultivation.

Before the advent of modern archaeological research, it was generally assumed that the history of agriculture in tropical Asia started with the domestication of root crops and their cultivation in swidden fields, progressing later to the cultivation of dry rice in swiddens, and eventually to growing wet rice in irrigated fields. Ecological facts make this unlikely: some ancient root crops, such as most varieties of taro, must be grown in inundated fields. Rice is also originally a water plant; its use in dry fields must be a later adaptation. It is likely that swidden cultivation originated in the seasonal tropics where it is relatively easy to burn vegetation during the long dry season. Wetland cultivation, however, seems more suited to the humid tropics, where swampy areas abound. Archaeological evidence is still meager.

When Chester Gorman raised the possibility that some eleven thousand years ago Southeast Asian peoples experimented with raising plants, it stirred a debate that has so far not been settled. The earliest known remains of cultivated plants are those of rice found in mound sites from the third or fourth millennium B.C. in northeastern Thailand, which is today a zone of tropical parklands but at that time was probably wetter than it is now. In sites like Non Nok Tha and Ban

Chiang (the latter is known for very extravagantly painted pottery), the rice occurs primarily in the form of chaff used for tempering clay in the manufacture of pottery. Even earlier remains of rice have been found farther to the north in sites located in the swampy Yangtze delta dating to about seven thousand years ago. Intriguing findings have been reported from Kuk Swamp in the central highlands of New Guinea, where an extensive system of drainage canals was first constructed about nine thousand years ago and intermittently used and reconstructed until a few hundred years ago. Unfortunately, no actual plant remains have been found, so what was grown at Kuk Swamp is not known, although taro is a strong possibility.

As I argued earlier, with the advent of agriculture, a pattern of interaction developed between groups specializing in farming and others specializing in the exploitation of the forest by foraging. Not surprisingly, sites of hunter-gatherers dating to the fourth millennium B.C. and later almost invariably contain some evidence for domesticated plants and animals, while farming settlements usually yield remains of resources derived from the forest. There is some supporting archaeological evidence, then, that farm and forest economies developed interdependently.

Most tropical soils are relatively poor and ill-suited for agriculture. Until the rapid expansion of populations and agricultural technology in the nineteenth and twentieth centuries, permanent field cultivation was mainly limited to coastal lowlands and river bottoms enriched with nutrients by annual floods and some areas with volcanic soils. Elsewhere, swidden cultivation predominated. Although swiddening did have a definite impact on the forest, this was not very different in principle from natural forest dynamics of tree fall and regrowth. It is only in our age that forests are being cut rapidly and extensively; expanding farming populations move in behind the loggers to settle upland areas and establish permanent field farms there, preventing forest regeneration. The results are devastating. Not only are thousands of rare tropical species lost forever (without even having been classified) but farming systems are put in jeopardy; shallow tropical soils erode in a few years; rivers are clogged with sediment; monsoonal flooding is worse than anybody remembers; local climates are affected; and valuable forest products disappear forever.

Forests and Empires

Roughly around 500 B.C., major kingdoms and empires began to develop throughout Southeast Asia. Pyu (Burma), Champa (southern Vietnam), Funan (Cambodia?), and Srivijaya (Malay Peninsula and Sumatra) are some of the more important (or better known) among them. Much of their cultural accouterment in terms of religion, art, dance, and literature shows strong connections with India (and, to a lesser extent, China), eventually finding its most vivid expression in the great temple complexes of Pagan (Burma), Angkor Wat (Cambodia), and Borobudur (Java). Among an earlier generation of scholars, this connection raised the suspicion that civilization was brought intact to Southeast Asia from India. Archaeological research has now demonstrated that this is not accurate but rather that the so-called "Hinduized" empires are built on the foundations of highly developed indigenous cultures and that the Indian cultural influences were strongly remolded in Southeast Asia into local forms.

One of the great puzzles has always been how and why these strong Indian influences penetrated the Southeast Asian region. Was it conquest? Did the Indians send missionaries? Did Indian traders, who sought in Southeast Asia exotic products to suit the refined tastes of princes and merchants, incidentally transmit some of their culture? Both ancient texts and archaeological findings make it clear that it was in the context of trade that Indian culture became known in Southeast Asia. Spices, particularly cloves, nutmeg, and cinnamon grown in eastern Indonesia and desired throughout the ancient world from China to Rome, attracted traders. As long as two thousand years ago, for instance, it was good form in China to suck a clove to sweeten the breath while approaching the emperor.

Trade in spices was an enormously lucrative business, and control of trade provided the economic basis for some of the early Southeast Asian empires. Srivijaya, for example, sat astride the straits of Malacca and effectively controlled much of the maritime trade with India and the Mediterranean region. It is likely that Southeast Asian rulers of the time, grown wealthy and powerful through trading, adorned themselves not only with material goods from foreign countries (ornaments from India, silk umbrellas from China), but also deliberately adopted the immaterial symbols of the state religions of powerful foreign civilizations in an effort to provide supernatural legitimacy for their new power and status.

Eventually, other Southeast Asian goods became important trade commodities as well, chief among them resins from tropical trees, which substituted for the rare and exorbitantly expensive frankincense from the Arabian Peninsula. Besides valuables and delicacies found in the sea (such as pearls and sea cucumbers) and along rocky shores (birds' nests, for example), forest products dominated trade: scent glands of wild animals for perfume, beeswax, aromatic woods, cinnabar, placer gold, and others.

Many of the trade valuables were collected by hunter-gatherers in the interior forests who exchanged them for rice and local products with traders from coastal principalities who, in turn, traded them to Chinese, Indians, and Arabs. This new venue of exchange both complemented and expanded the trade between hunters and farmers discussed earlier. Through it, forest hunters became indirectly connected with lowland princes and even with the potentates and markets of China, India, and the Western world.

Not all the early empires of Southeast Asia relied on trade as their major economic base. Others derived their economic strength and power from farming localized regions of rich agricultural soils. Early kings of the Khmer empire, for instance, built extensive irrigation systems along the shores of the Tonle Sap (great lake) of Cambodia. Still, even the agricultural states were tied into the great trading networks: many of the trading states did not produce enough food to sustain the large populations of their coastal port cities and had to import food from agricultural regions.

Even in ancient times the tropical forests of Asia were an important resource not only for local populations but for the whole world. The fine hardwoods cut in these forests today with chain saws and hauled out by great machines are still major elements in international trade. The hunger of industrial nations for these goods and the economic pressures on Southeast Asian countries has so accelerated the consumption of the once grand and vast forests that their complete exhaustion is possible within a few more years.

5

INDIANS
OF THE
AMAZONIAN FOREST

ROBERT L. CARNEIRO

When Charles Darwin first saw the rain forest of Brazil a century and a half ago, it so affected him that he wrote:

> Among the scenes which are deeply impressed on my mind, none exceed in sublimity the primeval forests undefaced by the hand of man. No one can stand in these solitudes unmoved. . . . Epithet after epithet was found too weak to convey to those who have not visited the intertropical regions, the sensation of delight which the mind experiences. . . . The land is one great, wild, untidy, luxuriant hothouse, made by nature herself.

The rain forests that Europeans viewed so reverentially were, however, regarded with a bit less awe by the Indians who lived in them. After all, they had not only lived in the forest from birth but in their quest for subsistence they had to cope with the forest every day of their lives.

While not many more than a quarter of a million Indians survive today in Amazonia, when the basin was first discovered around 1500, perhaps six million Indians were living there. They dwelt, as their descendants still do, in pole-and-thatch houses in small, politically autonomous villages. Technologically simple, their principle cutting tool was the stone axe, their main weapon was the bow and arrow, and their primary form of river travel was by dugout canoe. Village organization was simple and egalitarian, with a headman who generally lacked much real authority and a shaman whose function was to cure the sick. Few if any clothes were worn, so that in this respect as in many others, the Indians were free denizens of the forests that surrounded them.

Just how large were these forests? Late in the nineteenth century the French geographer Elisée Reclus put the size of the Amazonian rain forest at 5,000,000 square kilometers (2,000,000 square miles).

Since then deforestation has made relentless inroads, and a recent estimate places the remaining area of this rain forest at 2,000,000 square kilometers (898,000 square miles). Although only half its former size, the rain forest still occupies a vast area, some twenty-two times the size of Ohio.

Running through this huge region of rain forest is the mighty Amazon River. The Amazon is not a single river, but a vast and intricate network of watercourses with more than one thousand tributaries, seventeen of them more than sixteen hundred kilometers (one thousand miles) long.

The almost incalculable amount of water carried by the Amazon—it discharges at its mouth some 200,000 cubic meters (7.5 million cubic feet) per second—derives in part from the melting snows of the Andes. But most of it comes from the torrential rains that fall on the Amazonian rain forest. Averaging some two meters (80 inches) a year, rainfall increases to

BELOW LEFT: A Kuikuru woman squeezes the poisonous juice from grated manioc pulp using a flexible mat strainer made of leaf midribs. Many varieties of manioc contain deadly prussic acid, which must be removed before the starch contained in the root can be eaten.

BOTTOM: Yanomami Indians felling a large tree in clearing a garden plot. The scaffold built around the base of the tree enables the men to chop above the plank buttresses.

BELOW RIGHT: An Amahuaca woman plants corn in a newly burned garden plot. She pokes holes in the ground with a long digging stick and deposits two or three kernels in each hole. Her necklace is of monkey teeth and her crown is of split bamboo.

A Kuikuru shaman and his assistants leaving the village on their way to recover a patient's soul, which was said to have been stolen by an evil spirit living at the bottom of a lake. The shaman holds his gourd rattle in one hand and a sprig of magical *kejite* leaves in the other.

An Amahuaca man makes arrows. He is attaching a bamboo point to a short hardwood foreshaft imbedded in a length of arrow cane. Feathers for fletching the arrows are kept in an insect-tight basket.

nearly four meters (150 inches) or more at the foothills of the Andes where the prevailing easterlies are intercepted and forced to surrender much of their remaining moisture.

Of course, rain does not fall all the time. Rainy and dry seasons alternate over the year. This seasonal variation in rainfall is more marked—and much more important in the life of the Indians—than the slight fluctuations in average daily temperature that occur between the seasons. Ask Indians of any tribe and they will assure you that they prefer the dry season to the wet. The Mekranotí of central Brazil, for example, call the dry season *amex kam,* "good time," while the wet season is just *na kam,* "rainy time."

The downpours of the rainy season send water racing into the rivers, causing the smaller ones to rise as much as ten meters (thirty feet) or more overnight. Such flooding has led some tribes, like the Shipibo and Conibo of eastern Peru, to build houses with palm wood floors raised one meter or more above the ground, allowing the flood waters to pass harmlessly underneath.

During the rainy season large areas of low, flat land are inundated, creating *igapós*—tracts of flooded primary forest. Through these flooded forests the Indians can pole or paddle their canoes, finding fluvial shortcuts between places otherwise connected only by winding trails.

Because of the unpredictable and drenching rains, the rainy season is a time when Indians prefer to stay home. Social and ceremonial activities are turned inward, and village life is more self-contained. The rainy season is also a time of heightened agricultural activity when planting, fencing, and weeding are given needed attention.

When the rains finally cease the Indians are ready to travel. Now they can walk long distances through the forest with reasonable certainty of not being caught in a downpour. The dry season is thus a time for visiting relatives and for tendering or accepting invitations to intervillage feasts, dances, and ceremonies.

The dry season is also a time for trekking—going on long expeditions to gather such wild food or raw materials as Brazil nuts or arrow cane that may not be available in the immediate vicinity of the village.

It is the heavy rainfall coupled with warm temperatures that create and sustain the giant forests of the Amazon. The forest, of course, consists preeminently of trees, but it is more than trees. It is a biological cornucopia, a biome of incredible richness and complexity. The waters of the Amazon and its tributaries teem with fishes, astounding not only in their amount but also in their variety—altogether some two thousand species, eight times as many as in the Mississippi. A wealth of animal life is likewise found in the upper reaches of the forest. At least twenty-seven hundred species of birds inhabit Amazonia, more than three times the number in all of North America.

Sunrise awakens a village of Angotere-Secoya Indians along the Napo River in the Peruvian Amazon. About fifty people live in this community.

ROBERT L. CARNEIRO

Amazonia is estimated to have at least fifty thousand species of vascular plants. The territory of the Aguaruna and Huambisa Indians of eastern Ecuador alone contains some twelve hundred species. In just one-sixth acre (.07 hectare) of forest near a Yanomamö village on the Upper Orinoco, I found fifty-two different kinds of trees. These figures take on special meaning when we realize that the whole state of Michigan, with an area of 150,000 square kilometers (58,000 square miles), has only eighty-nine native species of trees.

The great botanical diversity of Amazonia gives the Indians a spectrum of plant resources from which to make the many artifacts that constitute their material culture. They have taken full advantage of this wealth. To be sure, Amazonia does not offer unlimited resources. Certain materials normally useful to primitive peoples elsewhere in the world are lacking or in short supply here. Chief among these is stone. So thick are the sediments covering the Amazon basin that stone is often very difficult to find. A well sunk in 1954 at the Indian Service Post of Capitão Vasconcellos (now Posto Leonardo Villas Boas) in the Upper Xingú reached ten and one-half meters (thirty-five feet) without coming across even a good-size pebble. The French traveler Alcide d'Orbigny journeyed by canoe from the stoneless llanos of Bolivia up to Cochabamba in 1832. He reported that on reaching the section of the river where the first stones were to be found, his Mojo Indian boatmen gathered them up excitedly, "as if they were gems."

Since stone for spear points and, later, for arrowheads was so scarce in Amazonia, the first Indians to enter the basin were soon forced to begin looking for substitutes. Fortunately they were readily available. Sharpened monkey bones, stingray spines, hard palm wood, and bamboo were found to be acceptable replacements for stone for projectile points. Indeed, so effective did these substitutes prove to be that they seem to have replaced stone for this purpose even in those few areas in which it was available. According to the Swedish ethnologist Erland Nordenskiöld, by the time Europeans arrived not a single tribe in Amazonia still tipped its arrows with stone points.

When Indians first entered Amazonia ten thousand or more years ago, the habitat they found was not entirely unfamiliar. Their ancestors had traveled through the rain-forest regions of southern Mexico and Central America. During the centuries it took to work their way through these areas, these early Indians no doubt discovered and began using many of the resources of the rain forest. When they finally arrived in Amazonia, the early migrants found plants and animal species in greater profusion than they had known before.

This new habitat, however, presented certain

problems. The large rivers of Amazonia were a barrier to further migration, since these early migrants probably lacked watercraft. Lacking the bow and arrow as well, they likely found the taking of game and fish more difficult than it later became.

For every problem it posed, the rain forest also offered a solution or at least the means of achieving one. Over the ensuing millennia Amazonian Indians worked out many successful ways of adapting to life in the tropical-forest environment. These living patterns or adaptations make up what anthropologists call *Tropical Forest Culture*.

A major element of this culture is watercraft. When the dugout canoe was introduced into—or invented in—Amazonia, it no doubt had a profound effect. Large rivers ceased to be obstacles to travel and became instead avenues of communication. It is conceivable that the very idea of the dugout was suggested to the Indians by a tree, the *barrigudo,* "big belly" palm (*Iriartea ventricosa*), which has a pith-filled engorgement half-way up its trunk. Hollowed out, this engorged section makes a trough somewhat like a bathtub, which can be used as a rough-and-ready craft for river travel.

Perhaps Amazonian Indians had found earlier that the tough, inch-thick bark of certain trees, such as purpleheart (*Peltogyne paniculata*) and *jatobá* (*Hymenaea courbaril*), could be cut away from the trunk in a single, large, curved piece, which could then be shaped into a very serviceable canoe. Later, when true dugouts began to be made, Spanish cedar (*Cedrela odorata*), became the wood of choice for such craft. It is at once strong, relatively light, and easy to carve, and it resists both insect attack and rot.

Trial and error also led to the discovery of the strongest, most resilient woods for their bows: *pau d'arco* (*Tecoma violacea*) in eastern Amazonia, and the peach palm (*Bactris gasipaes*) in northern and western Amazonia. Similarly, they found that the longest, straightest, lightest shafts for their arrows came from the giant grass, *Gynerium sagittatum*. Similarly, woods that best resisted decay when put into the ground, like *huacapu* (*Voucapoua americana*), came more and more to be used for house posts. The knowledge that Indians acquired of the rain-forest trees was extensive and intimate; the forest became less an adversary and more an ally.

The first migrants into Amazonia came as hunters, fishers, and gatherers. Their food was thus limited entirely to the wild plants and animals the forest and rivers had to offer. Edible fauna was found in considerable abundance in Amazonia: game animals, including deer, tapir, peccaries, monkeys, capybaras, and many other species are distributed widely throughout the forest, making hunting, if practiced skillfully, a rewarding activity.

Fishing was and continues to be even more productive. The many hundreds of fish species that occur in such abundance in Amazonian waters, especially along the major rivers, provide a vast supply of protein. Unlike hunting, which gradually thins out the game and requires villages to pick up and move every so often, fishing, at least along large rivers or lakes, allows villages to remain in the same place almost indefinitely.

Sometime around 3000 B.C., agriculture appeared in Amazonia. When it became fully incorporated into subsistence, the impact was profound. Over the course of time, small, simple, nomadic bands of foragers were transformed into larger, more settled, and more complex villages of agriculturalists. Adopting agriculture did not mean that Amazonian Indians gave up all reliance on wild foods. They continued to consume fruits, nuts, and roots from the forest to supplement their diet. In doing so they became more and more familiar with the rain forest and what it had to offer. As this knowledge broadened and deepened, the Indians became more effective exploiters of the forest not only for food but also for raw materials to make their tools, weapons, utensils, adornments, shelters, and watercraft.

Only recently have we begun to glimpse the full depth of the Indians' knowledge of the forest. Working in what is now Guyana, the botanist P. W. Richards found that his Arawak Indian guide had a native name for more than three hundred different trees. In almost every case, Richards found, each native name designated a single taxonomic species.

Moreover, an Indian may not need to see the entire tree to know its identity. "On numerous occasions," Brent Berlin wrote of the Aguaruna, "we were presented with a piece of bark taken from a tree that could barely be seen in the dim forest light. Our guide would smell it, taste it, and then firmly provide us with the plant's correct name."

The Kuikuru of central Brazil were able to name 191 different trees I asked about, but beyond that, they could cite a use—and often multiple uses—for at least 138 of these trees. Further inquiry would, I am sure, have elicited even more uses. Some trees, like *tafaku* (*Xylopia* sp.), had half-dozen uses: the bark was used for lashings, the straight trunks for wall posts, the trunk split into long pieces for firewood, and the resin for medicine. A stack of tafaku firewood placed outside the door of a prospective mother-in-law was a formal request for her daughter's hand in marriage. Some trees, however, had limited and specialized uses. The sole use that I could elicit for a tree called *netufe* was that its roots were used to poison dogs.

Beyond identifying the names and uses of plants, Amazonian Indians understand their roles in the web of forest life. For example, a Kuikuru can tell you that the tapir likes the seeds of the *aku* tree, that monkeys eat the fruit of the *inui* or *egeikajï,* and that the fruits of the *fingugi* are relished by the toucan. They say that *fakuasa* (a kind of grasshopper) likes the roots of the *takisi* tree, while *augigo* (another grasshopper) eats the leaves of the *tifa* (*Calophyllum brasiliense?*) tree. The subject having turned to tifa leaves, they might add that these leaves are also favored by a certain species of leaf-cutter ant.

Over the centuries that they lived in the Upper Xingú river basin, the ancestors of the Kuikuru gained a thorough knowledge of the properties of the hundreds of tree species that surrounded them. Their descendants are the inheritors and beneficiaries of this knowledge. Any Kuikuru can tell you what use (if any) is made of the wood, bark, sap, resin, roots, limbs, leaves, fruits, and seeds of perhaps three hundred different species of trees.

For some purposes, a Kuikuru will use any of several species of trees. Many different trees are used for house timbers, although certain ones are favored for center posts, others for rafters, still others for wall posts. Many (but not all) trees make suitable firewood, and a Kuikuru generally selects these for burning. In fact, he may even girdle or fell such trees as iñui, kuó, or ñongiñongi, which make especially good firewood, so the dried trunk will be ready for use when needed.

A number of artifacts, however, are made from only one kind of wood. The sharpened stick used in piercing a boy's ear lobes, for example, is always made from the wood of the *angá* tree (*Genipa americana*). Here it would seem that tradition plays more of a role in the choice of *Genipa* wood than do the qualities of the wood itself.

The connection between particular tree species and their uses by the Kuikuru has had interesting linguistic consequences. Thus certain artifacts bear the name of the tree from which they are customarily made: the *kofï* tree has given its name to the mortar, the *tungifï* to the digging stick, the *tafaku* to the bow, and the *kïntï* to one type of fish trap.

In their vast knowledge and wide use of forest trees, the Kuikuru are, of course, not unique. In all probability every Amazonian tribe has an equally thorough knowledge of the trees of its habitat and makes correspondingly broad use of them. Recent studies of four Amazonian tribes, the Urubú-Kaapor and Tembé of Brazil, the Panare of Venezuela, and the Chácobo of Bolivia, found that on the average these groups used at least two-thirds of the tree species growing in their forests.

Of all the botanical families of trees, palms are the most extensively used. Some three hundred species of palms grow in Amazonia, from the *iú* palm (*Bactris* sp.) with a stem no thicker than a goose quill, to the mighty *Mauritia* palms with trunks A. R. Wallace de-

scribed as "huge columnar stems rising undisturbed by branch or leaf to a height of eighty or a hundred feet." This large, water-loving palm is exploited extensively by many tribes, especially those on the Orinoco. Father José Gumilla, a missionary who lived among the Otomac of the lower Orinoco in the early 1700s, called the moriche palm (*Mauritia flexuosa*) the Indians' "tree of life." From its leaves the Otomac obtained fiber for cordage; from its pith, edible starch; from its fermented sap, palm wine; and from its fruit, a refreshing beverage.

The Warao of the Orinoco delta make even greater use of *Mauritia*. The palm's wood serves for house posts, canoes, bowstaves, and spear and arrow shafts. From its leaves they obtain thatching and from the cuticle—the thin layer stripped from the underside of the leaf—fiber for their clothing, nets, and hammocks. The Warao make an edible flour from the pith they extract from inside the trunk much like the famous sago of the Pacific. To this list the Kuikuru could add at least two more uses for *Mauritia*: material for skirts from the upper part of the leaves (after the cuticle is removed) and the stiff elements for their manioc strainers from the leaf midribs.

Slash-and-Burn Cultivation

Hardly a tribe exists in Amazonia that does not derive most of its subsistence from agriculture. The method of farming employed is that known as slash-and-burn, swidden, or shifting cultivation. Although many variants exist, the essential outlines of the pattern are similar throughout the wet tropics. A section of the forest is felled, the slash is allowed to dry and is burned prior to the start of the rainy season. Varying combinations of crops are planted before or after the burn. The same plot may be replanted two or three times, but diminishing yields finally lead to its abandonment and a new plot is cleared.

Although slash-and-burn agriculture is well suited to tropical rain forests, it is by no means restricted to it. Where the forest is extensive, it is a productive system of cultivation. In the deciduous forest of North America, slash-and-burn agriculture most likely preceded the permanent field methods in current use. When Charles Dickens traveled through thinly settled western Pennsylvania in 1842, he observed slash-and-burn methods being practiced.

The first step in swidden cultivation is clearing the forest. Before the large trees themselves can be attacked, the undergrowth has to be cleared. Under aboriginal Amazonian conditions no machetes were available, so the small seedlings and saplings that make up most of the undergrowth were either pulled up by hand, bent over and broken, or cut through with a piranha jaw or a palm-wood knife.

When the undergrowth is cleared the Indians turn

Dugout canoes are the most common form of river transport for native Amazonians. A man of the Kalapalo tribe, neighbors of the Kuikuru, makes a canoe.

CENTER: Gathering forest edibles is important to most native Amazonian agriculturists. A Yanomami man picks a tree fungus.

RIGHT: A Yanomami woman returns from her fields with the fruits of an *Inga* tree in her basket.

While large game animals may be preferred by many, ▷ fish, small animals, and birds often are more frequently caught and are more important in the diet. A Kayapó man with the day's catch.

their attention to the trees. Before the arrival of the Europeans the stone axe was the principal tool used for the job, but felling trees with a stone axe was no easy task, especially in a forest of trees with some of the hardest woods in the world. It involved many days of sweat, blisters, and aching muscles. The technique was different from that used with a steel axe. Instead of notching one side of a tree and then hacking at the opposite side until it falls, Indians using stone axes preferred to cut all the way around a trunk. A tree cut in this way looks as if it had been felled by a beaver.

The extremely hard work involved in using a stone axe was graphically described to the German ethnologist Karl von den Steinen many years ago by the Bakairí Indians he had discovered:

> How tired a Bakairí gets cutting down a single tree! Early in the morning when the sun rises he begins wielding his stone axe. The sun climbs the sky and the Bakairí continues to chop: *tsok! tsok! tsok!* His arms get wearier and wearier. The Bakairí rubs them and then lets them hang limply at his sides. He lets out a deep breath. . . . He resumes chopping, but no longer *tsok! tsok! tsok!* Now it is accompanied by deep groans. The sun reaches zenith. His stomach is now nothing but folds of skin—it is empty. How hungry the Bakairí is! . . . Finally, when the sun is right near the horizon, a tree falls!

Pretty much the same lament might have been heard from the lips of almost any Amazonian Indian

before the steel axe was introduced. For example, when I asked the Amahuaca to tell me about the days of this archaic tool, one informant, too young to have used the axe himself but recalling vividly what he had heard from his elders, told me: "They say it was always breaking. They say it was always getting dull. That stone axe is no good!"

Forced to use this axe for lack of anything better, the Indians found ways to reduce the amount and intensity of the work required. Very large trees were often not felled at all but merely girdled. This killed the tree, causing it to shed its leaves, so that while it remained standing, at least it cast less shade. Fire was often used to ease the process of felling. Firewood or dry palm leaves were placed against the trunk, or resin daubed around it, and the flammable material set afire. When the fire burned down, the charred parts of the trunk, being relatively soft, were more easily hacked away. A fire was again built around the tree, the charred parts chopped out as before, and the procedure repeated until the tree fell.

By far the greatest labor-saving device in clearing the forest is the driving tree fall. The smaller trees directly in the path of a larger one are notched, and when the big one is felled, down come the others with it, domino fashion. This technique is especially effective because tree crowns are often interlaced by vines and sometimes by thorny bamboo, so even trees lying outside the direct path of a large tree may be pulled

down by it or have their crowns snapped off.

Felling the forest is done as soon as the rains stop, allowing the slash to dry for several months. When it is time to burn, the Indian cultivator walks through his plot, torch in hand, setting fire to the dried vegetation every few feet. Each small fire gradually enlarges until all coalesce into a single mighty conflagration.

The fire burns quickly, consuming the dead leaves and smaller branches but leaving the larger trunks and stumps only charred. Many tribes then practice what in Brazil is called *encoivarar*—piling up the slash that failed to burn well the first time and setting fire to it again.

Even with reburning many logs and stumps remain, giving a new swidden a rather messy appearance. Charred logs are strewn everywhere, often crisscrossing one another; between the fallen logs unburned stumps protrude. During the three or four years that a plot is cultivated, though, many of the logs are cut up and hauled off for firewood or used for fencing. Moreover, the weeds pulled up in a garden from time to time are often piled against logs or stumps to dry and then burned. In this way after three or four years, a swidden may take on the cleared look of a permanent field with only the growing crops to be seen.

With the first rains and sometimes even before, planting begins. Manioc, the main subsistence crop of Amazonia, is planted entirely from cuttings, which are inserted into mounds hoed up in the spaces left between the logs and the stumps. For corn, which is planted from seed, holes are punched in the ground with a digging stick and one to three kernels dropped in each. Some tribes leave the holes open, others cover them over with the foot. Several other food crops are grown, including sweet potatoes, yams, various aroids, beans, peppers, and, since contact with Europeans, bananas and plantains. Peanuts are planted by some tribes, usually on sandy beaches along rivers.

Forest soils are soft and friable and thus easy to till. The only impediment to tillage is the tangle of roots from the trees that have been felled. The Kuikuru sometimes dig out masses of small rootlets and place them on top of freshly planted manioc cuttings to shield them from the sun.

In some parts of Amazonia herbivores pose a serious threat to the crops, and fields must be fenced. In Kuikuru gardens deer eat the manioc leaves while agoutis and white-lipped peccaries gorge themselves on the roots. Without a stout fence surrounding his plot, a Kuikuru could easily lose his entire crop.

With warm temperatures throughout the year and abundant rainfall much of the time, growing conditions in Amazonia are nearly ideal. Corn, the fastest growing of all Amazonian crops, can be harvested in as little as two months. Manioc tubers take at least six or eight months to reach edible size but will continue to grow underground without rotting for long after that. Since the roots store themselves so conveniently, manioc does not have to be harvested until needed, which may be eighteen months or more.

When manioc tubers are finally pulled from the ground, the stems of the plants that bore them are cut into sections about thirty to forty centimeters (twelve to fifteen inches) long. These cuttings are often replanted immediately in the same mound from which they came, or they are set aside for replanting at some future date, perhaps in another plot. Shielded from the direct rays of the sun, manioc stems may last for weeks or even months without dying. A manioc garden is usually replanted two or three times. By this time the yield has decreased so substantially that an Indian prefers to abandon the plot and clear a new one. A garden's diminishing yield is due partly to lower soil fertility and partly to the choking effect of weeds.

Weeding is, for many tribes, a necessary practice. How thoroughly a garden is weeded varies from tribe to tribe. The Kuikuru, for the most part, are fastidious weeders, but the Amahuaca hardly weed at all. There is good reason for the difference. The chief crop of the Amahuaca is corn, which ripens in just two months, so the field is harvested before the weeds have gotten much of a start. Moreover, since the Amahuaca usually abandon a plot after only one year of cultivation, they care little how weed-choked it may become once the crop is harvested. On the other hand, since the Kuikuru grow manioc in their gardens for three or four years, they must weed carefully if they are to get adequate yields over that length of time.

When Amazonian Indians do move their agricultural plots, it is, however, not only in response to weed infestation. Chemical analyses have shown most Amazonian soils to be poor in the nutrients that plants need for growth. Cutting and burning vegetation prior to planting improves the growing environment temporarily. During the several years of cultivation, crops in a swidden plot draw largely upon nutrients previously locked away in the forest and freed once the trees were felled and burned. These are added to by later burning the weeds and the remaining stumps and logs. Under continual heavy rains and high temperatures, however, the small amount of organic matter decays and soluble nutrients are washed from the soil. The nutrients added by the ash are thus critical to the success of the garden, but their effects last for only a short time.

It would seem, therefore, that in looking for land to clear and plant, an Indian cultivator should pay at least as much attention to the trees overhead as to the soil underfoot. If the trees in a prospective swidden are sufficiently large and if they burn well, a garden made there should yield a reasonably good crop. This is especially true if the crop is manioc, which makes less demand on the soil than such crops as corn.

In clearing the forest several choices have to be made: first, whether to clear primary or secondary forest. As a rule Amazonian Indians prefer the former. It is more work to fell large, hard, primary-forest trees than the smaller, softer trees of secondary forest, but there are compensations. Soils under primary forest are usually more fertile, and fewer weeds spring up in plots cleared in old rain forest than in secondary forest. Thus the tedious, back-breaking labor of weeding is considerably reduced. And though felling primary forest is hard work, it is also exhilarating. There is something almost thrilling about watching a forest giant, hacked at for a long time, finally come crashing to earth—a feeling that even the most creative weeding cannot approach.

What happens to an Amazonian swidden after the last manioc tuber has been picked? That depends on several things. If the plot was cleared in or near secondary forest, a ready source of weed seeds, the invasion of weeds after abandonment is likely to be rapid and intense.

The way a plot is treated while under cultivation also affects its fate. If a Kuikuru keeps his garden well-weeded throughout its lifetime, a dense stand of grass—called *sapé* in Brazil—will become established and effectively exclude all other vegetation for five years or so until secondary forest trees begin to shade it out. Another twenty years or more may have to pass before primary-forest trees overtop the faster-growing secondary-forest species.

As a rule plant succession is a matter of no immediate concern to the Kuikuru cultivator. After all, he lives in a tiny village surrounded by large expanses of forest. With so much forest available from which to clear his next plot, why should he care how long it takes his old one to regain its original cover? Even to call the old plot "his" is misleading. A piece of land is "owned" only as long as it is cultivated. Once abandoned it reverts to the common property of the whole village, just as it was before it was cleared. Indeed among the Kuikuru it is highly unlikely that someone will clear and plant the very same plot of land twice during his lifetime.

These remarks about an abandoned plot, while characteristic of the Kuikuru, do not necessarily apply to other Amazonian tribes. Among some other groups a garden plot is not abruptly abandoned. For example, before abandoning it, Indians may plant a swidden with fruit trees that will not begin to bear until several years after the plot has ceased to be cultivated. Such plots will be visited and harvested by their owners for many years.

In northwestern Amazonia, the peach palm is useful not only for its nutritious fruit but also as a source of excellent bow wood. It is often planted in gardens and is harvested for fruit or felled for bow staves only years later. Bananas, plantains, and papaya are other fruit-yielding crops that continue to yield for several years after a plot is abandoned. The person who plants such trees continues to own and harvest them until they are finally choked out by the encroaching forest. The Kuikuru sometimes plant in their gardens a tree called *piqui* (*Caryocar brasiliense*), the fruit of which they will only begin to pick six or eight years later.

Certain wild plants that may invade an old plot as part of the succession to secondary forest are edible and serve to prolong the useful life of the plot. One such plant, which springs up in abandoned Amahuaca gardens, is *cocona* (*Solanum sessiliflorum*), a shrub that has fruit the Indians enjoy. Moreover, certain invading species as well as remnant crop plants may attract deer and agoutis to an abandoned plot, making an old garden a good place to hunt. Abandonment of a swidden is rarely abrupt; it is instead a long process proceeding from a swidden dominated by cultivated annual plants to an old fallow composed entirely of natural vegetation.

As long as the forest is large and the population small, slash-and-burn is a system of agriculture well-suited to the coexistence of man and forest. The portion of the forest cleared and planted by a village is usually but a tiny fraction of the whole, and after three or four years each clearing is allowed to revert to forest. As long as populations remain small, the ratio of swidden to forest remains low and fallow times can be long. Thus there is little threat of long-term degradation of the soil.

Slash-and-burn agriculture is both conservative and productive. At least this is true if we measure productivity per unit of human effort. Nonmechanized, permanent-field agriculture, which is labor intensive, may yield more food per unit of *land,* but it rarely does so per unit of *labor.* Since, as a rule, people work no harder than they have to, the intensification of agriculture from swidden to permanent fields is rarely freely chosen but rather forced on a community by circumstances.

The evolution of agriculture from its simple, slash-and-burn beginnings thus seems clear. As human numbers increase villages encroach on each other, and the amount of forest available to each village diminishes. Continued population growth eventually makes it impossible to allow an abandoned plot to remain fallow for the twenty to twenty-five years necessary to restore soil fertility. Instead it becomes necessary to clear a plot again after only eight or ten years of fallow before the forest has grown again. Eventually, if population pressure continues to increase, fields may be tilled almost continuously with only occasional short periods of fallow.

Given sufficient population pressure and insuf-

A Yanomami hunter removes an arrow from a giant ant-eater. Although they are not a favored food among most native Amazonians, anteaters, like most forest animals, are not scorned by Yanomami as sources of meat.

BOTTOM: Hunting wild animals provides animal protein for many forest peoples. Yanomami boys cut up a tapir. Like many Amazonians, the Xikrin, a Kayapó group of east central Brazil, use *Genipa* fruit mixed with charcoal to paint their bodies.

BOTTOM: A Yanomami woman prepares cotton for spinning.

A Kuikuru village is surrounded by old fields, fallows, and forest.

ficient technical advances, an agricultural downward spiral may result from a shortened fallow. This spiral eventually leads to the degradation of the land and the impoverishment of its inhabitants. But until population pressure becomes acute, slash-and-burn must be judged a rational system of subsistence. The primitive farmer borrows land from the forest and mineral nutrients from the trees growing on it which enable him to feed himself and his family. After a time he returns the land to the surrounding forest, somewhat depleted. But as the forest again takes over, it begins to heal its wounds and to restore its fertility.

As practiced in Amazonia, slash-and-burn has proved to be a long-term system. It has provided the basis for a distinctive and successful culture that, wherever it has been left untrampled by the outside world, continues to flourish.

But such pristine areas of Indian occupation are being reduced and threatened with extinction. The survival of native Indian culture is now very precarious. In a few areas of Amazonia, like the Upper Xingú in central Brazil, a reservation affords substantial protection to the Indians living there. But this kind of protection cannot prevent—and in some ways actually encourages—a certain amount of acculturation. Thus in cases of serious illness the Xinguanos have come to rely more and more on modern medicine. In most parts of Amazonia, however, surviving Indians have no such protection.

In the 1950s after completing my first field work among the Kuikuru, I wondered where I might work next. Looking at the map of South America, I saw between the Aripuaña and the Rio Roosevelt in west-central Brazil a completely unknown area. Although no one had any inkling of it at the time, it seemed to me that there had to be Indians living there. It became my fantasy that someday I would be the first outsider—or at least the first anthropologist—to visit these mysterious Indians and record their culture.

The intervening years proved my surmise correct. There were Indians between the Aripuanã and the Roosevelt, including such tribes as the Cintas Largas, Gavião, and Zoró. But modern methods of surveying through magnetometers carried aloft on airplanes made it possible to discover mineral deposits in the area, which turned out to be cassiterite, a tin ore. The inevitable result was that mining companies sent parties into the region. Once-unknown Indians quickly found themselves displaced and disadvantaged, the first stage in a long spiral of decline.

The sad fact is that these Indians, even if their individual lives are spared, face the death of their culture as a coherent way of life. Attempts to stem the tide of outside influence are being made. A reserve of some five thousand square kilometers (two thousand square miles) was recently set aside by presidential decree for the exclusive use of the Zoró, but a quarter of this land is already occupied by Brazilian squatters. Thus, here and elsewhere in Amazonia, the struggle for the survival of the Indians and their culture continues with the odds against the Indians growing longer with each passing year.

THE LACANDON MAYA

JAMES D. NATIONS

On both sides of the trail stand giant trees dripping with rain. Thick lianas twist down from a forest canopy that blends into a green wall of vegetation. Overhead a flock of red and green macaws feed on jungle fruit, tossing aside pieces that fall thirty meters to the forest floor below. Insects whine and buzz with a thousand different voices, and a tiny brocket deer flashes across the trail into undergrowth, disappearing into shadow. The air smells like a mixture of rot and genesis.

Moving silently through the forest, a lone hunter spots the deer and freezes. Insect sounds cease as he slowly raises his rifle. With the crack of the bullet, the macaws burst into flight and scatter above the canopy. The hunter pulls the lifeless deer from the understory and binds its legs with vines he strips from the buttresses of a nearby tree. He hefts the deer onto his shoulders and heads down the trail for home.

The hunter is one of 450 Lacandon Maya Indians who inhabit the remnants of the Selva Lacandona in Chiapas, Mexico, the largest remaining tropical rain forest in North America. Once covering thirteen thousand square kilometers (five thousand square miles) of eastern Chiapas, the Selva Lacandona now consists of six thousand square kilometers (twenty-three hundred square miles) of forest patches interspersed with pastures and agricultural clearings.

Until the 1960s the immensity of their rain forest environment isolated the Lacandon Maya from the forces that produced such rapid change in the lives of other Mayan peoples. As a result, they managed to preserve a life-style intimately adapted to the tropical forest that surrounds them. When timber companies bulldozed logging roads through the region in 1965, the twentieth century arrived in force. Backed by government policies designed to bring the Selva Lacandona into the Mexican national economy, the roads prompted the immigration of 150,000 peasant colonists and a wave of cattle ranchers who burned huge stands of forest for pasture. By 1987 more than half of the Lacandon rain forest had been eradicated.

For centuries the Lacandon Maya lived in isolated family settlements in an almost uninhabited wilderness of lower montane rain forest. Today the population is concentrated into three villages of more than one hundred people each and a dozen families who hide in compounds dispersed throughout the forest. Although the ancient Lacandon systems of hunting, fishing, and agriculture are being rapidly altered by daily contact with the outside world, the Lacandones still preserve an ecological heritage passed down to them, generation by generation, from pre-Columbian ancestors. From the biological diversity of their rain-forest environment the Lacandones gather fruit, wild animals, natural insecticides, fish poisons, fiber for clothing and ropes, incense for religious ceremonies, wood for houses, furniture, and canoes, and medicinal plants that may cure a toothache or a snakebite.

The central feature of the Lacandones' traditional rain-forest management is a system of agroforestry that produces food crops, trees, and animals on the same plot of land simultaneously. Lacandon agroforestry combines up to seventy-nine varieties of food and fiber crops on single-hectare (two and one-half acre) garden plots cleared from the tropical forest. Like forest farmers throughout the tropics, Lacandones create these garden plots by felling and burning the forest to clean the plot of insects and weeds and to create a temporarily fertile soil by transforming the nutrients of the tropical-forest vegetation into a nutrient-rich ash.

To absorb these nutrients before they escape through leaching and soil erosion, the Lacandon farmer plants fast-growing tree crops and root crops, including chayote, papaya, bananas, plantains, manioc, sweet potatoes, and a tarolike root crop called *macal* or *Xanthosoma.*

After these initial nutrient-grabbing and soil-protection crops have taken root, the farmer and his wives and children plant other food and fiber crops during the course of the agricultural year—corn, onions, garlic, pineapples, chilies, watermelons, limes, grapefruit, coriander, squash, cotton, tomatoes, mint, tobacco, rice, parsley, beans, plums, guavas, sugar cane, ginger, and cacao. Planting times for some of these crops are keyed to seasonal signals, like the flow-ers dropping from natural forest species. When the flowers of the mahogany tree fall, the farmer knows it is time to plant the spring corn crop. The falling of the wild tamarind flowers indicates the days to plant tobacco. Following this system of natural indicator species, the Lacandon farmer plants his crops according to local climatic conditions rather than by a fixed agricultural calendar.

In addition to the crops the family actively plants, the Lacandon garden plot has a second major component—spontaneous, natural forest species that sprout in the garden and are recognized by the farmer and allowed to grow. These spontaneous crops include such food plants as *mamey,* sapodilla, wild pineapple, wild dogbane, and wild sugar vine, and such raw materials as balsa and corkwood used in house construction and for making bows and arrows.

By maintaining a variety of domesticated and spontaneous crop species scattered throughout his garden plot, the Lacandon farmer helps prevent the mass outbreaks of plant diseases and insect pests that plague crop monocultures in the tropical-forest biome. This diversity also provides a wealth of food and fiber crops throughout the agricultural cycle because different crops produce useable parts during different times of the year.

The biological diversity of the Lacandon garden plot has a corollary benefit: pacas, peccaries, brocket deer, and other forest animals are drawn to certain food crops, so the farmer purposely plants an abundance of these foods to attract edible animals. He knows that his agricultural plot is also a productive hunting zone that will provide his family with high-quality protein. Several studies in the Latin American tropics indicate that the presence of garden plots in a tropical forest can actually increase the populations of certain wild animals.

To conservationists and government planners the most intriguing aspect of the Lacandon farming system is the fact that Lacandon families maintain this food, fiber, and animal production on the same plot of cleared forest land for five to seven consecutive years. In contrast, most immigrant colonists in the Selva Lacandona clear new plots from forest yearly.

Lacandon farmers are the first to point out that aggressive, almost daily, weeding is the key factor that allows them to cultivate the same garden plot for so many years in a row. After five to seven years they clear a new forest plot, not because the soil has lost its fertility but because the labor required to weed the garden finally outweighs the labor required to clear a new plot from forest or regrowth.

Even then the Lacandon farmer does not abandon the old cultivation plot. Instead, he plants it with such tree crops as rubber, cacao, citrus, and avocado and continues to harvest the area for another five to fif-

A young Lacandon Maya boy crosses his father's newly cleared swidden field.

teen years while it regrows with natural forest species. Lacandones call these regenerating plots *pak che kol,* "planted tree gardens."

When the natural forest finally overtakes his tree crops, the farmer clears and burns the plot again and begins the cycle anew. Thus the Lacandon agroforestry system cycles food and forest continually on small plots of forest land. The tropical forest becomes a garden plot, which becomes a planted tree garden, which becomes tropical-forest regrowth, which becomes a garden plot again, and so on through time. Using this system, a Lacandon farmer may clear as few as ten hectares (twenty-five acres) of virgin tropical forest during his entire agricultural career—from the ages of seventeen to seventy.

Several years ago I tried to explain the potential benefits of the Lacandon system to an agronomist hired to develop sustainable agricultural systems for the Selva Lacandona. He listened politely, but it was obvious that his mind was already filled with visions of agribusiness and cattle production. He told me that the Lacandon system was very interesting, but it wasn't modern. Instead, he told me, "We must teach the Lacandones how to farm in the tropical forest."

My answer then was the same that it is today: that rather than eradicating indigenous systems like that of the Lacandon Maya, we should be working with traditional forest farmers as their students. For in the end they will teach us how to farm in the tropical forest without destroying it.

KAYAPÓ INDIAN
NATURAL-RESOURCE
MANAGEMENT

DARRELL POSEY

South of the Amazon's main stream in the basin of the Xingu River, the rain forest intergrades with drier savanna. In this diverse environment the Kayapó, a traditionally seminomadic Amerindian group, survives the encroachment of the developed world. A quick look at the Kayapó would identify them as typical shifting cultivators like most of their Amazonian neighbors. In the course of several years of research, however, a multidisciplinary team of researchers have found that their resource-use practices are far more diverse and complex than had first been assumed.

Kayapó Indians do not separate management strategies into the neat categories of agronomy, forestry, agroforestry, wildlife management, and forestation as Western thinkers try to do; instead, they have a unified view of plant-animal management and conservation. Even traditional scientific concepts of agriculture and domestication are challenged by the complexities of Kayapó plant manipulation. For example, agricultural plots are simply the beginning of a long-term process of planting and sequential management that ends with a mature forest filled with medicinal and edible plants, as well as plants used in building and crafts and useful animals. Many crops are planted and survive only due to the care of their cultivators, but the majority are transplanted from the wild to make a concentrated resource bank in the modified microenvironments created by the Indians. Other useful species are simply allowed to grow in these gardens. Plants known to be favorite foods of wildlife are likewise introduced into fields and these old fields are thought of as hunting reserves for future generations. As gardens grow into forests, they are dominated by fruit and nut trees that bear as long as thirty to fifty years after they were planted.

Crop management is the result of carefully integrated strategies of soil management, ground cover preservation, temperature and humidity control, natural pest management, and well-timed intercropping. The process begins with selection of good agricultural land, which depends on the Kayapó farmer's knowledge of the soils, based on their color, texture, organic matter, drainage, and temperatures. Ground cover is also indicative of surface and subsoil types. Underbrush is cleared and some planting of tubers (sweet potatoes, yam, taro, manioc) and bananas occurs be-

fore the trees are felled to dry and be burned. When burning does occur some two to three months later, the preburn plantings have already developed a healthy root system. A controlled, "cool" burn kills the aboveground vegetation and sterilizes the soil surface; it does not, however, adversely affect the tubers and bananas, which can then take up the nutrients released from the ash during the first rains. Planting time is based on lunar phases; the Indians say destructive mammal and insect pests are least active during moonlit evenings, thus planting is preferred at the onset of a new moon to protect new shoots.

Planting is anything but random. Distinct concentric circles or zones can be observed in Kayapó plots; each zone is managed differently and has a different complement of crops. For example, the center zone is reserved for sweet potatoes and taro, where the soil is frequently aerated by hand and enriched constantly by the addition of ash and organic matter. A second circle is reserved for such nutrient-demanding crops as beans, papaya, melons, pumpkins, yams, cotton, and tobacco.

One of the most interesting zones of a Kayapo field is the surrounding *atykma,* a buffer zone between the plot and the surrounding forest. It is full of useful medicinal plants, some of which may lure would-be pests from the more valuable cultigens. A high proportion of these atykma plants have nectar-producing glands on their foliage. These nectaries attract aggressive ants, which also deter leaf-cutting ants and termites. Several species of parasitic wasps nest in bananas that ring the fields; these wasps feed on herbivorous caterpillars, thereby also contributing to the natural protection of the Kayapó plots.

An important key to the successful ecological management system of the Kayapó is their preservation of natural corridors of old forests between field plots. These corridors serve as biological reserves that can also facilitate the reforestation of the old fields.

The Kayapó do not limit their resource management to forest areas; savannas are also modified by fire and by the creation of "islands" of forest (*apêtê* in Kayapó). Fires may be set fifteen to twenty times a year in savannas near village sites to keep trails open and reduce snake and scorpion populations. Fires also alter the flowering and fruiting times of savanna plants.

The Kayapó, like many other Amazonian groups, use a variety of plant and animal materials to adorn themselves for festivals.

A woman brings home a load of bananas. The Kayapó cultivate fourteen varieties of bananas.

based upon their plant knowledge; it is never just haphazard. Some plants are fire-tolerant and even stimulated by burning; others are damaged by fire and need protection. The Kayapó may stand guard in their apêtê to beat out any flames that threaten fire-sensitive species.

The apêtê themselves are some of the most ingenious aspects of Kayapó resource management. These forest islands are actually created by the Indians in piles of a planting medium prepared from termite and ant nests mixed with compost. Into this rich earth are planted hundreds of useful plants. Small apêtê are expanded to many hectares over the decades. A complete survey of sample apêtê revealed that 98 percent of the plants found in them had at least one use; well over two-thirds had multiple uses. Equally amazing is that these forest islands are composed of botanical resources taken from an area the size of western Europe. Many of the species are used to attract wildlife and are included in the forestation process so that older apêtê will abound in useful birds, reptiles, rodents, and other mammals.

The thread of uniformity to these strategies—and the great lesson that can be learned from the Kayapó—

is that biological diversity is fundamental to sustained management of the humid tropics. In sharp contrast to the dominant modern pattern of forest destruction for the establishment of single-species plantations, the Kayapó actually increase biological diversity through their concentration of useful resources.

Native peoples have had much time to discover uses for the natural resources around them and to develop strategies to exploit and manage them. If those who plan the future of tropical areas would follow some of the fundamentals of the Kayapó system, we would be well on a path to a socially and ecologically viable alternative for the humid tropics. The world is threatened not just with the loss of tropical ecosystems but with the loss of the peoples who know how to use them, whose ideas and knowledge may be the richest of all tropical resources.

Funding for the Kayapó Project was provided by the Brazilian National Council for Science and Technology (CNPq), the Wenner-Gren Foundation for Anthropological Research, the National Geographic Society, The National Science Foundation, and the World Wildlife Fund.

Brazilian highway BR-80 cuts through the mature rain forest of the Xingu National Park, an Indian reservation.

A wealthy businessman from São Paulo offers candy to Txukarramae Indians in Brazilian Amazonia.

INDIAN RIGHTS IN AMAZONIA

KENNETH I. TAYLOR

And everyone will come here and will finish off with everything, with game, fish, with pigs, with everything that we use to sustain ourselves. You will contaminate, you will bring a lot of sicknesses, a lot of malaria, sicknesses we have never seen, that we never have suffered. Because, without the white man, we never suffered from the sicknesses that people are suffering today.

HAMO OPIKTERI, 1986

(Yanomami Indian who lives in the Catrimani Valley, Brazil, which is transected by the Perimetral Norte highway)

The accelerating destruction of the world's remaining tropical rain forests is a matter that concerns us all, but most directly affected are the millions of indigenous peoples who live in these forests. In Amazonia, for example, the resources and the livelihood of the Indians are being destroyed along with the forest. Some cases of deforestation are occurring inside recognized Indian areas, destroying not only their forests but also the animal and plant resources they depend on for their survival. Even when the deforestation occurs outside designated Indian areas, the impact on the animal and plant resources, the water supply, and the rivers in and near the Indian areas can be devastating.

Deforestation in Amazonia follows both traditional frontier expansion and large-scale, internationally financed development projects. In both cases, there is an influx of outsiders into regions that had been sparsely inhabited, in part by Indian populations. Their isolation is broken overnight as land-hungry settlers invade their lands. In Brazil colonists purposefully settle on Indian lands. If a settler can establish a small holding on Indian land (the least protected of all categories of land in the interior of Brazil), then by squatter's rights he will be virtually guaranteed a substitute plot of land through government-sponsored colonization programs.

The Indians lose control of their natural resources as these are destroyed both within and around their traditional territories. The result is impoverishment and dispossession, migration to regional towns and cities, and a wretched future of unemployment, begging, homelessness, prostitution, and disease.

The situation of the Indians has to be seen in the context of: (1) the defense of their historical, moral, and legal rights; (2) the policies and practices of the agencies that fund international development; and (3) the recent emergence of their own articulate and increasingly powerful representative organizations.

As the original inhabitants, indigenous peoples might be said to have a historical right to their lands. As our fellow human beings, we would also grant them a moral right to them. Over the years the countries within whose boundaries they live have recognized their legal rights to their lands, in terms of both national and international law.

In only a few historic cases have invaders recognized the sovereignty of indigenous peoples. Examples are the treaties established between the British and the Maori of New Zealand, the British and the Indians of North America, and between the federal and state governments of the United States and the Indians. Such treaties typically provide for the formal cession of land areas to the newcomers. In most cases, however, Indian sovereignty was not recognized and newcomers acquired the lands they wanted by conquest, formal annexation, or illegal encroachment and dispossession. In virtually all cases guardianship by the national government was imposed.

National laws affecting indigenous peoples are sometimes explicitly destructive to ethnic groups. For instance, the Chilean Decree Law 2568 of 1979 provides for the division of the community lands of the Mapuche Indians of southern Chile into parcels of private property as family plots. In addition, however, this law denies the status of Indian to the Mapuche occupants once the lands are divided. On paper at least, Brazil recognizes that Indians have a constitutional right to the permanent possession of their lands and an exclusive right to use their natural resources. The 1973 "Statute of the Indian" reaffirms these rights and provides for the protection of the customs and traditional ways of Indian populations, except when considerations of national security or national development take precedence.

Relevant international law is found in a series of conventions and declarations of the United Nations, the Organization of American States, and the International Labor Organization (ILO). These statutes, however, primarily concern individual human rights and not collective or communal indigenous rights. The United Nations Working Group on Indigenous Populations is currently preparing a new convention specifically on indigenous rights. The ILO convention is now under revision and it is hoped that the new version will not include the outdated assumption that indigenous people will, sooner or later, be fully assimilated into the national societies of the countries where they live.

The main funding agencies of international development that have U.S. financial support are the multilateral development banks (MDBS), especially the World Bank and the U.S. Agency for International Development (AID). The World Bank has recently set new policy for the treatment of those indigenous peoples affected by development projects that it funds. One of its key provisions calls for the recognition,

demarcation, and protection of indigenous lands "containing those resources required to sustain the . . . people's traditional means of livelihood." Demarcation is to be completed before any funds are disbursed. Unfortunately no project funded by the Bank has yet respected this provision and, in fact, several current projects are allowing the opposite process to occur, with considerable loss of land and natural resources as a result.

Demarcating lands (or titling them as communal property where the national legislation provides for this) as a precondition for disbursement of loan funds is a realistic requirement. It was done, for example, in the U.S. AID-funded Palcazu Valley sector of the Pichis-Palcazu Special Project in Peru. At the urging of a number of nongovernmental organizations including Survival International USA, AID held the Peruvian government to this requirement for the fifteen months that it took for the titling process to be completed.

Recent oversight hearings held by the U.S. Congress on the performance of the MDBS have led to some relevant legislation. While this falls far short of full protection for the rights of indigenous peoples, it does increase U.S. pressure on the MDBS to pay proper attention to the problems these people face as a result of international development.

Organizations formed and staffed by indigenous peoples themselves are becoming increasingly well established, vocal, and effective. For example, UNI (The Union of Indian Nations), a pan-Brazilian Indian organization, has recently set up an alliance with the rubber tappers' union of the Brazilian Amazon. Together with Indian organizations of Peru, Ecuador, Colombia, and Bolivia, UNI is a cofounder of the recently created Coordinating Committee of Indian Peoples of the Amazon Basin (La Coordenadora), which advocates sustainable development sensitive to specific ethnic needs in that region.

As they continue to strengthen their own organizations and federations within the legal framework provided by international law and, in a very few cases, more or less favorable national legislation, indigenous peoples will be able to insist that their rights and their traditional, sustainable systems of resource management be taken into account as a necessary part of the agenda for the future of the tropical rain forests.

I would like to acknowledge the hospitality, tolerance, and helpfulness of the Yanomami of the upper Auaris River valley. Their ecological knowledge and wisdom have amazed me forever. My thanks and appreciation go to Dr. Peter Seitel of the Smithsonian Institution's Folklife Program for the initial contact that led to participation in the project.

6

HILL PEOPLE
OF NORTHERN
THAILAND

PETER KUNSTADTER

It was September 1963, and monsoon rains had been pelting down steadily throughout northern Thailand for over a week. For a day and a half after leaving the district town my guides and I had crossed and recrossed the Amlan River, swollen to chest height with brown water, and picked our way balancing precariously on narrow clay dikes in flooded irrigated fields. We climbed the mud-slick trail up the mountain slopes, through forest and swidden (slash-and-burn) fields and past an occasional Karen village. We were walking on a narrow trail through swidden fields of nearly ripe rice and had almost reached our first destination, Pa Pae, a Lua' village in the hills of Mae Sariang district, northwestern Thailand, when my cleated boots lost their grip and I landed on my back, muddy but unhurt. The hills rang with the laughter of the barefoot women and men who had paused in their weeding chores to watch our progress along the narrow trail. Two decades later the villagers still sometimes remind me of their first sight of me when we talk about the "old days."

In the early 1960s Pa Pae was a village of about 195 people who depended almost entirely on what they produced to provide their food, medicine, clothing, and shelter. Most of the men and all of the women were dressed in clothing the women had woven from homespun cotton they had grown in the swiddens. The newly built school and teacher's house contrasted strongly with the houses of the villagers, which all stood above the ground on sturdy teak pilings and were roofed with large shingles woven of *Imperata* grass. Only the houses of the more affluent had wood-plank walls or floors, carefully hewn from teak trees; most had bamboo floors and walls. All but one of the village houses was built in the traditional pattern, with a large front porch and a single, large enclosed room with a clay-lined fireplace set in the middle of the floor. The grass-shingled roofs extended nearly to the ground on three sides and covered half the front porch. Under the overhanging roof on one side of each house was a wooden, foot-powered pestle and mortar used for removing the husk from their staple rice. Every evening after the villagers returned from their fields, the slow thumping of these rice pounders rang throughout the village. Only occasionally, when the Border Patrol teacher was in the village and his batteries had not yet run down, could you hear the sound of a radio.

I visited a number of other villages, but found that Pa Pae best suited our research purposes. After harvest I returned to Pa Pae with my wife, Sally, and we asked the headman, Kae Ta Kham, for permission to move into Pa Pae. We hired our soon-to-be next-door neighbor, Ai Po, to build us a house for $35, and we settled in to begin to gain an understanding of how

Pa Pae, a Lua' village in the hills of northwestern Thailand, is surrounded by a sacred grove of trees with fallow irrigated fields in the foreground and recently burned swiddens in the background.

the villagers used and protected the forest where their ancestors had lived for many generations.

Loong Ta, who was then in his late sixties, became one of my most helpful teachers. He told me that most of the present Pa Pae residents were descendants of people who had lived in villages within a kilometer or two of the present village site. He showed me the sites of the old villages, where broken Chinese Ming period pottery could still be found. During his youth Pa Pae villagers grew all of their rice on swidden fields. He also recounted that in the days of his father Pa Pae villagers used to walk 200 kilometers (120 miles) across the mountains to pay a tribute of forest products, including orchids and roofing grass, to the prince of Chiang Mai. In return the prince recognized their claim to the hill fields they farmed and lectured them on the need to conserve their forest and soil resources.

In the 1920s, Loong Ta said, some Pa Pae villagers hired lowlanders to teach them the necessary techniques and rituals for farming irrigated rice. In the early 1960s Pa Pae villagers still grew most of their rice with traditional swidden techniques, using only a few metal tools, which they made themselves. These included the long-bladed knives they used to fell trees that grew on fields during nine fallow years following one year of cultivation. Since the 1960s the villagers have had to respond to an increasing number of cultural, economic, and religious changes imposed from the outside.

Human Cultural Adaptation in Tropical Asia

Mainland Southeast Asia is occupied by a great variety of ethnic groups whose members have taken widely varied approaches to using what was once a largely forest-covered area. The highland Lua' villagers of Pa Pae are similar to a declining minority of people who lived more or less in a state of balance with the forest. Until the past decade or two, their way of life has been relatively unchanged by contact with the modern world, while the majority of the Thai population who live in the lowlands has seen very rapid development.

Most of the lowlands of tropical Asia, where the majority of the people live, are densely settled by people who traditionally depended for their subsistence on cultivation of wet (irrigated) rice. Populations here have increased and expanded rapidly in what were two centuries ago sparsely settled, poorly drained, densely forested areas. Wherever the lowland plains were large and well-watered—throughout the broad lowlands of Java, the Philippines, Vietnam, Kampuchea, Laos, Thailand, Burma, Bangladesh, India, and Sri Lanka— watercourses have been channeled and rivers have been dammed to control the flow of water. The lowland forest has been cleared, land has been leveled, diked, and drained were necessary, flooded, plowed, and harrowed to remove the last vestiges of native vegetation, and planted with vast fields of rice. Only a few trees remain to shelter water buffalo or provide shade to farmsteads. Soil fertility is renewed primarily by

A path leads into the village of Pa Pae in Mae Sariang district of northwestern Thailand.

the irrigation water, which carries dissolved and suspended minerals from soil erosion and vegetation decay at higher elevations, rather than by decay of vegetation from the field itself. These farmers have followed a strategy of environmental homogenization and control. Lowland native forests persist only on some coastal and brackish-water estuaries where mangrove forests remain.

In recent years larger-scale irrigation systems have allowed farmers to grow several successive crops more or less continuously throughout the year. This has been accomplished with increased dependence on external sources of energy for farm machinery and on farm chemicals. The rich species diversity of the forest has been replaced by a few crops with diversity related primarily to water regimes ("floating" rice, brackish water-tolerant rice, etc.). The genetic diversity of these super crops has been diminished by widespread adoption, sometimes as a result of governmental edict, of improved "miracle" varieties, which require even greater control of water level and often large-scale use of chemical pesticides and fertilizers to maintain productivity.

At slightly higher elevations, usually near the coasts, native forests in some of the warmer, rainy areas of Peninsular Malaysia, southeastern Thailand, parts of Kampuchea, and southern Vietnam have been turned into managed monocrop plantations of oil palm or rubber or into orchards of tropical fruits (durian,

mango, mangosteen, rambutan). These supply national and international commodity and urban food markets. Demand for these products has led to the rapid conversion of natural forest into plantations, especially on the Malay Peninsula. These plantations also require heavy inputs of energy and chemicals from external sources.

Drier upland areas above the floodplains of major rivers and away from the coasts have traditionally been sparsely populated, primarily due to shortage of water for agriculture. Lowland farmers have used these areas to collect firewood, for grazing, and as places where those who had insufficient irrigated land could grow a subsistence crop using a bush-fallow swidden system. In some places swiddening has been followed by conversion of forest to more or less permanent (annual) cultivation of cash crops (manioc, corn, sugarcane), which often require extensive use of farm machinery and chemicals. In other places, for example, in eastern Thailand where rainfall is sufficient, the forest was cleared in the 1960s for manioc but has now been converted to rubber plantations. In some places lowland migrants or imported plantation workers have replaced traditional forest people, as on the Malay Peninsula.

These upland areas are closer to markets than the rugged highlands and generally did not support a dense, permanent farming population, but their forest resources have long been exploited by lowlanders for

The distribution of Lua' and Hmong villages in
Thailand.

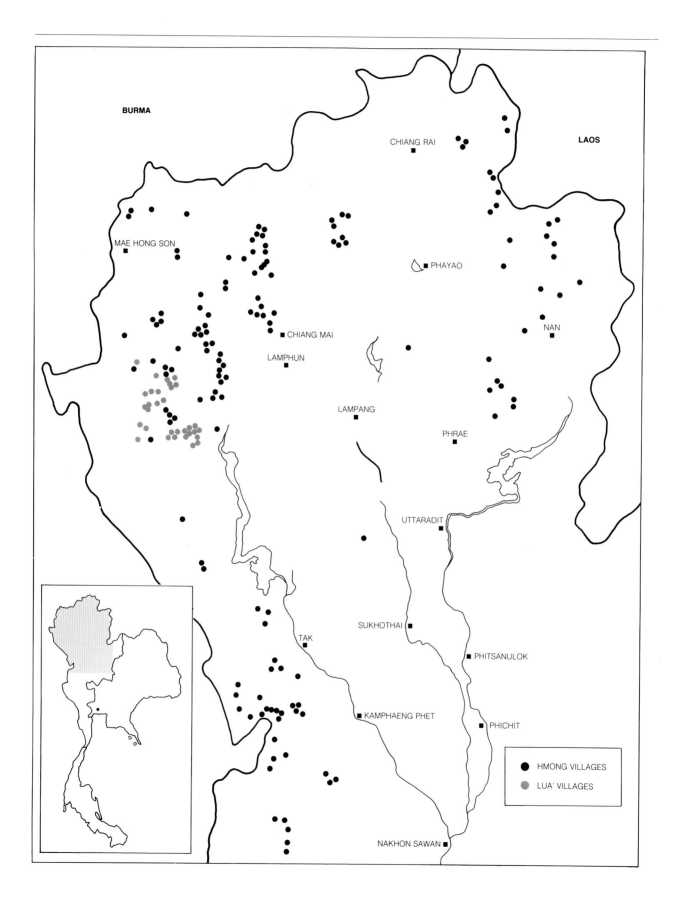

BURMA

LAOS

CHIANG RAI

MAE HONG SON

PHAYAO

CHIANG MAI

LAMPHUN

NAN

LAMPANG

PHRAE

UTTARADIT

SUKHOTHAI

TAK

PHITSANULOK

KAMPHAENG PHET

PHICHIT

● HMONG VILLAGES

● LUA' VILLAGES

NAKHON SAWAN

lumber. Initially this was usually done by highgrading (removing only mature valuable trees), which left a forest depleted of mature trees of a few species, but still composed of a large number of species. More recently, as national and international demand for all kinds of wood has increased and chain saws, bulldozers, and other machinery have become available, the tendency has been to clear-cut trees of all species in large blocks. Clear-cutting is followed either by abandoning the area or establishing plantations of a single species such as teak.

At elevations above four hundred meters (twelve hundred feet) where rainfall is generally more plentiful, native vegetation changes from mixed deciduous-evergreen forest to moist evergreen, and at the highest elevations to montane forest. The highland forests of tropical Asia were traditionally occupied by small scattered villages of a wide variety of ethnic groups. They make up only a small percentage of the total population in Kampuchea, Malaysia, Thailand, or Vietnam, but are much more important numerically in Burma and Laos. Many of these people—such as the Khmu, Lamet, and Htin in Laos, Lua' in Thailand, Wa in Burma, and Korwa in India—speak languages distantly related to the language of the majority population of Kampuchea. Their ancestors lived in the area long before the ancestors of the now-dominant majority ethnic groups in Burma, Laos, Malaysia, Thailand, and Vietnam. Unlike South American and African forest dwellers who lived in areas remote from major centers of civilization, most of the minority people in the Southeast Asian highlands have strong cultural ties to ancient centers of great civilizations. The culture of the Lua', for example, shows influences from the ancient civilization of India. Other forest-dwelling highland minorities, such as the Hmong (Meo) and Mien (Yao) who number in the tens of thousands in Thailand and hundreds of thousands in Laos and Vietnam, are related to large minority groups numbering in the millions in China and have cultures strongly influenced by Chinese civilization. Other groups, such as the Akha, Lahu, and Lisu, speak Tibeto-Burmese languages. The large Karen minority (several million in Burma and about one-quarter million in Thailand) live in both the lowlands and hills of Burma and Thailand and speak a language that may be distantly related to languages spoken by the majority populations in Tibet and Burma. A few groups, such as the Rhade in southern Vietnam, speak languages that are related to Malayo-Polynesian languages found throughout the Pacific. A very small minority of the highlanders, such as the Mrabri of northern Thailand (numbering only in the hundreds) and aboriginal groups on the Malay Peninsula including the Semang and Sakai, are nomadic hunters and gatherers, but most are farmers who make their living by slash-and-burn agriculture.

Upland farmers in tropical forest areas must contend with an environment in which soil fertility is low and the most easily obtained fertilizer is decayed or burned vegetation. This contrasts with the great plains and delta regions in temperate zones, where most of the fertility is held in the soil. Tropical forest highlanders use two major strategies to extract the nutrients: a relatively conservative self-renewing system, used by such people as the Karen in Burma and Thailand, Lua' in Thailand, and Mnong Gar in southern Vietnam; and an extractive system that is followed by replacement of the forest by grassland, practiced by Hmong and Mien in Laos, Thailand, and Vietnam. In the conservative system, farmers clear fields in secondary forest and cultivate them for a short period in a manner that encourages forest regrowth. They fallow their fields long enough to allow regeneration of a secondary forest before clearing and cultivating again in a regular rotation. Farmers using this conservative system often live in permanently settled villages. Farmers who use the extractive system traditionally fell and burn mature forest. They clean cultivate the same fields for several years in succession until the soil is exhausted or until dense regrowth of *Imperata* or *Saccharum* grasses makes further cultivation difficult. Villages are generally temporary and farmers move when there is no more cultivable land close to the village.

Tradition and Change among Highland Lua' Farmers

Pa Pae, the Lua' village where we have done research intermittently since the early 1960s, is located at an elevation of about seven hundred meters (twenty-three hundred feet) in rolling forest-covered hills. There are about twelve thousand Lua' living in the mountains of northern Thailand who are the descendants of a group that was more widespread in the highlands and valleys of northern Thailand prior to the arrival of Thai-speaking people during the eleventh or twelfth century. Most of the Lua' population in the lowlands has intermarried and become culturally assimilated, indistinguishable from other lowland Thais. Traditional Lua' villages now remain only in the forested highlands where archaeological and historical evidence shows they have been settled for many hundreds of years.

The diet of Pa Pae villagers is composed mostly of rice supplemented by small amounts of meat from pigs and chickens raised by every household. Although in the 1960s about half the Pa Pae households had irrigated fields, economic and religious activities of the villagers were organized around the requirements of swidden cultivation. Traditionally all households of a Lua' village cut their swidden fields in a designated block of secondary forest. Aside from practical prob-

Men jab the loose soil of a freshly burned swidden with their long, iron-tipped planting sticks.

lems of clearing and burning an isolated field and protecting it from the depredations of wild pigs or bears, our Pa Pae friends often told us that it would be too lonely to have a field without Lua' neighbors. They farm each large block for only one year after it has been cleared and then fallow it for about nine years. When I asked them about planting for more than one year in the same place, Loong Ta, and his son, Ai Toon, told me that the yield would not be good in the second year. The soil would lose its fertility and there would be too many weeds. The Lua' know that burned immature vegetation will not produce enough ash, and the soil after the burn will not have enough fertility for good crop growth.

Swidden blocks around the village are cultivated in a regular rotational sequence with a ten-year period. The villagers know this cycle so well that they may reckon a child's age by counting the sequence of fields back to the one they were cultivating when the child was born. Swidden land has traditionally been considered the property of the village and was reallocated as necessary by village religious leaders. Cutting, burning, and planting of swiddens was traditionally controlled by the chief priest of the village. Villagers customarily were obliged to pay him such nominal tribute as the leg of any such large game animal as wild boar (*Sus scrofa*) or barking deer (*Muntiacus muntjak*) that they killed in symbolic payment for the right to cultivate. In return, he along with other religious leaders

would confirm the selection of the swidden block to be cultivated, set the day for burning and planting, and lead ceremonies essential to appease the powerful spirits of the forest whose land the villagers would use temporarily for their swiddens. The households that belong to the village normally have rights to use the same plot of the village swidden land each time it is cultivated, but villagers are not allowed to sell swidden land.

Each household normally returns to the same field it cultivated ten years previously. They mark their swidden-field boundaries by placing a row of charred logs along its borders after it has been cleared and burned. Traces of these logs remain to guide placement of new markers ten years later. Thus, every household has an interest in seeing that the fertility of each of its field sites is maintained for future use. Practitioners of this land-use system consciously attempt to sustain a balance between themselves and the forest in both their farming techniques and their rituals.

Every January village elders go to inspect the next swidden block on the field-rotation schedule to see if forest regrowth has been satisfactory for cultivation. Since a fire during the fallow period will reduce soil fertility, they check that the site has been free of fires since the last time it was cultivated. Pa Pae villagers are careful to prevent fires, but if a fire should occur, each household must work to put out the fire or pay a fine for failing to do so.

Swidden planting is an occasion for courtship. Maidens, dressed in their finest clothing, throw a few rice grains in each hole made by the men.

In 1967 we cultivated our own swidden field and went through the appropriate ceremonies with the help of our Lua' friends. Poo Sook, one of the village elders, sacrificed a chicken on our behalf and showed us that the gall bladder was full and shiny, a good omen indicating that the spirits would bless us with a good harvest. If the omen had not been good we would have had to try to trade sites with another household and sacrifice another chicken at the new site to see if our luck would be better there.

The villagers clear their fields using only long steel-bladed knives to fell the small trees, leaving stumps about one meter high. Cutting trees is mostly men's work. Loong Ta showed me how to start at the bottom of the slope and work uphill, so that the falling trees knocked down the smaller vegetation. He told me that the Pa Pae villagers are careful to leave a strip of trees along watercourses and at the tops of ridges to prevent erosion and provide seed sources for forest regrowth during the fallow period. The men also leave the larger trees standing but trim their branches so they will not shade the crops. They cut their fields in January or February and allow the slash to dry until the end of March, which is the hottest, driest time of the year. Kae Ta Kham, after consulting with other village elders, set the date for the fields to be burned. If two villages are cutting adjacent swidden blocks they try to coordinate their activities so that the fires will be burned on the same day; if the blocks are not adjacent they try to arrange to have people available to prevent the accidental spread of fire into unburned slash or forest reserved for future cultivation, and to prevent flying cinders from igniting the grass or dried-leaf shingles with which their roofs are covered.

A few days before the swidden fire scheduled for March 30, we went out with representatives from every Pa Pae household to help clear a firebreak four to six meters wide around the swidden block. All the low-growing vegetation was removed from the firebreak, which is swept clean in order to prevent the fire from burning adjacent parts of the forest that would be cultivated in future years or retained as seed sources or as the homes of various spirits.

On the day the fields were burned, Kae Ta Kham, Loong Ta, Poo Sook, and the other old men of the village led a ceremony to honor the spirits of the fields, and the old women made sacrificial offerings in honor of the villagers' ancestral spirits. At noon on a hot dry day before the afternoon winds sprang up, the younger men used torches of split bamboo to ignite the fire in the tinder-dry slash. Poo Yaeh explained why he spit a mouthful of home-brewed rice liquor on the end of his torch: he was praying that the fire would burn over the fields just as the raw alcohol burned his mouth. The men started the fire at the top of the swidden block and then ran down to light the slash at the sides and the bottom. The fire burned toward the center creating a strong indraft, which prevented the fire from escaping on the sides of the block. The slash was quickly consumed by a roaring fire, which burned tons of fuel within an hour.

The men who burn the swiddens usually carry their muzzle-loading guns with them, hoping that game animals will be chased toward them out of the blazing fields, but only very rarely does an animal appear these days. As soon as the flames die down, while the ashes are still smoldering, the field owners go to the spot where they will build a field shelter. They call out to the spirit owners of the forest and chant to inform them that they are claiming the place temporarily for human use, planting a sign woven out of split bamboo in the ground to symbolize this claim. At the same time they scatter seeds of red and yellow *Celosia*, marigolds, and cosmos, which will bloom at harvest time, because they believe that spirits are afraid of these flowers. Meanwhile the children run about the fields looking for any edible snakes or small rodents that may have been roasted by the swidden blaze.

The first crops the farmers plant are cotton and corn, which they sow on the slopes of the fields, and yams, which they plant in lower, wetter areas. The next ten days or two weeks they spend in propping up unburned logs along the contours of the fields (to reduce hillside erosion), marking their field boundaries, gathering larger logs for firewood, and piling and reburning the small bits of unburned slash, and building fences to keep the livestock out of the fields.

In mid-April on a day selected by village religious leaders, Kae Ta Kham was the first to begin planting the main subsistence crop, upland rice. In order to ensure a good harvest and to prevent illness of family members who are working in the fields, each household sacrifices a dog and a chicken or pig to appease the spirits of the forest and streams whose realm they are invading. Poo Dee told us that at planting and harvest times he was glad to have two eligible daughters because that made it easier for him to attract a large number of young men to help plant his field, so the seed would have a chance to take root and sprout before the heavy monsoon rains began. Planting season is a customary time of courtship. Youths and maidens joke with each other throughout the day, especially when they stop work for the noontime meal. The boys try to force the girls to drink liquor, while the girls try to force more food into the boys' mouths than they can eat, much to the amusement of onlookers. The joking usually escalates into water throwing, and everyone joins in the laughter as unwary victims are soaked.

Teams of men, often encouraged with bottles of rice liquor supplied by the field owner, chant as they jab the loose earth with three-meter (ten-foot)

long, iron-tipped planting poles. Bachelors traditionally dress for the occasion in their best traditional white homespun clothes, heads wrapped in bright pink silk cloths, and in recent years wearing sunglasses and store-bought straw hats (if they can afford them). When the planting begins, the men are followed by maidens dressed in their finest and wearing all their silver jewelry with flowers attached to their earrings, and by older women and youngsters who throw a few rice seeds into each of the shallow holes. They do not cover the rice seeds, but some of the loose soil and ash falls over the seed. The field owners direct the planters to sow different rice varieties in different areas of the field: quick-ripening types near the field shelter where they can watch it easily; drought-resistant types on the drier, sandier tops of the slopes; and a quantity of glutinous rice, which reflects whether their household prefers it to the nonglutinous types. Over the years each household has selected the strains of rice they prefer to eat, so each household grows slightly different varieties.

Each household plants tall-growing sorghum to mark boundaries of adjacent swiddens. They plant mustard greens, peppers, several varieties of beans, and other vegetables in gardens near their field shelters and viney plants in potential erosion sites along creases in the hillside fields. They also plant millet with the rice. By mid-May they can distinguish rice and other seedlings from weeds and begin the dreary task of weeding with a short-handled, L-shaped tool. Bending at the waist, the weeders scrape and hack the weeds at the surface of the soil but do not try to pull or dig out the weeds. Weeding is work for everyone, but most often women and older children trudge up muddy paths to weed their swiddens every day, rain or shine, throughout the rainy growing season. It is times like these when mothers are happiest to have daughters to help them.

Lua' farmers harvest their rice with a small hand-held sickle. Men and women cut the stems of each bunch of rice close to the ground, leaving stalks about one meter long. They lay the stalks on stubble to dry for a few days before threshing. Each household tries to assemble a large number of helpers—relatives and members of other households—on the day it begins to thresh. All the help received will have to be paid back when the other households thresh. Maidens and older women go around the field gathering large bundles of rice stalks, which they pile carefully around a threshing floor. The floor has been leveled on the hillside, lined with threshing mats woven of split bamboo, and decorated with flowers to ward off the spirits. Poo Sao showed me how he circled his field, carrying a chicken in a rice-measuring basket covered with a winnowing fan, calling the soul of the rice to come to the threshing floor and make the yield increase, and promising the rice soul a meal of the sacrificial chicken.

Usually it is young men who beat the rice stalks against the threshing mat to knock the grain loose. Other men beat the rice stalks and broken straw with bamboo threshing sticks to separate the rice grains as completely as possible. As the pile of grain and chaff grows they shuffle through it with their feet, fanning it with a woven-bamboo winnowing fan to blow away as much of the dirt and debris as possible. Periodically they load the rice into baskets and carry it to a mat-lined winnowing platform. Usually it is young women who carry the baskets up a ladder, which has been built into the winnowing floor, and slowly pour the grain onto the mat, while a young man standing below uses a winnowing fan to blow away more debris. Then they load the cleaned rice into baskets and carry it to a temporary barn, usually built on the site of the field shelter.

When all households have completed their harvest and carried their rice back to the village, they hold a ceremony to call the souls of the people and the souls of the rice back to the village and to return the fields to the spirits who normally live in them. Except for a few peppers, tobacco leaves, or cotton that may be gathered in the old swiddens in the year after harvest, the swiddens are left to fallow until their next turn comes in the field-rotation schedule.

After the souls have returned, the villagers hold a new year's ceremony led by the chief priest. If the swidden area that they will use in the next year is believed to be the home of a particularly powerful spirit, all the village households contribute to the cost of a large animal (water buffalo, cow, or large pig), which is sacrificed to appease that spirit. Traditionally all households participated in this ceremony, bringing specially prepared food to the hillside at the edge of the village where the animals are sacrificed. Thereafter the annual cycle begins again.

Ecological Effects of the Traditional Lua' Swidden System

The traditional Lua' rotational system maintains a series of vegetation zones around the village, which are used by the villagers in various ways. Mature forest was preserved as the home of spirits or as a cemetery, where villagers were forbidden to cut lumber or make swiddens or gardens. Uncut strips were also maintained between swidden blocks, around the village, along streamcourses around headwaters, and at the tops of ridges. In addition to reducing erosion, these serve as seed sources for revegetation of the fallow swiddens and shelters for wildlife.

Because there is enough soil moisture, regrowth on the fallow swiddens is vigorous following harvest. Herbaceous growth covers the soil surface even before the start of the next rainy season. The villagers use the grassy vegetation of swiddens during the early fallow years for grazing. Sprouts grow from many of the tree stumps that were left in the fields and not killed by the swidden fire.

By about the seventh fallow year a forest canopy shades and suppresses most of the grasses. After nine years of fallow the forest has grown to about the same size and species composition that it had when it was last cut and burned, with trees ten to twenty cm (four to eight inches) in diameter and up to nine meters (thirty feet) high. Soil conditions also return to approximately their condition prior to the previous cultivation period. Forest regrowth on fallow swiddens contains some species found in the mature forest, but most of the species are fire-tolerant or fire-resistant and adapted to a drier, more open environment.

In addition to the species they cultivate, Lua' villagers use many plants from the regrowth on their fallow swiddens and from uncut forest for house construction, for weaving baskets, as traditional medicines, dyes for their homespun clothing, and supplementary foods ranging from wild fruits to wild yams and tubers especially important during times of food shortage. With the help of Ai Toon, Ai Dam, Ai Pho, and other Lua' friends we collected and identified about two hundred uncultivated species used by Pa Pae villagers for food, over thirty used for animal food, over seventy used for medicine, and over twenty used for weaving and dyeing.

Forest products are very important for home consumption, but they play little role in the Pa Pae cash economy. Villagers occasionally gather traditional medicinal plants or vines used for a traditional shampoo for sale in the lowland markets, but for the most part to earn money they sell pigs, water buffalo, cattle, or their own labor.

Chickens are given a few grains of rice and penned up every night. They are released to hunt and peck for themselves during the daytime, and householders who are sunning their rice before pounding it to remove the hulls must keep shooing the chickens away from a tempting meal. Pigs were traditionally penned at night and allowed to scavenge during the daytime, but this is changing. They are fed on leftover cooked rice, usually mixed with the boiled trunks of wild banana and wild taro leaves gathered in the forest. Traditionally meat was eaten only on ceremonial occasions. When I asked Ai Dam why he was having a wrist-binding ceremony if no one at his home was ill, he said they just wanted to eat meat, but did not want to eat the chicken without having a ceremony.

Conservation of watercourses was important both to control erosion and because streams often provide human food. Nia Kham, an ancient but lively lady when we first lived at Pa Pae, told us that when she was young the villagers used to catch fish as big as her arm, but by the early 1960s the big fish were all gone. Fish were still avidly pursued in the late 1960s for their food value as well as the sport. Small groups of women and older children took their dip nets to fish in the turbid waters of the rain-swollen stream, and groups of men, women, and youngsters would join together to dam off sections of the stream in the dry season. The men groped under rocks and grabbed the small fish hiding there and then drained the dammed-off pools using nets to filter out the fish that had been trapped. Fishing was still a good way to cool off in the hot season, but the yield was disappointingly small—only a few finger-sized fish, tadpoles, and water insects. The villagers attributed the loss of fish to use of poisons and agricultural chemicals downstream, but we also noted that teams spraying village houses against malaria dumped out their unused insecticide and rinsed out their spray pumps in the stream.

Pa Pae men often go hunting with their antique muzzle-loading guns, but they only rarely kill a dog-sized barking deer and even more rarely a bear or wild pig. Usually they come home empty-handed. They tell us that although barking deer, pigs, and even bears occasionally get into their fields, there has been very little game since the end of the Second World War. They are more successful with traps and deadfalls, which they set in the swiddens to catch birds and rats that are attracted to the newly sown seed and the ripening crops.

Archaeological and historical evidence as well as village traditions suggest that this system has persisted for many hundreds of years, representing many swidden-fallow cycles. Perpetuating this system of living with the forest required both stability of population size and adherence to the traditional norms of behavior backed by religious sanctions. Lua' population appears to have begun slow sustained growth only in the mid-1950s. Population growth was controlled by mortality, which remained high until smallpox and malaria were controlled in the 1950s, by delay of marriage, which controlled fertility, and by customs restricting migration. It takes time for bachelors to accumulate the necessary brideprice, so Lua' tended to marry in their twenties. Children were considered valuable because they helped with the farm work, but limitations on the amount of swidden land meant that there was no long-term economic advantage in large family size. Because in-law households are supposed to help each other in farming tasks if they live nearby, Lua' prefer to marry within the village, but customs that restrict marriage between close relatives reduce the number of eligible partners in the small Lua' villages and might further delay marriage.

Tradition also encouraged or required outmigration of villagers who broke the marriage taboos or other village customs. Migration into Lua' villages was restricted by land-use customs, which gave access to village swidden lands only to descendants of founding families who inherited this right from their father's household. Normally the only migrants were brides moving into a village one at a time, and their number was roughly balanced by daughters who married and moved out to their husband's village. As a result, villages were composed of people who were relatively successful in the traditional economic and socioreligious system and had an interest in maintaining village stability.

Changes in the Traditional Lua' Swidden System and Their Consequences

A series of changes has upset the stability of both the traditional Lua' land-use system and the socioreligious system that maintained it for many generations. Non-Lua' population in the area of Lua' villages began to grow gradually in the early nineteenth century with the arrival of small numbers of another ethnic group, Skaw Karens. The first Karen migrants stayed in Lua' villages, but as the Karen population grew they formed villages in what had previously been exclusively Lua' territory and paid rent to the Lua' villages on whose land they farmed.

Early in the twentieth century the Bangkok government took control of Northern Thailand and imposed a head tax to be paid in cash by all ethnic groups. Karens stopped paying rent to the Lua' villages and continued to expand their population and territorial control. Karens use a swidden system similar to that of the Lua', but they are less careful in controlling fire and conserving land and forest resources and not tied as tightly to specific farm sites. Lua' cut large cohesive swidden blocks in which each household has its own field, but Karen cultivate swidden fields wherever land is available even between two Lua' fields. When a Karen village grows too large for the available land, groups of villagers leave to seek new land. In this way Karens filled all the spaces between Lua' villages and began encroaching on traditional Lua' swidden land holdings, forcing Lua' villagers to reduce the length of their swidden fallow.

By the middle of the twentieth century a few Hmong were beginning to settle in the midst of Lua' and Karen villages, disregarding traditional Lua' claims of land ownership and often cutting fields on ridges and at the tops of watersheds. In the late 1960s Hmong from Mae Tow began to cut the forest at the headwaters of the stream running through Pa Pae, an area that Pa Pae villagers considered sacred and had left undisturbed in order to protect their watershed. They asked the Hmong to stop cutting there to no avail. They protested to district officials that destruction of the forest at the headwaters of their stream would cause flooding in the first year, followed by low water

Corn fields now surround Mae Tho, a Hmong village in western Chiang Mai Province, Thailand, where forest grew in 1960. The land immediately around the houses has been prepared for opium poppies.

The Lua' harvest rice with a short, hand-held sickle and carefully lay it to dry on the stubble.

in the years after the water-holding forest had been removed. The government officials declined to intervene, and the villagers' predictions proved correct.

The Thai government considers that all forested highlands belong to the Royal Forest Department. According to Thai law (as distinct from Northern Thai custom), all swiddening in the Royal Forest is illegal regardless of who does it. Thai government officials do not recognize traditional claims to swidden land and will not intervene in land disputes between highlanders. Thus, the Lua' now have no legal claim to the land granted to them hundreds of years earlier by Northern Thai princes and have no power to protect the watershed upon which their livelihood depends.

Lumber is important in the Thai economy. It was traditionally a major export, but by the 1970s Thailand had become a major importer of lumber from Burma and Laos and of wood products from industrialized countries. The government began giving lumbering concessions in the nineteenth century but took little control over other uses of the forest until the middle of the twentieth century. By the 1970s the Royal Forest Department was engaged in widespread reforestation projects including some on fallow swiddens. The result of these changes was to decrease the amount of land available to Lua' villagers for swiddening and to reduce the security with which they held this land. When some of the major diseases were controlled after the Second World War, the Lua' population began to experience sustained growth, which further increased the land pressure.

Although they were rarely visited by lowlanders, Lua' highlanders were never truly isolated, even one hundred years ago. They went to market to sell a few pigs, a little rice, and a few forest products, to buy a few manufactured items (salt, metal tools, Chinese pottery, silver), and occasionally to pay tribute to the Northern Thai princes in Chiang Mai or Lamphun or to honor famous Buddhist monks. In order to earn money to pay their taxes, they carried goods between Northern Thai and Burmese markets before roads were built and worked in mines or the lumbering industry. Outside influences increased rapidly in Lua' villages starting in the late 1950s; roads and schools were built; health, welfare, and other governmental services became available; agricultural development projects were initiated; and Buddhist, Catholic, and Protestant missionary activities increased. Access to an increasing variety of manufactured goods (kerosene, flashlights and batteries, matches, radios, watches, sunglasses, rubber sandles, and clothing) increased the demand for cash. Temporary jobs in development projects provided money and increased villagers' contacts with the outside world.

The authority of traditional Lua' leaders was based on their relationship with spirits and the common belief in their ability to control those spirits for the benefit of all the villagers. In return the villagers accepted the direction of the religious leaders in location and timing of swidden cutting, burning, and planting. The conversion of a number of Pa Pae households to Christianity has broken down the community. Now in addition to sanctions against marriage between close relatives, there are obligations to marry within one's own religion. Because this seriously reduces the number of eligible mates within the village, more Pa Pae villagers are getting mates from outside the village including some Karen and Hmong. The influx of new people and ideas, the presence of teachers and development workers in their villages, and the development of alternatives to swiddening were associated with a decline in power of the traditional leaders. Until the late 1960s households that had converted to Christianity continued to pay their share for the purchase of pigs, cows, or water buffalos used in village ceremonies and ate their share of the meat after the animals had been sacrificed. Ai Tit, an early Catholic convert, told me that later the Christians decided it was sinful to eat meat from a sacrificial animal. By the late 1970s they stopped contributing to the cost of village ceremonies but continued to live in the village. Consequently the remaining animist villagers can no longer afford to hold villagewide ceremonies requiring large animal sacrifices. Without agreement on traditional religious sanctions and the beliefs on which they were based, village leaders can no longer coordinate the swidden activities of all the village households or constrain use of the forest. By the early 1980s a road was bulldozed through the sacred grove south of Pa Pae and villagers had cut many of the remaining trees to plant coffee, an action that once would have cost them a stiff fine. After Kae Ta Kham died his successor, Kae Boon La, could no longer control the location or timing of the swidden burn.

Lua' villagers have long been aware of alternative land-use systems, especially permanent irrigated (wet rice) fields. These have a far higher yield per unit area than swidden fields when the land in fallow is considered. Some highland Lua' villages had extensive irrigated fields by the 1880s. As pressure on swidden land increased in the 1960s and 1970s Lua' villagers (and their Karen neighbors) began to invest their labor and money to increase the number and size of irrigated fields. Thus, their land-use system is coming to resemble that of the lowlanders, and the balance of rice production at Pa Pae has now shifted from swidden to irrigated fields.

Instead of maintaining the diversity of their environment with their swidden-rotation system, they are increasing its homogeneity by leveling the land into terraces, building larger irrigation systems, and permanently changing the land from forest to farm. This has also resulted in reducing the variety of crop plants. Some of the traditional supplementary crops (beans, chili peppers) are grown on the margins of the irrigated fields, but others (sorghum, millet) are not. Because of the increased pressure on land from the growing human population and the large number of cattle grazing in the highlands, few Pa Pae villagers grow their own cotton now and most purchase clothing or thread for weaving. By 1985 some Pa Pae farmers began substituting modern, improved rice seed for their traditional irrigated varieties. Increasing numbers of Lua' villagers have begun to seek wage work, at least in the dry season.

Unlike swidden fields, which traditionally could be reallocated among village households by village religious leaders, irrigated fields are subject to the customs and laws governing irrigated fields in the lowlands. They can be registered, bought, sold, and mortgaged, and disputes over ownership are settled by government officials, not village leaders. Land that once belonged to the village as a whole has become personal property and in some places has been sold or lost to outsiders through foreclosure. Location and timing of activities on irrigated fields does not require ceremonial blessing by village religious leaders or villagewide coordination and cooperation for fire control. Thus, the increased dependence on irrigated rice further eroded the authority of village leaders over land use.

Increase in amount of irrigated land has expanded the need for water buffalos for plowing and harrowing, and improved transportation has made it easier for lowlanders to send their livestock to be raised on shares by Lua' highland villagers. Grazing pressure has increased greatly in the fallow swiddens. The most noticeable consequence of this, aside from the complaints of farmers whose fences or crops are damaged by these beasts, has been the decreased availability of roofing straw (*Imperata cylindrica*), traditionally gathered from fields in the early fallow stage. Until the 1960s all Pa Pae houses were roofed with shingles made of *Imperata,* but by the late 1970s roofing straw had become scarce, and villagers were making their roofs either out of dipterocarp leaves or, if they could afford the price and the cost of transportation, out of corrugated metal.

Increase in dry-season irrigation for such cash crops as soybeans has changed the quality of the stream running through Pa Pae from clear and free-flowing to muddy and foul-smelling, and the villagers are reluctant to bathe and wash their clothes in it because it makes their skin itch. Year-round irrigation also means year-round mosquitoes in the village.

Tradition and Change among Highland Hmong Farmers

My first visit to a mountain Hmong village was also in 1963, when I walked to Mae Tow a few days after

A Hmong swidden cleared in a large forest in Chiang Mai Province, Thailand.

I first visited Pa Pae. At that time the walk to Mae Tow from the nearest road took about a day and a half, and the villagers were relatively undisturbed by outsiders. In about 1961 a few families had piled their portable possessions onto ponies and moved from near Chiang Dao, about 200 kilometers (120 miles) to the north, to establish Mae Tow in a forested area near the site of an ancient Lua' iron mine. The traditional Hmong economy was based on swidden farming of rice as a subsistence crop, corn (which they used mostly for pig feed), and opium as a cash crop.

Hmong speak dialects of the Miao-Yao language family. Chinese historical records suggest that in pre-Han times Hmong were lowland irrigated-rice farmers in what is now central China. Han Chinese pushed the Hmong out of the valleys and into the mountains of southern China. For several hundred years the Hmong population has expanded to the south into northern Vietnam and Laos. They first crossed from Laos to the Thai side of the Mekong River in the 1880s and are now as far south as Kanchanaburi Province near the Burma border, or some 600 kilometers (370 miles) from where they first entered Thailand. Unlike the Lua', who have lived in permanent villages and whose population grew slowly until recent years, Hmong have adapted to a series of natural and social environments and have sustained rapid population growth and territorial expansion for over a century.

Instead of working on a swidden-rotation system, Hmong households traditionally farm the same sites until the soil is exhausted or grass and weeds become so thick that it is too difficult or time-consuming to continue to cultivate. When this occurs, individual Hmong households seek new farm sites. If the available area is large enough to accommodate them, several households or the whole village may move together to a new site. On the advancing southern front of the Hmong population, villages are often only temporary groups of households whose farms and dwellings are located in the same area. Villages often split up when soil in their area has become unusable.

In contrast with the Lua', little economic cooperation exists among Hmong households in the same village. Hmong religious leaders and ceremonies are concerned primarily with curing illness and with services for the ancestor spirits of household and clan from whom they believe physical well-being and agricultural blessings flow. They have little interest in agricultural ceremonies for spirits attached to specific land areas. Our host, Lao Tha, and Wan Chai, the spirit doctor whom he had invited to perform a household spirit ceremony, explained this to us when we visited them in 1987 in Pang Ung, a Hmong village with about one thousand residents located seventy-five kilometers (forty-six miles) north of Pa Pae.

For such major ceremonies as marriages and funerals, Hmong maintain ties with lineage and clan members who trace relationships to a very remote ancestor through the male line. Clan membership is so important to the Hmong that they try to prevent anyone from dying in a place where they do not have at least some clan relatives. We learned this when we went to a postburial ceremony for Chai Sae Yang at the Pang Ung home of Wan Chu Sae Yang. Chai and Wan Chu were members of the Yang clan. Although they were members of the same clan and had occasionally smoked opium together, they were not true relatives. The dead man had no children, and there were no members of the Yang clan in Pang Tong, the village where he lived. Since only members of one's own clan know the proper ceremony for conducting the soul of a clan member to the land of the dead, the day before he died Chai was brought to Pang Ung by Pang Tong villagers, so his clan relatives could arrange his funeral. The Hmong believe that if this ceremony is not done properly the dead person's soul might wander around and cause trouble both in the village where the death occurred and for the living members of his clan.

Hmong maintain kinship networks that include people who calculate relationships through many generations, over several centuries, and across great distances, even across international borders. This network makes it easier for them to exchange information about farming conditions and to move in search of new farm sites.

Hmong look for swidden sites with deep soil that can be cultivated for several years in succession. They usually cut their swiddens in mature evergreen forests with large trees, often at a higher elevation in a cooler, wetter environment than the mixed deciduous-evergreen secondary forest in which Lua' cut their swiddens. Unlike the Lua' whose villages collaborate in clearing and burning swiddens, the largest regularly cooperating land-use unit among the Hmong is the extended family household. Households may clear small isolated fields, or several households may clear a large area together. When the fields are burned they make little effort to control the spread of the fire into abandoned fields outside those to be cultivated in the current year, and fire discourages rapid regrowth of forest on abandoned swiddens.

After burning the felled vegetation Hmong farmers dig out the tree stumps and hoe the fields before planting or hire Karens or sometimes Lua' workers to do this heavy work. Hmong plant their rice and corn in April, often in separate swidden patches, carefully spacing between each planting hole and covering the seeds with soil. If they plan to intercrop opium with the corn, they will select a site with suitable nonacidic (limestone-based) soil. They try to clean-weed their fields with hoes three times during the growing season, and deep cultivate rather than just scraping the soil's surface as the Lua' do. They may plant an early crop of opium between rows of corn in August at about the time of corn harvest and leave the corn stalks for protection of the young poppy plants. A later opium crop may be planted in September or October. They harvest their rice in October and November. The early work in opium fields may overlap with the final weeding and harvest of rice, which increases Hmong need for labor.

Opium poppy cultivation was learned by Hmong in China early in the nineteenth century and has subsequently spread with the Hmong wherever they have migrated. They need much labor to clear all the vegetation from the fields, to hoe to a depth of 25–38 cm (10–15 inches) before planting, to keep the fields hoed and clean-weeded during the growing season, and for harvest. The environmental and labor requirements of this major cash crop have profoundly influenced Hmong settlement patterns and the organization of their households. Poppies grow best on a deep, rich, limestone-based soil in a cool climate with moisture from dew but little rainfall. This combination of conditions occurs at the end of the rainy season in small patches at higher elevations in southern China, northern Vietnam, Laos, Thailand, and Burma, where opium-growing groups such as the Hmong are now settled. Hmong traditionally also chose sites for new settlements near villages where they could hire labor and buy rice, often in exchange for opium.

Hmong traditionally grew opium for home consumption (as a pain medicine and treatment for diarrhea and as a narcotic) and for sale. Unlike harvesting a rice field, which may be completed in a few days, the opium harvest may go on for several weeks in a single field as new seedpods mature on the poppy plants. Each ripe seedpod is incised repeatedly and revisited after the tarry sap has oozed out so that harvesters may scrape off the raw opium. Because the opium is very valuable and the work goes on for a long time, it is not practical to hire workers or to exchange labor between households for the opium harvest. Each household tries to maintain a large labor supply of its own by encouraging high fertility through early marriage and by keeping all married sons, their wives, and children in the same extended-family household with their parents. Hmong households, averaging nine or more people, are about twice the size of Lua' households.

Cultivation, possession, and consumption of opium have been illegal in Thailand since 1957. Between the early 1960s and the early 1980s the Thai government and international narcotics agencies attempted to wean Hmong and other opium-growing groups from production of opium by promoting substitute crops and by detoxifying the addicts. Opium production was reduced and, perhaps as a result of

U.S. pressure, a hard-line policy of poppy eradication has been followed since 1985. Hmong villagers have been ordered to reduce cultivation by one-third every year over a three-year period until production is stopped, except for home use by addicts over the age of 50. This policy appears to have further reduced the amount produced but has resulted in serious economic concern because of economic and ecological problems with the new crops. The demand and price for opium has remained high, substitute crops require at least as much land as opium, and the price declines as soon as large numbers of farmers start to grow them. Hmong farmers in several villages told us the substitute crops were not economically rewarding: they were promised forty cents per kilogram (2.2 pounds) for cabbages, but when they were ready for sale they could only get ten cents and could not even afford to send them to market; potatoes, red kidney beans, carnations, and strawberries have suffered similar declines in price with increased production. Khru Boon Sri, a Hmong teacher in Khun Klang, a Hmong village with over one hundred households located about seventy kilometers (forty-three miles) southwest of Chiang Mai, told us there were other problems with strawberries. For maximum yield strawberries require costly fertilizer and pesticide, and runoff from strawberry fields pollutes fishponds down stream.

Hmong have traditionally grown hemp (a variety of the marijuana plant), the stalks of which the women laboriously soak, peal, soften, spin, and weave into long narrow strips. In 1986 government officials began to suppress the growing of hemp because of its resemblance to marijuana (it is called by the same name in Thai), although Hmong neither use it as a narcotic nor sell it. Lacking hemp to weave, Hmong women now frequently buy cotton fabric and dye it in the traditional fashion to make their skirts.

Ecological Consequences of the Traditional Hmong Land-Use System

The Hmong system involves clearing the swidden fields of all natural vegetation and cultivating the same field for several years in succession. Perhaps because of the care with which Hmong prepare and weed their fields, the yield of rice the first year is probably 1,250 to 2,000 kilograms per hectare (1,100 to 1,750 pounds per acre), up to twice as high on Hmong swiddens as the amount harvested by Lua' farmers. Yields on Hmong rice swiddens apparently decline each successive year that the field is cultivated without fallow. Opium yield is much lower, only about five to twelve kilograms per hectare (four to nine pounds per acre), but it can be sold for a much higher price.

One old Hmong lady in Khun Klang told us she thought the government was right to forbid the villagers to cut more forest. She first moved to Khun Klang when she was eight years old, about sixty years ago. She said that the soil was good and the area was covered with dense forest at that time. There were many wild animals and birds, including hornbills when she came. The wild animals are all gone and she hasn't heard or seen any hornbills in at least twenty years. She fears that if the people don't stop cutting the forest there will be no birds left at all.

Hmong fields usually extend over ridgetops and are cleared of all trees and clean cultivated, destroying sources for tree seeds and coppice regrowth. Secondary vegetation following Hmong cultivation consists mostly of such grassy species as *Imperata cylindrica* or *Saccharum spontaneum* or such weedy species as *Eupatorium odoratum* or *Lantana,* which persist until they are shaded out. Forest regeneration is slow. If left undisturbed it may take a century or more for mature vegetation to return. Because Hmong traditionally start with a mature forest, which has much more wood than the secondary forest used by the Lua', and because of the much lower regeneration in the early years following cultivation, the Hmong system appears to produce only about half as much rice per kilogram of forest trees per year of a 100-year cycle as does the Lua' system. Annual burning of fields continues in each successive year of cultivation, and accidental spread of fires to the abandoned grassy areas further delays the regeneration of trees on abandoned Hmong swiddens.

The result of the traditional Hmong cultivation system has been to create large patches thickly covered with fire-resistant grasses. Species diversity in the vicinity of Hmong villages is more limited than around Lua' villages. Rather than geographic stability and maintenance of environmental diversity, the Hmong way of life involves periodic migration and adaptation to new sites and new environments. Rather than wait for the forest to regrow, Hmong households have traditionally abandoned their grass-choked swiddens and looked for new forested farm sites. They traditionally viewed the forest not as a renewable resource to protect and perpetuate but as a consumable resource and an obstacle to farming soil that lies below.

Unlike the Lua' system, which has been associated with a balance between population and secondary forest in fixed village locations over the past several centuries, the Hmong population has grown rapidly and expanded into new territories at the expense of large areas of mature forest. Because of their mixed subsistence and cash economy, Hmong households are able to farm economically and productively for about three months more during each year than the Lua' who spend about eight months a year on swidden activities. Hmong traditionally have produced a valuable, nonperishable, readily marketed product—opium. They could convert their extra months of work into cash

BELOW: A Hmong woman planting beans in a tractor-plowed field, Chedikho, western Tak Province, Laos.

RIGHT: A Hmong woman harvests opium by scoring the poppy capsules with a knife and then collecting the resin that oozes from the cuts.

OPPOSITE: Using a bamboo stick as a spacing guide, an elderly Hmong woman in Pang Ung uses a wax-filled *janting* to draw the outline of her batik skirt pattern. The wax with which she fills her janting is kept hot and liquid in the socket of an iron plow blade, heated by a charcoal fire.

and accumulate wealth much more easily than the Lua' who concentrate on subsistence rice production. In traditional times this allowed Hmong to accumulate more pigs and silver jewelry than the Lua' and to buy ponies for transportation. In recent years a sizable fraction of Hmong households have acquired motorcycles or pickup trucks, and some even have battery-powered television sets and VCRs.

Hmong use forest products in their own subsistence economy for food, fiber, construction, medicine, weaving, and dyeing as do the Lua'. They get most of their meat from domestic pigs and chickens but are avid hunters, even though the number of game animals is now very small. They are quick to pick up new ideas including the use of diving masks and spear guns for fishing.

Hmong are also quick to pick up ideas for commerce and are rapidly organizing themselves for life in the modern economic world. Some Hmong still sell such traditional forest products in the Chiang Mai market as pitch pine (used by lowlanders to light their charcoal fires), wild banana stalks (for pig food), or green parrots and parakeets, which they trap in the jungle and sell as pets. In recent years an increasing number of Hmong have begun selling needlework and other crafts directly to tourists at the night bazaar in Chiang Mai and occasionally on street corners in Bangkok.

Changes in the Hmong System and Their Consequences

Large numbers of Hmong villagers have been subject to especially severe dislocations in recent years as a result of warfare and insurgency in Southeast Asia. Many of the Hmong living in Laos were directly involved on one or the other side of the Indochina wars starting in the early 1950s and continuing until 1975. Since then many of them fled to refugee camps in Thailand, and some have been relocated to the United States.

In addition to roads, schools, and health services similar to those being provided to Lua' villages, many Thai-government and international programs have attempted to persuade Hmong to stop growing poppies by substituting nonnarcotic cash crops, including potatoes, red kidney beans, coffee, peaches, apples, and other fruit trees, strawberries, cabbages, carnations, and other cut flowers. Mae Tow is one of the Hmong villages where these projects have taken place. The houses, some made of cement blocks, are no longer set in corn, rice, and poppy fields but are now lined up on either side of an all-weather road. There are several government buildings on a nearby hill. All the trees are gone, and no opium poppies are in evidence. The fields are planted to red kidney beans, cabbages, and gladiolus. One young man, asked why his family had moved away from there, replied, "They are just growing red beans all over Mae Tow now, and it is

not a pleasant place to live anymore."

In the 1970s the Thai army relocated many Hmong villages and established development projects in an attempt to separate them from the influence of the rebels. Many relocation projects seem not to have been as socially disruptive or psychologically disorienting for Hmong as for other ethnic groups who are less well adapted to migration.

Hmong responses to changes in recent years suggest the resilience of their socioeconomic system, their willingness to innovate, and their entrepreneurial talents when land is available. In areas where mature forest is not available or where it has proved difficult to relocate to new village sites, Hmong have developed longer-term crop-rotation systems to make more intensive use of land to which they have access and have begun to use larger amounts of hired labor, farm machinery, and herbicides, in order to farm grass-covered areas. Some Hmong have bought or cleared and leveled their own irrigated fields and have begun cultivating irrigated rice.

Since the mid-1970s many Hmong villagers in Tak Province who lived or moved near roads have abandoned poppy cultivation and have become large-scale growers of corn as a cash crop. Chediko is a relocated village in western Tak Province where, at least temporarily, Hmong farmers have access to large amounts of land. Chediko villagers contract with low-

land Thais for the services of tractors to prepare large fields for corn cultivation. Tractors temporarily prevent or solve problems of grassification and allow more or less permanent conversion of forest to cultivated upland fields. In the presence of ample farm land Chediko farmers seem to be doing well without opium. In addition to labor from their own households and from nearby Karen villages, some Hmong living near the Burma border now hire undocumented migrants from Bangladesh to work on their farms.

Despite this agricultural modernization, Hmong fertility, associated with early marriage and low use of contraception resulting in rapid population growth, remains high but this may be changing. One man in Chediko told us that he was going to stop having children because it cost too much to send them to school. His father, who was listening to the conversation, said that wasn't the way it used to be. When his children were growing up and they still lived in the mountains where there were no schools, he would put them to work in the fields. But that was before they had been moved to Chediko, which is located on a paved road, and where there is a school, and they can hire tractors.

Other relocated Hmong have not been as fortunate as Chediko villagers. For example, Song Kwae, Pang Puei, and Huai Baw Hoi in Nan Province were resettled in lower elevations of dry forest areas where soil is poor and land and water are in short supply. Their economic prospects have been worsened by recent enforcement of laws against poppy cultivation and against cutting swidden fields in the forest. In the mid-1980s Hmong have found themselves unable to grow their traditional cash crop or to follow their traditional response to land shortage.

The extent to which Hmong population growth and expanded use of forests can be stabilized without major economic problems is uncertain. Residents of Huai Nam Chang and the Mawn Ya cluster of villages, about seventy kilometers (forty-four miles) west of Chiang Mai, can easily see that there is no more land around their villages for their children to farm. The future looks bleak for them. As in the Nan villages, government officials have told them to stay where they are and not grow opium or cut new fields in the forest. In the past four or five years many of them have decided that they cannot continue to have more children because their sons will not have enough land to feed their children, and many now take advantage of family-planning services.

Conclusion

For several centuries Asian tropical forests have been sacrificed to human demands for forest resources and farm land, starting with easily irrigated areas of the lowlands, most of which were cleared and leveled at least one hundred years ago. As lowland populations grew, the demand for land increased, and forests were cleared at higher elevations.

Traditional land-use systems have survived most frequently in forests of relatively remote, sparsely settled highland areas. There are now very few hunter-gatherers, and their impact on the forest is minimal. Most of the people living in the highland forests are swidden farmers whose land-use systems may either be cyclical, conservative and self-renewing, or extractive.

Conservative systems like that used by Lua' farmers of northwestern Thailand result in the development of a secondary forest composed of rapidly growing trees, which are fire resistant. Compared with permanent wet rice fields this system is inefficient, but it allowed rapid regeneration of forest and production of a subsistence crop large enough for permanent settled villages to persist in the same location for hundreds of years. This system now faces collapse because of strong challenges to the traditional land-use system and the socioreligious customs that support the system including increased population, declining land base,

increased amount of irrigation and associated changes in land tenure, cash cropping, and increased demands for cash. The authority of traditional village religious leaders has been undermined by failure of the government to recognize traditional claims to swidden land, substitution of Thai regulations for Lua' customs concerning irrigated land, and by the presence of teachers, government workers, and missionaries as alternative authority figures.

Extractive systems, such as that practiced by Hmong in northwestern Thailand, involve cultivation of fields cut out of mature forest that are cultivated for a few years and then abandoned. Because grass not forest is the secondary vegetation that for many years follows cultivation with the Hmong method, the Hmong system is associated with impermanent villages and the need to search for more forest-covered land. On average Hmong farmers using their traditional system have been able to provide themselves with a better standard of living than Lua' farmers, both because they have not confined themselves to a limited land base and because of their more extensive involvement in the cash economy.

With modern farm machinery Hmong farmers can clear larger areas of forest and cultivate commercially profitable amounts of corn. It is too soon to say whether this will increase the speed of forest destruction, or because tractor-drawn plows, herbicides, and chemical fertilizers may allow permanent cultivation, whether this may lead to permanent settlement and a reduction in the demand for land. The outcome will depend on the growth of the Hmong population, development of alternatives to agricultural occupations, and enforcement of laws against cutting of the forest. To an increasing extent, however, the future of forests in tropical Asia depends not on the traditional land-use systems of indigenous forest people but on national and international markets for products derived from the forests.

In preparing this chapter I have drawn upon research supported by grants from the National Geographic Society, National Institute of Child Health and Human Development, National Institute of General Medical Sciences, National Science Foundation, Princeton University, and the University of Washington. In addition to the people we have named from Pa Pae and the many Hmong villages we have visited, special thanks are due to Nai Saman Khamhuang of Pa Pae, Chupinit Kesmanee of the Tribal Research Institute, Chiang Mai, and Sally Kunstadter. Their assistance is gratefully acknowledged.

7

HUNTERS AND FARMERS
OF THE
AFRICAN FOREST

DAVID S. WILKIE

With bow and arrows in hand Karambodu ran quickly and quietly through the sparse undergrowth of the forest. Finding a suitable spot he carefully bent over several shade-stunted saplings to give himself a better line of sight. Placing an arrow against the bowstring he waited ready to ambush any game flushed from hiding by the other men of this Pygmy hunting group and myself. The relative cool of the forest, its dappled light filtered through the leafy canopy some fifty meters (160 feet) above our heads, was a relief from the scorching equatorial sun. Waiting was no burden; we were entertained by the steady buzz of cicadas, a colorful mixed troop of blue and mona monkeys, and the reverberating "akoru-toku-toku-toku" of a pair of great blue turaco.

How different this scene, which took place in the rain forest of the Congo River basin of Zaire, is from our stock images of Africa: broad sweeping savannas covered with grazing herbivores constantly watchful of powerful and ever-present predators. We usually equate Africa with the immense grasslands that sweep in a huge arc from West Africa, east to Sudan and south through Tanzania, and we can readily picture African pastoralists such as the Masai eking out a subsistence by following their herds of cattle and goats as they exploit seasonally available forage. Yet tropical Africa also contains over 2 million square kilometers (840,000 square miles) of rain forest, which is home to thousands of shifting cultivators from hundreds of tribes and supports one of the last cultures of hunter-gatherers remaining in Africa, the Pygmies.

Location and Evolution

Africa, the second largest continent after Eurasia, contains over 20 percent of the world's remaining rain forest, the largest and least disturbed section of which lies within the Zaire (Congo) River drainage.

As the giant granitic block that became the African continent slowly warped and its edges uplifted, its equatorial center formed a broad, shallow bowl some 1,600 kilometers (1,000 miles) in diameter. By the Tertiary period (65 to 1.6 million years ago) this depression was a vast lake that, as a result of the inexorable forces of erosion, slowly drained through a narrow outlet to the Atlantic, exposing what is now the forested Congo basin.

The Congo basin covers some 3.6 million square kilometers (1.4 million square miles), an area a little less than half the size of the United States, and contains over 80 percent of Africa's tropical rain forests. It extends in a contiguous zone from Gabon on the Atlantic seaboard through the People's Republic of the Congo, Cameroon, Central African Republic, and Zaire. Other sections of rain forest still remain in Nigeria, in areas west of the Dahomey Gap in the Ivory Coast and Guinea, and on the eastern edge of Madagascar.

Although rain forests are thought to be one of the oldest of all forests, having remained unchanged for millennia, recent pollen studies clearly show that much

of the area now covered by tropical rain forest in Africa is, in geological time, of very recent origin. When Europe and North America were under miles of glacial ice, tropical Africa's annual temperature and rainfall were less than they are today, and the Congo basin forests shrank in size until only three remnant patches of forest existed. These Pleistocene refugia sustained and preserved the plants and animals that depend on a constant hot (27 degrees Celsius or 80 degrees Fahrenheit), humid (80 percent), rain-drenched (1,800 millimeters or 72 inches per year) environment and are now unique to Africa's rain forests. As the last ice age gradually receded rainfall increased, and the boundaries of the refuge forests in Guinea, Gabon, and eastern Zaire expanded to fill the vast central basin. That the central region of the Congo forest was recently (in a geological sense) savanna scrubland is reflected by its much lower variety of plants and animals compared to the Pleistocene refuge areas such as the Ituri forest of northeastern Zaire.

The Ituri was the largest and most ecologically diverse of the three Pleistocene refuges and consequently now contains the greatest number of plant and animal species of any African forest, over 15 percent of them endemic to that area. The forests of the Congo basin now appear to be at equilibrium with the environment and are neither exhibiting a natural expansion nor contraction of their domain.

Flora and Fauna

Tropical rain forests of Africa, like their counterparts throughout the globe, are most often seen from the rivers and roads that cross them. These roadside or riverbank strips of forest form impenetrable thorn-vine tangles of vegetation, which give the traveler the impression that all rain forest is like this. On the contrary, the Ituri forest, the home of Pygmies, is an open, easily traversed landscape. Unlike roadsides or riverbanks, which receive constant and intense levels of sunlight, much of the rain forest is kept in relative shade by the leaves of mature forest trees, which capture most of the light. Below this canopy very few plants are able to secure enough light with which to grow, and those that do grow extremely slowly. The rain forest is in reality a layered environment. Tall, 100 to 300-year-old hardwood trees such as the African ironwood (*Cynometra alexandri*) and mahoganies (*Entandrophragma* species) form a varied and nearly continuous leafy canopy that shades the forest floor, which is sparsely covered with stunted saplings, shade-tolerant shrubs, and broad-leaved herbs. The forest only resembles the vine-entangled jungles of Tarzan films on riverbanks, roadsides, and where a giant forest tree has died, fallen down, and opened up a large gap where the sun once more beats steadily to the ground prompting the frantic growth of vegetation in competition for light.

Because most of the sun in tropical rain forests is captured by the trees that dominate the high canopy, most of the edible leaves, flowers, and fruits available to animals and humans is also at the tops of the trees. Not surprisingly, rain forests have large numbers of birds, bats, and arboreal mammals (the most conspicuous being monkeys) that exploit these abundant, treetop resources. African rain forests, unlike the forests of South America and Southeast Asia, also have a wide variety of ground-dwelling animals. These animals range over the forest floor in search of fruits and seeds that, once ripe, have either fallen from the canopy or have been dislodged or discarded by feeding bats and monkeys. Other than rodents, the most abundant of the forest floor fauna are the forest antelopes called *duikers,* an Afrikaans word stemming from their habit of ducking into the nearest brush pile when startled. Duikers probably moved into the forest, as did elephant, buffalo, and the forest giraffe (okapi), from the enormous neighboring savannas. These vast grasslands are generally not found surrounding the world's other rain forests.

The Earliest Human Inhabitants

The Congo basin is inhabited by more than two hundred different tribes speaking as many languages and dialects. It is unclear how long the forest has been home to humans. Although evidence of a Stone-Age culture (Sangoan) of hunter-gatherers has been found within today's forest boundary, it has neither been shown that the region they inhabited was forested at that time nor that the hunter-gatherers of today, the Pygmies, are their descendants. Regardless, there is archaeological evidence that Stone-Age humans were foraging for food within the Congo basin more than forty thousand years ago. By studying the linguistic patterns of today's forest dwellers we have been able to trace the occupation of the forest back at least two thousand years. If we are to believe the accounts and drawings made during the reign of Egyptian pharaoh Nerfrikare of the sixth dynasty, Pygmies have been seen living south of present-day Sudan in the Congo basin rain forests for at least five thousand years.

Three main groups of people now live in the rain forests of the Congo basin: Bantu- and Sudanic-speaking shifting cultivators and Pygmy hunter-gatherers. More Bantu inhabit the Congo than the other two groups combined, which is not really surprising as Bantu peoples are the most widespread culture in Africa south of the Sahara.

An Abundance of Plants, a Scarcity of Food

Karambodu's Pygmy ancestors were probably the first inhabitants of the forest; they lived in small, highly mobile bands ranging over the forest in a seasonal pattern, foraging for fruits, roots, and leaves, damming small streams to trap crabs and catfish, and hunting forest duikers and monkeys. The prehistoric Pygmies may not have spread over the whole Congo basin, for their present distribution indicates they may have avoided the central basin, preferring instead the species-rich refuge forests of Gabon and eastern Zaire. The rain forest's enormous diversity would have provided the early Pygmies with a wonderful variety of foods from which to choose; however, a diverse resource often means that no individual food species ever occurs in great numbers at any one location. Unlike temperate-zone foragers, who could harvest a whole hillside of wild grain, gather an abundance of acorns from a forest of oak, or hunt herds of deer and bison, the Pygmies of the rain forest would have to range over several kilometers to find two or more fruiting trees of the same edible species or to capture more than a couple of forest duikers, which either live alone or at best in mated pairs. Rain forests, which may appear to offer lush and abundant foods, actually do so in a very dispersed, patchy manner. Foragers are thus forced to roam widely to find enough to eat and must move camp frequently to exploit the forest's dispersed, seasonally available resources.

Advent of Forest Agriculture

The nomadic, hunting-gathering life-style of the Pygmies changed dramatically around two thousand years

Map showing the present extent of rain forest in Africa, the forest during the Pleistocene, and the homeland of the Ituri Forest Pygmies.

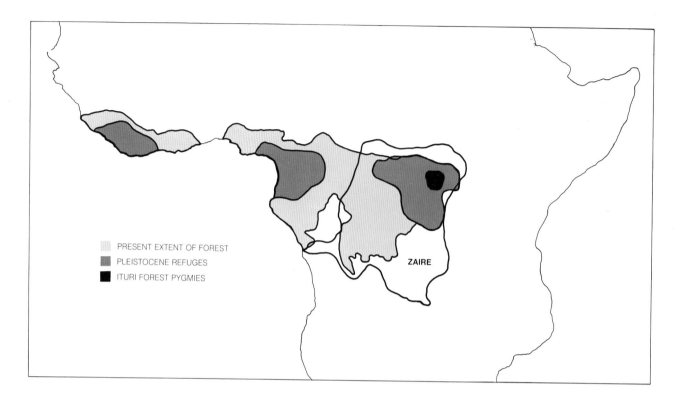

PRESENT EXTENT OF FOREST
PLEISTOCENE REFUGES
ITURI FOREST PYGMIES

ZAIRE

ago when farmers from the more densely populated bordering savannas entered the forest along the innumerable watercourses that drain into the Ubangi and Zaire rivers. What prompted this invasion of the forest? Africa's main native cultivated crops are millet and sorghum, neither of which can tolerate the constant humidity of the rain forest. The only native crop species of the rain forest are oil palms (*Elaeis guineensis*), which provide oil-rich fruits and seeds but only do so three to five years after planting, and herbaceous vine yams (various *Dioscorea* species), which produce rather bitter, unpalatable tubers. Extensive farming within the rain forest only became feasible with the introduction by Arab traders of rain-loving crop plants such as bananas from Southeast Asia and, much later (sixteenth century), when the Portuguese brought manioc, corn, sweet potatoes, peanuts, beans, and squash from the Americas. With the increased cultivation of bananas, primarily the hard, green plantain, came the progressive introduction of agriculture into the Congo basin.

The rain forests of Africa have therefore been altered by the human hand for well over one thousand years. Tropical forest ecologist Dr. Paul Richards contends that what has always been considered to be primeval, uncut rain forest in West Africa is actually the ancient, abandoned gardens of early forest farmers. However, as all forests of the world are mosaics of young, old, and dying trees, after a few centuries

it becomes very difficult to tell what were natural tree falls or a result of felling by humans. The rapid growth and decay characteristic of rain forests makes Richards's conclusions even more difficult to prove. Nonetheless, African rain forests have been altered by humanity for a considerable time. Forest farming methods have changed little since becoming established within the Congo basin. Very few tools are used, no draught animals exist, and crops are only produced in sufficient quantities to feed the family and provide seed for the next year.

Contemporary Forest Farmers of the Congo Basin

The Lese Dese of the Ituri forest of northeastern Zaire are forest farmers, and Ngodingodi is a typical Lese village. Mupenda built the village on its present site when he was a newly married young man and needed to find suitable land to clear and cultivate. His step-father's village is less than a kilometer away, and the two villages work and socialize with one another daily. Mupenda lives in the village with the families of his three married sons. He now has two wives; he took a second wife when his first wife failed to conceive—a common occurrence in this region of Africa. Of his three daughters, only Manjeke survived through puberty. She has recently married an industrious young Lese man, who, as tradition dictates, gave her father a bride wealth that included a *kitunga* (basket made from forest materials) of seed peanuts and several chickens. She will soon move to a nearby village to live with her new husband.

Gamiembi, Mupenda's youngest son, is building a new *mafika* (kitchen shelter) at the entrance to his mud hut. Each family has its own hut, mafika, and cooking fire. The women of Ngodingodi have been out in the forest all morning cutting the broad *tilipi* leaf (*Megaphrynium macrostachyum*) with which to shingle the roof of the mafika. Huts, mafika, and the men's social-gathering shelters (called *baraza*) are all made from small trees and saplings tied firmly together with tough, flexible strapping; this binding is made by carefully splitting a palm vine that grows more than thirty meters (one hundred feet) in length. The mafika has open sides, whereas sleeping and food storage huts have latticework sides covered completely with mud. Huts are usually built in December at the end of the heavy rains when the soil is still wet and easily mixed into mud, which, when applied to the hut walls, will have time to dry over the next two months of the annual dry season. The dry season is never totally dry, but at least it rains less often and less heavily.

By early afternoon the women are back with their bundles of leaves. Alimoya, the oldest woman in the village, sits down with legs outstretched beside the pile of leaves. She methodically splices leaves together in wads of five with the aid of a small knife fashioned locally from metal smelted by the Zande in the northern savannas. Next morning, before the sun rises high in the sky and before the leaves begin to dry and curl, Gamiembi and his brothers will climb on top of the mafika. Starting from the bottom, they will overlap the leaves into a waterproof roofing that, once held down with saplings or split bamboo, will last for three to five years. As Alimoya works on the leaves her co-wife, Uboobi, sets out again for their *shamba* (garden) to dig up some manioc and cut down some plantains for tonight's dinner and tomorrow's breakfast. Her task complete, Uboobi adjusts her sling slightly to let her baby Tofi nurse, places four or five large pieces of firewood on top of her already laden food basket, and, with the expertise of a weight lifter, hoists the cargo onto her back and adjusts the tumpline across her forehead.

As I follow Uboobi back to the village, I am reminded how hard Lese women have to work to provide for their families. Uboobi's days are always busy with child care, food preparation (which includes gathering, cleaning, peeling, pounding, and cooking), cutting and hauling firewood, carrying drinking water and her husband's washing water, washing clothes and cooking items, and working in the fields. In contrast, the men have few demands on them other than field clearing and live a much more leisurely existence.

In late November or early December Mupenda and his sons Gamiembi, Kenikungu, and Itude search for a section of forest to clear for cultivation. They are looking for an area as close to the village as possible because the women will work there each day and will have to return with heavy loads of firewood and foodstuffs. Like most shifting cultivators living in the Congo basin, Mupenda prefers sections of forest that he or his relatives cleared fifteen to twenty years previously. The forest growing in these patches is composed of softwoods such as *kere,* the parasol tree (*Musanga cecropioides*), which can be fairly easily cut down and cleared with their simple tools. This secondary succession tree species, which never exceeds a height of eighteen meters (sixty feet), colonizes four to five years after fields are abandoned by farmers and dominates the canopy for the next fifteen to twenty years. (In South America *Cecropia* occupies a very similar niche.) If Mupenda chooses an area of forest younger than this, the dormant weed seeds stored in the soil from the last cultivation would still be viable, and his wives would spend much time weeding. Moreover, competition by the weeds for limited nutrients in the infertile soil would substantially reduce crop yield. Forests older than this contain progressively more mature forest trees, such as African ironwood, characteristic of uncut forest. These trees are extremely difficult to cut down, since the axes available to most forest farmers are frequently made from suspension springs of old Renault trucks or Land Rovers.

Once a suitable area has been found that satisfies these requirements and is located within Mupenda's usufruct, all the men of the village, usually with the help of Pygmy men, begin the arduous task of cutting and clearing the forest. Mupenda's usufruct is a region of the forest that he and his relatives have hereditary rights to cultivate. The land is not actually owned by Mupenda; he only holds it in trust for future generations. This traditional system of land tenure promotes conservative use of the rain forest as individuals would not degrade a resource that their children and children's children will inherit and upon which they will depend for subsistence.

While Gamiembi cuts part of the way through several of the smaller trees, Kenikungu, braced on a scaffold above the huge buttress roots of a *kobokobo* tree where the trunk is narrower, chips away to form a slowing enlarging **V**. If their plans work out, Kenikungu's tree will fall across Gamiembi's trees, bringing them down with it. This time they weren't so lucky, and Gamiembi went back to finish the job. After continuing this process for a week or so, the trees are down and the field crisscrossed with fallen timber. As the remaining branches are lopped and added to the debris on the ground, the women and adolescent girls move through the tangle planting manioc cuttings and plantain sprouts. For two months the sun beats down

on the field, drying the dense cover of debris that protects the fragile soil from hardening and eroding. During this hiatus the women of the village start to shell and sort the seed peanuts and remove the dry corn kernels from their cobs. In February, on a windy day if possible, firebrands, carried from the village, are used to torch the field, which is as dry as it ever will be. The fire is not very hot, and the debris is never completely burned. The soil stays remarkably moist and cool, which allows the already sprouted banana and manioc plants not only to survive but to make the most use of the limited wood ash fertilizer. Unburnt debris is cut, piled into mounds, and burned until scattered boles of large trees are all that is left.

The field is now ready to be planted with peanuts, the first crop of the year. Planting is a communal affair, and Mupenda calls friends and relatives from other villages and the nearby camp of Efe (Pygmies) to come and help. All the women and girls down to the age of three or four drop seed peanuts from leaf cornets into shallow holes dug by the men using long-handled hoes. Some women carry corn seeds and intersperse them with the peanuts, while two adolescent girls plant small mounds of a climbing squash called *kokoliko* close to several of the tree stumps. Once finished, the field is a patchwork of sprouted plantains and manioc surrounded by a mixed planting of peanuts, corn, sugarcane, and squash. Mixed cropping in this way closely emulates the way vegetation grows in

a natural tree fall clearing in the forest. Combining crops that require different levels of scarce nutrients and that grow at different heights and rates utilizes efficiently the available sunlight and wood ash fertilizer, in a manner that resembles natural successional vegetation. Moreover, mixed cropping means that the fragile soil is quickly protected from the destructive effects of direct sunlight and heavy rains, and crop diseases and insect pests are kept to a minimum.

At the end of peanut planting, men's work for the year is all but over. Other than hut building every five to ten years and tool and basket making, Gamiembi and his brothers have a full nine months of inactivity before next year's field clearing. Lese men spend this time socializing around *libondo* palms, drinking the mildly alcoholic sap, visiting neighbors, and idling away the days in endless games of *mali*.

Unlike the men of the village, Alimoya, Uboobi, and the other women and girls have only begun a grueling work schedule. Girls begin working as soon as they can fetch items or carry a basket (when they are two to three years old) and women's work continues unrelentingly until elephantiasis, leprosy, or death excuses them. The women of Ngodingodi will weed the field each day until the peanut leaves cover the soil and inhibit excessive weed growth. In late June the peanuts are uprooted and laid in a specially built baraza to dry. The field is then broadcast with upland rice just in time for the heavy rains of August through

◁ Weeding peanut fields is an onerous task until the leaves cover the soil and impede the growth of many weeds. A Lese woman toils in the tropical sun.

Rice is planted in Lese fields during the wet months of August through November. Children help with the harvest.

November. Bananas and manioc are ready for harvest after twelve to fifteen months, although Uboobi will start gathering manioc leaves as soon as they appear. She'll use these to make *sombe,* the Ituri's most flavorful dish: boiled and pounded manioc leaves mixed with palm oil and searingly hot red pepper. Sombe is one of the forest's few good sources of vegetable protein, essential vitamins, and minerals available to the Lese, but Uboobi must be wise in her use of these nutritious leaves because without them the plant is unable to produce the starchy tubers that provide most of the calories in her family's diet. Each new garden is used for about two years, by which time most of the crops, all planted within the first six months, have been harvested. A few plantains and oil palms will survive after the garden is abandoned to the already colonizing natural succession vegetation of the rain forest.

The Lese way of life is intimately synchronized with the environment and the annual cycle of field clearing, planting, and harvesting that are all integral to their shifting-cultivation subsistence economy. Unlike all other Congo basin inhabitants, barring perhaps the forest elephant, the forest farmers have been a major force in restructuring the natural rain-forest landscape such that the sea of mature, high-canopy forest is now dotted with islands, 5 to 50 hectares (12 to 125 acres) in size, of active cultivation and regrowth vegetation of various ages. As long as mature forest predominates, the impact of subsistence-level shifting

cultivation is negligible and may actually increase ecological diversity and provide more food resources for forest animals.

By six in the evening the sky turns a spectacular red, and the sun plunges out of sight. Here at the equator days and nights are always twelve hours long, and the beautiful twilights last only a few short minutes. Uboobi crosses to where her sister-in-law Melinea is cooking and returns with a hot ember with which to rekindle her fire; neither the Lese nor the Pygmies know how to make fire and must carry hot embers with them or extract them from smoldering remains of giant forest trees felled by lightning. This evening as always Uboobi leaves a bowl of hot wash water for Mupenda and returns to her hut to sit with her children and co-wife Alimoya; she later moves the fire into the hut and rolls out the sleeping mats. As her older children fall asleep and her baby, Tofi, fusses, the sound of Lese voices is punctuated by the crescendo yell of a tree hyrax. This small mammal is not much larger than a house cat, but remarkably it is most closely related to the elephant. It screams its territorial imperative each night at dusk. There's no moon tonight and city lights are thousands of miles away. The stars seem that much closer, and beyond the red glow of the fire the night is dark indeed. Tofi is still fussing as the village quietens for the night. Uboobi mentions that she must visit the Efe camped nearby tomorrow and get them to find some stomach medicine in

Efe men and boys at leisure in their camp in the Ituri forest.

the forest, so that she can *changa* Tofi and cure her stomachache. Patients are treated for sicknesses of all kinds by changa: small cuts are made in the skin over the area where it hurts with a knife or arrowhead, and a herbal potion is rubbed into the shallow incisions. Lese medical histories can be read, much like a map, by examining the extent and location of past changa marks.

The Pygmies: Hunter-Gatherers of the Rain Forest

The Pygmies Uboobi sets off to visit in the morning are camped in the forest at the far side of the Kero River, only a short distance from the village. The Andiokbo are a clan of Efe-Mbuti, one of the two tribes of Pygmies now living within the Congo basin. The Mbuti live throughout the Ituri forest of northeastern Zaire, whereas the other tribe, the Binga, forage in Gabon, Cameroon, and the Central African Republic. So-called pygmoid groups also inhabit central Africa: the Tswa, a fishing tribe of the lower Ubangi and Zaire rivers, and the Twa of Rwanda. Both groups have extensively intermarried with Bantu farmers and no longer maintain their traditional subsistence practices. The Mbuti of the Ituri remain the largest and least acculturated of all tribes of hunter-gatherers within Africa's rain forests.

Mbuti (Pygmies) of the Ituri Forest

Karambodu is an Andiokbo Efe. Efe are bow hunters and live in the northeastern Ituri; they are one of four subgroups of Ituri forest pygmies collectively called the Mbuti. One subgroup, referred to only as Mbuti, hunts with nets and lives in the southern and central Ituri. The Sua and Aka are also net-hunting Mbuti living in the northwestern and northern forest-savanna edges; however, both these subgroups have all but abandoned their traditional way of life and subsist as plantation laborers or as guides to ivory poachers.

Why two different hunting techniques should have persisted in the same rain forest is a puzzling question, especially as both bow and net hunters are aware of the other group's technique and when members of the two groups meet, they will occasionally hunt together. Surely if one hunting technique were better than the other, it would have eventually supplanted the less-efficient method. As this obviously has not happened, there must be some other reason for the establishment and perpetuation of two such unique subsistence economies.

Efe Bow Hunters

Karambodu, Ima-chabo, and their toddler Chabo (Karambodu's wife's name means *mother of Chabo*) live with his uncles, cousins, and their families in a camp

know where their dogs are but also to provide additional noise to help flush hiding game. Pygmy dogs are probably descendants of the basenji and although they are not mute, they do not have a resounding bark. Karambodu, Kebe, and the rest of the men of the band go hunting with their dogs three to four times a week.

Men's Work: A Bow Hunt

In the relative cool of the morning hunters sit close to the fires filling small clay pipes, which they attach to the meter-long hollowed midrib of a banana leaf. A concerted draw on the pipe produces a blast of very strong tobacco smoke. As the exhaled cloud clears around Kebe's face he grins a chisel-toothed smile. Efe prefer the look of pointed teeth and they chip their children's incisors and canines with an arrowhead and a small stone. Kebe hands the pipe to me and says that he hopes to kill an *iti* today. The iti is one of seven species of forest duikers that make up 90 percent of all game captured by Efe bow hunters. The smallest, the blue duiker or *medi*, weighs a mere 5 kilograms (11 pounds), an iti about 20 kilograms (44 pounds), and the largest, the yellow-backed duiker *tochi* a comparatively heavy 50 kilograms (110 pounds). Compared to a white-tailed deer (100 kilograms or 220 pounds) of North America or red deer (400 kilograms, 880 pounds) of Scotland, forest duikers are remarkably small ungulates.

As the sun rises above the trees and the day begins to warm, the men string their bows and harden and straighten their arrow shafts over the fire. One of Kebe's metal arrowheads has become loose on the shaft, so he melts a piece of *ando,* tree resin, over the fire and uses it to reattach the barbed arrow point. Efe mostly hunt terrestrial animals, although they will shoot at primates with untipped poison arrows if they come low enough in the trees or if a sick or aged monkey, foraging on the ground (as do crested mangabeys), is slow to flee. The poison is slow acting, and the prey probably die more often from blood loss than the poison's toxicity.

Just when I thought they had decided not to go hunting today—hunts are often cancelled because of bad omens, which are more prevalent when it's raining—Kebe jumps up, calls his dogs, and heads out into the forest. We walk west at a steady pace, fording rivers, climbing hills, crossing precarious log bridges, obviously going somewhere known to the hunters. Within an hour we come to a clearing, where an Efe named Matiasi is sitting next to a small fire. I had not even seen him leave the camp that morning. He said he had left before dawn to sit in a fruiting tree to wait in ambush for any duikers that might find the fallen fruits a tempting food source. This hunting technique, called *ebaka,* is not as haphazard as it first seems. The

located in a small gap in the canopy next to a clear, gravel-bottomed stream. The camp includes eight adult men, six adult women, four adolescent girls and boys, one toddler, and one newborn. For most of the year the Andiokbo camp remains within two kilometers (1.2 miles) of a Lese farmers' village; at other times they may settle a day or two days' walk away, deep in the forest. Karambodu and his family live in a simple but effective hut constructed from saplings imbedded in the ground and bent and woven into a dome. The lattice of saplings is shingled with the ubiquitous and ever-useful *tilipi* leaves. Each family constructs a hut, and they arrange them in a rough circle with the hut entrances facing inward, thus enclosing a communal social space. If arguments break out in camp a hut entrance can be quickly repositioned, thus effectively separating the antagonists. Arguments are usually short lived, however, and camp life is usually harmonious. Bokbau, the leader of Karambodu's camp, calls me over to show me a new dog bell that he is in the process of carving out of a block of *hoye* (*Alstonia boonei*), a semi-softwood. Although all Efe men learn to make bows, arrows, and bowstrings, Bokbau is renowned as a master craftsman. He no doubt adopted this specialization when he lost his left leg below the knee after having been bitten by a Gabon viper and was no longer able to accompany the other men on hunts. The bells are used not only so that the hunters

The Efe home is a simple but effective, domed hut made from forest saplings and leaves. A camp within the Ituri forest.

A young Efe woman. ▷

Efe only practice it during the dry season when few forest trees are in fruit and duikers have few other food sources. After another quick smoke, the archers set off to form a rough semicircle at the head of a short watercourse. Eyalu waits by the fire with the dogs for about fifteen minutes until he is sure that the archers are in place. Calling "aas aas ibu aas" to beckon the dogs, we start up toward the archers through the much more dense riverine vegetation yelling, beating the brush, and making as much noise as possible.

A game drive or *mota* like this can take anywhere from thirty minutes to over an hour and is completed once the beaters have reached or passed the archers. Several mota are conducted until the hunters feel they have caught enough game or it is time to give up and return to camp. If an animal is flushed close enough to an archer for him to get a clean shot, the hit animal is seldom killed outright and must be chased down by dogs and hunters. The dead animal, usually a duiker, is butchered on the spot and the meat and innards wrapped carefully in the utilitarian tilipi leaves. Who gets what parts of the animal is fairly rigidly determined. The man who shot the first arrow gets the largest and most prized portions (the hind quarters and liver), while the man who owns the dogs gets the head and one forequarter. If a second arrow hit the animal or if the arrow that killed the duiker did not belong to the archer, the second hunter or arrow owner receives

the other forequarter. The rest of the carcass is divided in an amicable manner according to need. If few or no animals are killed, the men still return to camp with food they gather, such as forest mushrooms, tortoises, forest francolin eggs, and fallen fruits. The Efe are also remarkably attuned to the sound of bees; beehives provide honey as well as pollen and grub comb (honeybee comb with larvae in it). When cooked, grub comb tastes rather like loose scrambled eggs.

As I strained to keep up with the swift pace of Kebe and the rest of the band, a *borokboro,* dark mongoose, broke from the undergrowth and ran within two feet of Matiasi. Although he followed it with a feathered bow until it was out of range, he never tried a shot. I asked him why he let an easy kill escape him. He replied, "Don't you know that my wife is pregnant and that there is a taboo against expectant fathers killing or eating this animal?" Again I realized just how little I knew about this forest and the people who live within it.

I was hot, dripping with sweat, and bone tired by the time we got back to camp, but the hunters looked as though they had not broken sweat all day. Small body size means a greater surface area-to-volume ratio; the Efe are thus far more efficient at radiating excess body heat in the humid forest than Europeans and consequently do not overheat as easily.

As we had caught two blue duikers, the camp was

filled with chatter and the excited expectation of meat for dinner. Ima-chabo unwrapped a tilipi leaf parcel to show me a pile of *opi,* the oily, olivelike fruit of the *Canarium schweinfurthii* tree, and an equally large mound of *iswa,* fatty alate termites that she had gathered while we were out hunting. All forest game is extremely lean and one very quickly develops a craving for anything with oil in it. Iswa are delicious anyway, and I never needed to find an excuse to eat them. I asked Karambodu when he intended raiding the honey tree that he had marked on our way back from the hunt, and he said not until after the rofo had flowered. The two major canopy trees in the Ituri are *ato* (*Cynometra alexandri*) and *rofo* (*Brachystegia laurentii*), which flower from late February through March and from May to August. Honey produced by the rofo tree is the most flavorful, therefore honey is best during the months of July through September. At this time the Efe all but abandon hunting to focus solely on gathering honey, which during these brief months contributes 13.5 percent of the Efe's annual calories.

Honey Collecting
Honey gathering, like hunting, is man's work. Karambodu's honey tree is an old *ndau* (*Irvingia gabonensis*), and the hive is located in a rotten branch some twenty meters (sixty feet) from the ground. A colony of *Apis mellifera* bees lives in this tree, which is good

because hives of stinging bees always seem to contain more honey than the stingless variety (*Meliponula bocandei*). Gathering honey is a dangerous pursuit, but the rewards are potentially enormous. Kebe hands his twelve-year-old son Ndikpa an *apopau,* a small machete, with which to open the hive. He helps Ndikpa up to a notch on an adjacent tree that he will climb to reach the lowest branches of the tall ndau. As Ndikpa maneuvers across to the hive, smoke from the tilipi parcel of hot embers and green vegetation swirls around him and keeps the now agitated bees somewhat at bay. He cuts the hive open with three quick hacks and pulls out and throws down sections of honeycomb, which we catch in mitts of *sini* leaves, a smaller forest version of tilipi. The bees are everywhere, sticking to the comb, sticking to our skin. I keep my arms away from my body so as not to trap an irate bee under my armpit, and Ndikpa makes short snorts as bees sting his honey-coated hands and arms. It is a good hive, and we collect about five kilograms (eleven pounds) of honey and two kilograms (four and one-half pounds) of grub comb. As Ndikpa starts down, the Efe at the base of the tree are consuming what to me are huge sections of comb. After twenty minutes of gorging only about one kilogram of honey is left to take back to camp with the grub comb. This is one of the first trees of the season, and it is not uncommon for the men to eat nearly all the honey, leaving little for the women and children. In good years there is always plenty for everyone and even a large surplus for exchange with the villagers.

Back in Camp

In the evening the camp settles down to eat, although this doesn't prevent a fairly constant banter from hut to hut to fireside. Karambodu chops a small piece of boiled meat until it is tender, hands it to Akoro, one of the camp's toddlers, and is then himself handed Chabo to look after while Ima-chabo goes to get some more firewood. Efe children, like their Lese counterparts, are highly valued and are frequently passed from adult to adult to adolescent around the camp. Children therefore get to know all the band at a very early age and, with so many caretakers available, are quickly allowed free range of the camp. When Ima-chabo returns, Kebe starts to tell the story of today's hunt. With sounds and intricate motions he makes the wounded blue duiker sound real as it bleats and crashes through the forest in a desperate attempt to flee the dogs. The story ends, the camp chatter resumes, and, quietly at first, Bokbau beats out a cadence on a duiker-skin drum. Kebe joins him with a *likembe*, a finger piano, and the rhythms become more complex. Women around the camp gradually add their voices in a series of roundelays, and soon an impromptu dance is in progress. The drumbeat and singing become so insistent that it is impossible not to join the swaying circle of dancers surrounding the fire. The dancing never really stops all night, for as some dancers drop out others step in to take their place. Yet the approaching dawn finds most of the band either sleeping by the large dance fire or back in their huts.

Women's Work

Ima-chabo is up early, even after a night's carousing. She has a full day ahead looking after her children, carrying water, gathering firewood, and seeing to the welfare of the camp. Although hunting is hard work, Efe women have more subsistence-related responsibilities and spend more hours working than do the men. The demands of Efe women's work often require that they be out of camp in places where it is difficult or dangerous to care for small children. Even when Chabo was still nursing his mother would often leave him for short periods of time with another lactating woman who would breastfeed him if he got hungry or began to fuss while his mother was away. This type of multiple caretaking may be unique to the Efe, and it certainly contradicts many of the beliefs held by sociobiologists. It does, however, allow Efe women considerable freedom, safe in the knowledge that their children are being well cared for.

Efe women traditionally gather food and fish. Now they also labor in the fields of their Lese exchange partners, all in all providing over 60 percent of the calories within their family's diet. Efe men and women, unlike the Lese, share many of the day-to-day subsistence tasks. Efe men prepare and cook food when their wives are busy, a practice not sanctioned by the Lese who have a much more rigid sexual division of labor. Efe women do most of the gathering and fishing, but seldom help to raid a beehive and only accompany the hunters during the dry season when large *musilio*, a type of hunt that involves women, are conducted. These hunts are more like picnics, and the women are there only to carry food for the hunters and bring back any game that is killed.

The importance of women in the subsistence economy of the Efe is often overlooked. Although hunting is exciting to write about, it is both highly dangerous and an exceedingly unpredictable source of food. In contrast, within the rain forest plant food is generally more abundant, more reliably collected, and therefore usually provides more calories to the diet than animal food. Woman the *gatherer*, therefore, contributes more to her family's daily food supply than man the *hunter*. Thus *gatherer-hunter* may be a more accurate description of the Pygmies and indeed of most contemporary hunter-gatherers.

Mbuti Net Hunters

Unlike Efe women such as Ima-chabo, women of the Mbuti clan are a required component of net hunting, one of the major differences in subsistence economies between the Efe bow hunters and the Mbuti net hunters.

Tafe lives in a camp much like Karambodu and his family; however, the camps of net hunters are much larger, containing many more huts and many more people. It is not uncommon for fifty to eighty Mbuti to live in Tafe's camp whereas a camp of more than twenty-five Efe is rare indeed. The Mbuti style of making nets was probably adopted from Bantu farmers; net hunting is therefore considered to be a more recent technology than the more traditional bow hunting. Regardless of when nets were first made by Pygmies, net hunting is still practiced very much like an Efe bow hunters' game drive, or mota, but instead of archers waiting in ambush, an arc of nets is set to trap fleeing game. Nets are made from the tough skin of a forest vine called *sowdi* or *nkusa*, the epidermal hairs of which can give a very nasty friction burn if it brushes against skin.

The nets are about one meter high and 30 to 100 meters (100 to 330 feet) long. By linking nets together the trap can be up to one kilometer in length. As most game only get temporarily tangled in the nets, all the men of the camp are positioned at intervals along the barrier, ready to club or stab trapped animals. Not only does it require many men to secure a one-kilometer-long net but someone must still be available to drive the game. Not surprisingly, Mbuti women and children are always employed as beaters on hunts.

While Ima-chabo contributes to her family's subsistence by working in the Lese's fields, Obolu, Tafe's wife, does so by joining the hunt. Although a net hunt results in the capture of many more animals (less than ten) than a bow hunt (less than three), it requires many more participants, and the actual per capita success rate for the two techniques is similar. Why then does Obolu go net hunting and Ima-chabo go to work in the fields? The answer may partly lie in differences between the exchange partners of the Efe and the net-hunting Mbuti.

Efe Hunters and Lese Farmers of the Northeastern Ituri: A Complex Relationship

Kebe has a balanced reciprocal relationship with the Lese farmer Gamiembi. Kebe's father Achukpa had a similar exchange relationship with Gamiembi's father Mupenda. The Efe-Lese trading system is hereditary and complex. Exchange is not on an instantaneous basis; instead, repayment obligations extend over long periods and are even passed from father to son. Neither side consistently bests the other, and both players constantly vie for what they ascertain to be an equitable system. When Kebe arrives in the village with a *faruci*, leaf parcel, of meat and mushrooms from the forest to give to Gamiembi, these exchange items are usually in repayment for a past debt or a deposit to pay for future trade items rather than a specific request for some plantains or manioc. Kebe's wife may, however, return to the camp later in the day with some rice or peanuts given to her by Atosa, Gamiembi's wife.

The Efe exchange meat, honey, building materials, medicine, and, most important, field labor for such cultivated crops as manioc, plantains, peanuts, and rice, which now constitute over 50 percent of their diet. The Lese also trade metal (for knives and arrowheads), cotton cloth (which is more colorful and more durable than the traditional cloth made from the pounded bark of fig trees), and aluminum cooking pots. These pots are considerably less fragile than traditional biscuit-fired clay pots, although the latter are still prized for cooking sombe or roasting peanuts. The relationship between the Efe and Lese must have been going on for many generations because the Pygmies no longer speak their own language; instead, they speak a dialect of KiLese, which is the southern Sudanic tongue of their trading partners. Similarly, the Mbuti net hunters speak KiBira, the Sua KiBudu, and the Aka KiNgbetu. Interestingly, many Lese and Bira words for forest plants and animals are the same, suggesting that these may be the last remnants of an all-but-lost Mbuti language.

Although the Efe and Lese have been living in close association for hundreds of years, the Efe have maintained their genetic integrity. As the Lese consider Efe camps lower-class habitations, Lese women would never agree to marry an Efe man and thus have to move from a village to a camp. Efe women, on the other hand, have no such prejudice against marrying a Lese. The Lese buy their wives for a brideprice, whereas when an Efe man is ready to marry a woman from another camp, he must give a sister or cousin of his in exchange. In this way the sex ratio of Efe camps is maintained. Bokbau's camp has, however, lost two young women who left to marry Lese men, and now Baranga, a single Efe man in the band, is without "sisters" to exchange for a marriage partner.

Reduction in the number of women in an Efe camp is also important as Efe women provide the greatest contribution to the diet of the camp by laboring in Lese gardens. To continue this important aspect of the Efe-Lese exchange relationship, Efe camps must remain close to Lese villages for much of the year. This has restricted the nomadic existence of the Efe hunter-gatherers and sets up conflicts between Efe men and women. The women want to camp near the villages, and the men would rather be deeper in the forest where there is less competition for game and honey. Bokbau, Kebe, Karambodu, and the rest of the band only move the camp far from the village during the honey season, since honey is an exchange item more highly prized than field labor. They also move during the annual hunger season that occurs in May and June prior to the peanut harvest, which is the first harvest of the year. During a severe hunger season, the Efe will often move to areas adjacent to rocky outcrops that are several days' trek from the village. Here Ima-chabo and the other women will spend hours gathering the abundant tubers and *Dioscorea* yams. Wild tubers are definitely not a preferred food; they are unpalatable, laborious to prepare, and are only exploited in emergencies. Great care must be taken in selecting wild tubers; although the *njatu* and *kocho* varieties are very similar in appearance, kocho contains deadly concentrations of bitter and poisonous hydrocyanic acid.

The intimate and intricate relationship between the Efe and Lese has had profound effects on the nomadic life-style and health and welfare of the Efe. The Efe certainly gain substantially from their relationship with the Lese. Every day Ima-chabo returns from the village with kilograms of manioc and plantains, a quantity of food that would take many more hours or even days to gather, assuming that sufficient carbohydrate food was available within the forest. But this bounty of cultivated crops is paid for in the increased exposure of all Efe to a more sedentary, materialistic way of life, as well as a sharply increased incidence of disease.

Children are highly valued and are often taken care of, even breastfed, by women other than the child's mother. An Efe woman feeds an infant.

Rain-Forest Life: Not Quite Utopia

The Ituri forest, much like the Congo basin rain forests in general, is relatively benign. There are few occurrences of death from snakebite or from being mauled by a leopard. The hot, humid forest is, however, a perfect breeding ground for myriad insects, fungi, and microbes that are considerably more dangerous to Efe and Lese alike than even the deadly (albeit beautiful) black-and-white forest cobra. The seemingly easy-going, low-stress way of life of the Efe and Lese may seem enviable in contrast to the accelerating pace of modern technological society. It is not a paradise, however, and can at times be desperate and brutish in the extreme.

Mortality and morbidity among children are very high. Many children do not survive to puberty, and few adults reach the age of fifty or sixty. Malaria, infant diarrhea, bilharzia, filariasis, intestinal worms, amoebic dysentery, tropical ulcers, ringworm, pneumonia, leprosy, tuberculosis, sleeping sickness, and sickle-cell anemia are just some of the diseases that sap the strength of all forest dwellers. Although traditional cures are effective, they cannot hope to defend against such a concerted onslaught. Death and dying are commonplace. I felt so useless when despairing parents would bring their terminally ill children to me in the vain hope that the *Ude* (European) could effect a miraculous cure. It is a scandal that so little money is spent on these tropical diseases that destroy millions

of lives each year. Those children who do survive into adulthood seem to carry with them extraordinary immunities and the ability to recover quickly from trauma. After I sewed up Karakokbo's kneecap when he had nearly severed it falling on his spear, he amazed me by walking into camp the next week with an imperceptible limp. But even the most robust and vital people can suddenly fall sick and die. Karambodu, my Efe guide and friend, died recently from a sudden and undiagnosed disease.

Morbidity and death are often ascribed as the work of forest *bulozi* (witches), and accusations fly concerning who cast the spell. Villagers are more prone to disease than the Efe primarily because most diseases are water borne or depend on insects that breed in stagnant pools. Because Lese villages are permanent, and villagers use the same water in which to bathe and drink over a long period of time, their water supplies are almost always polluted. The Efe, who move camp regularly, are generally spared a contaminated water source but contract many diseases by drinking water while in the villages.

We have only just started to understand the complexity and mutual interdependence of the relationship between Efe like Kebe and his villager who is referred to as *muto*. It is unknown how long such relationships have been established, but we do know that the Lese would eat less meat and honey and would be unable to clear and maintain such large gardens without the Efe, while the carbohydrate diet of the Efe would be considerably more meager and unpalatable were it not for their relationship with the Lese. The future of these two populations is interconnected and changes in the life-style of one must necessarily affect the subsistence economy of the other.

The Mbuti and Bira of the South and Central Ituri

Tafe, of the net-hunting Mbuti clan, and his camp also have a trading relationship with forest farmers. The Bira are a tribe of Bantu who moved into the forest from the southeastern savannas fewer than four hundred years ago. The relationship between the net hunters and the Bira is more recent and in some ways different from that of the Efe and Lese. Tafe and his band go net hunting not only to provide meat for themselves to eat but to acquire it as their main trade item, which they exchange for Bira commodities and cultivated food. Net hunters like Tafe and their women seldom labor in Bira fields, and field labor is not a major item in the exchange relationship. Tafe's band heavily exploit the forest for game, traveling long distances and intensively hunting any areas that contain game. The unique importance of meat as a trade item may have prompted Tafe's ancestors to abandon bow hunting, in which only one or two animals are cap-

Efe (Forest Pygmy) men return from a successful hunt to their camp in the Ituri forest (Zaire) with a black-fronted duiker wrapped in leaf packages.

tured on a successful hunt, in favor of the large communal net hunts that secure upward of eight duikers a day. A shift in the exchange relationship from field labor to meat trade greatly increases the risk that Mbuti hunters will overexploit the forest, severely depleting the populations of duikers upon which they depend for subsistence. This is already occurring in the southern Ituri where farmer population densities are high and intensive net hunting occurs to satisfy the market for meat. Overhunting is occurring, but what else can Tafe and his band do? He and his ancestors have invested all their energies into satisfying their exchange partners' demands for meat and are now dependent on this system for nearly all the carbohydrate calories in their diet. Large bands of Mbuti net hunters need large amounts of manioc, plantains, and peanuts to survive—these must be provided by the Bira who in return demand large quantities of meat. Traditions are always hard to change, even though their continuation becomes increasingly difficult and may actually jeopardize their future existence.

Colonial Rule and the Ituri Forest

The arrival of Belgian colonialists accelerated the changes in the Mbuti way of life that had been started by the Lese and continued by the more recent invasion of the forest by the Bantu: the Bira, Budu, and Nande. Fifty years of colonial domination caused more change in both the hunter-gatherers' and shifting cultivators' economies than had occurred during the previous two thousand years.

By the 1930s the Belgian colonial authority was building roadways with the pressed labor of villagers and Pygmies and forcibly moving forest-dwelling farmers and their associated Mbuti to permanent villages adjacent to the roads. Mupenda's father was required to plant crops of rice and cotton for sale in the newly established market economy. Forest populations throughout the Congo basin were concentrated along the roads, and competition for land suitable for cultivation quickly intensified. Traditional usufructuary land-tenure systems collapsed in many areas as resettled farmers encroached on the *sapu,* home lands, of resident farmers. The cultivation period increased from one to two or more years, while fallow periods diminished from a nutrient-restoring fifteen years to a barely sufficient ten years or less. Clearing and planting larger fields increased the Lese's dependence on Efe labor, and the development of roadways and trading greatly increased the market for forest resources such as meat and honey. The traditional Mbuti-Bira relationship was often supplanted by merchants who traveled from urban centers where the high demand for meat produced a much higher exchange rate than the relatively poor forest farmers could pay. Net hunt-

ing solely for the market therefore increased and is still increasing.

The higher population density brought about by enforced resettlement resulted in more widespread disease. Water sources, used by growing numbers of people who were prohibited from moving to new areas, rapidly became rank and disease infested. Establishment of coffee and oil-palm plantations lured the young village and Mbuti men away from the camps and villages in search of wages and Western commodities. Acculturation often brought with it a breakdown in traditional values, an aping of wholly inappropriate European technologies and mannerisms, and an increase in alcoholism. Farmers started to cultivate their fields continuously and abandoned stable polyculture for monocultures of rice or corn. Within a decade or two huge tracts of the forest had been degraded from a productive, sustainable mosaic of active shifting cultivation and nutrient-restoring forest fallows to infertile ecological deserts of *Imperata* grasses. Intensive cultivation resulted in the development of a zone of regrowth vegetation and active fields two to three kilometers (one to two miles) wide on either side of the roadways. Only by the 1950s did Belgian agricultural experts realize that shifting cultivation as practiced for centuries by forest farmers was, and still is, the only really feasible form of sustained farming within the rain forest.

Changes Since Independence

When the Belgians abandoned the Congo on June 30, 1960, they left behind a legacy of confusion. A new bureaucracy had been established that replaced traditional chiefdoms, and a monetary economy had to a great extent altered the commodity barter system of old. Yet the Belgians had failed to educate Zairois in the new ways, and the early years of independence were chaotic. Successionist rebellions in the south and northeast in the 1960s and early 1970s forced many farmers to abandon their villages and flee with the Mbuti into the comparative safety of the deep forest. Rape, murder, and pillage all took their toll; the market economies of the Belgians collapsed; and the roadways quickly became rutted, potholed, and all but impassable for much of the year. Ironically, then, between 1965 and 1975 the Ituri inhabitants returned to more traditional subsistence economies.

As the young nation of Zaire grows older and gains experience it begins to look more toward the welfare of its people and the exploitation of its natural resources. The crash in the price of copper negated all of Zaire's optimistic economic forecasts, and the nation is now chronically in debt. Under such severe budget shortfalls the rain forests are in danger of being mined for their resources rather than being managed for sustained exploitation. A $280 million hardwood-pulp mill complex has been built in Gabon, and already huge areas of previously untouched forests have been cleared. All the Congo basin forest edges have been clear cut for lumber and, more important, charcoal. Resurgence of Zaire's agricultural market economy due to the increase in the world price of coffee has resulted in the expansion of coffee and oil-palm plantations and the rapid urbanization of adjacent villages. In addition, over the last few decades the Ituri forest has become a settlement frontier into which families from the rapidly growing, densely populated savannas and highlands on the north and east are immigrating in ever-increasing numbers. These immigrants often bring with them farming techniques that, although applicable to the fertile volcanic soils of the eastern highlands, are incompatible with sustained exploitation of the forest and result in the establishment of short-duration fallows, which are rapidly exhausting resources. Increasing population densities provide growing markets for forest resources; consequently, game hunting by the Mbuti solely for sale is expanding and risks cleaning out all animals from large areas in the forest.

All these developments threaten the integrity of the rain forest and put in question the continued existence of the traditional life-styles of forest farmers and hunter-gatherers. Clearly the future of the Mbuti is a precarious one. Changes that have occurred over the last sixty years have had a profound effect on their traditional nomadic hunter-gatherer way of life. These changes will only accelerate in the next few decades, resulting in the possible total acculturation of the Mbuti and consequently the loss of a unique and fascinating human culture.

The information in this chapter was obtained during a two-year field study funded in part by National Science Foundation grants (BNS-82-18791 and BNS-19629) and through numerous conversations with other Ituri Project researchers, primarily Drs. Gilda Morelli, Robert Bailey, Barbara DeZalduando, Nadine Peacock, and Steve Winn.

8

PEOPLE OF THE FLOODPLAIN AND FOREST

CHRISTINE PADOCH

The village of San Alejandro is hidden from view as we arrive on the *Jorge Carlos,* a cargo boat from the city of Iquitos. Disembarking on the muddy bank of the Ucayali River, we cross a field of ripening rice. The path then becomes a bridge of felled palm trunks that leads through a broad, shallow swamp. Ahead, barefooted children run along the bobbing logs, hopping from one to another. Red and yellow macaws scream as they fly from a towering *aguaje* palm (*Mauritia flexuosa*) across the river. The log bridge ends at a small rise where the first house stands surrounded by an orchard of fruit trees, each different, each unfamiliar to a North American.

This village in the Amazonian department of Loreto in northeastern Peru has 312 residents in forty-one families. Sixteen of the households are clustered on this small hill around a long ramshackle schoolhouse; the other twenty-five are strung out along four miles of riverbank. The houses are open, some with no walls at all, and stand on stilts. Palm thatch covers them and split palm trunks make up their floors and any walls. Diverse gardens of fruit trees and other plants can be seen behind each of the houses.

The village is quiet on this hot October afternoon. Several women look up to greet us as we pass by. A few are spreading cowpeas and rice to dry in the sun on large mats in front of their houses. One is making a palm-fiber net bag, another is cleaning fish. Our neighbor Rosalbina is chopping firewood; the afternoon meal of boiled manioc and *arahuana* fish (*Osteoglossum bicirrhosum*) is already on the earthen stove. Her eight-year-old daughter, Mirsa, sets an enameled basin full of *ungurahui* fruits (*Jessenia bataua*) soaking in water, to warm and ripen in the sun. Another daughter, Cleofe, is weeding the garden behind the house, careful that her machete only cut the unwelcome weeds and avoid the diverse collection of condiments, medicinals, and other utilitarian and ornamental plants her parents have assembled.

From our own palm-thatched house we can see some of the nearby swiddens, multicropped shifting cultivation fields, that dot the forested countryside. On the *barreales* (mudflats) along the river we make out a strip of golden rice. And toward the east, beyond this year's swiddens and the young growth from previous years' fields, we can see the edge of the tall rain forest. Cleofe tells us that most villagers have gone to harvest rice because the river is rising and some fields are flooding. Her family, however, harvested their rice early, and Emilio, her father, has gone to collect palm leaves to repair their leaking roof.

Rosalbina, Emilio, and their daughters, like all other San Alejandrinos, converse in Spanish and dress in the poor, patched clothing universal to the rural areas of tropical America. Most of them have straight

black hair, high cheekbones, and dark almond-shaped eyes, testifying to their Indian heritage. They plant manioc and dozens of other crops in swiddens; they hunt and fish; they cure with plants and incantations; they fear the forest demon with his feet reversed and the pink river dolphin. But neither Rosalbina Mayta-huari nor any of her neighbors would call themselves Amerindians or natives of the Amazon, and the government doesn't classify them as such. San Alejandrinos are *ribereños,* or *campesinos,* or *mestizos*; riverbank people, small farmers, mixed-bloods. They are mostly descendants of the Cocama Indians, peoples who lived along the greatest Peruvian rivers, the Amazon, Ucayali, and Marañon. Many San Alejandrinos also claim some European ancestry. All are inheritors, changers, and developers of the ancient ecological knowledge of floodplain Amazonians, whose large settlements and chiefdoms have long disappeared.

San Alejandro, Rosalbina, and Emilio are fictitious names, but the village and the people described here are real. Variations of this village exist along all the major rivers of the Peruvian Amazon as well as in the Amazon basin in Brazil, Bolivia, Colombia, Ecuador, and Venezuela. Counterparts of these Peruvian ribereños are to be found in thousands of settlements, with a population several orders of magnitude larger than that of tribal Indians. They are not officially natives, but neither are they recent immigrants. Their experience of the Amazonian environment is genera-

tions or even centuries older than that of the newcomers who in the last decades have followed Brazil's dusty roads and the rivers of the Andean foothills down to the lowlands.

But the ribereños of Peru, the caboclos of Brazil, the mestizos or campesinos of Bolivia, Colombia, Ecuador, and Venezuela, are curiously invisible to everyone but their neighbors. In the past few years even the international press has reported a good deal about the people of the great rural expanses of the Amazon and their problems. The plight of the last tribal groups, the land wars between immigrant squatters and large ranchers, and the enormous schemes for developing the Amazon have appeared in national newspapers and magazines, but the ribereños or caboclos have remained unknown. Even anthropologists have largely ignored them. In their own countries they have been confused frequently with colonists or unfairly labeled the oppressors of tribal peoples. Their own politicians often seem to be unaware of their existence.

The mere lack of national and international attention is not a problem for these rural people, but their invisibility has contributed to their often remaining legally unprotected, and the lack of studies of their environmental knowledge and resource-use patterns is a loss to us all. They are the traditional and, in many cases, exclusive users of certain important Amazonian environments, particularly the fertile floodplains. Their knowledge of environmental structures and pro-

◁ The ribereños of the Peruvian Amazon are largely the descendants of acculturated native groups and inheritors of many Indian traditions. A woman and her children along the Ucayali River in Peru.

The great rubber boom of the turn of the century brought much wealth into the Amazon. However, those who tapped the rubber, like this contemporary Brazilian caboclo, have rarely shared the riches.

BELOW: Rice is planted on seasonally flooded mudflats along the Amazon and its tributaries in Peru. Villagers from the lower Ucayali River winnow their freshly harvested rice.

BOTTOM: A wide range of medicinal plants and potions is used by both rural and urban populations of the Amazon. A vendor of medicinal plants displays her wares in Iquitos, Peru.

cesses may hold many keys to the sound and conservative exploitation of these agriculturally promising areas. Although in their families native languages may never be spoken, animist gods largely unknown, and native dress disdained, the caboclos or ribereños have not lost all Amazonian traditions. Even those most Iberian in their folkways largely farm, hunt, fish, and cure their everyday ills using technologies and products developed over centuries in the Amazonian forests.

Who Are the Caboclos or Ribereños?

It may be easier to define the caboclos or ribereños in negative rather than in positive terms: they are neither tribal Indians nor recent immigrants; their origins are varied. They are rural people, including detribalized Amazonian Indians and their descendants, the offspring of Amazonian-European and Amazonian-African unions, as well as the descendants of early immigrants from other areas of Brazil, Peru, and other Andean countries.

The processes that formed the caboclo or ribereño began centuries ago: destruction of many Amerindian cultures and more gradual change of others; European and other immigration; and intermixture of racial and cultural groups. Since the 1500s indigenous populations of Amazonia have experienced European incursions. Various periods have seen far more interest in Amazonian souls and resources than others, with con-

sequent greater destruction of indigenous cultures and heavier immigration flows.

Early missions created villages where Indians of various groups were often gathered and the detribalization process was effected. European tastes and markets for tropical forest products such as spices, waxes, and animal skins had an even more devastating impact on tribal groups. The Europeans and Ibero-Americans who came to the Amazon wanted both resources from Indian lands and the force of Indian labor.

The last great event that transformed the caboclo and ribereño populations, swelling their numbers, was the rubber boom, which lasted almost half a century and culminated around 1912. Many Brazilian and Peruvian caboclos and ribereños trace their ancestry to immigrants who ascended the Amazon and descended the great rivers of the Andean foothills in search of the "black gold" that was rubber. But other economic booms brought them also, some earlier and a few later than rubber.

The natives most affected by these invasions were those who lived along the major rivers, the flat and accessible floodplains. A great number succumbed early to imported diseases, to the abuses of slavery, to raids. But some survived, socially and culturally disenfranchised, and different from their mothers and fathers. These natives of the large Amazonian rivers, and the outsiders who migrated up those rivers, were the ancestors of today's ribereños and caboclos. And it is still

Cross-section of the Ucayali River and floodplain.

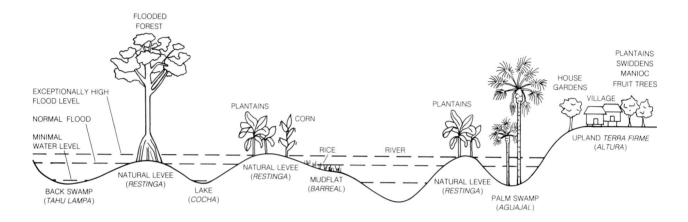

in the floodplains of these great waterways that their descendants live. The caboclos and ribereños thus are almost the sole rural residents of the *varzea,* the Amazonian lands that are seasonally or periodically flooded by silt-laden waters, where unpredictable floods can wipe out a season's production, but also where most of the region's fertile soils are found. It is on these narrow but rich strips of land that many experts believe future agricultural development in the Amazon must be focused. Neglecting the resource-use techniques of the caboclos and ribereños is folly indeed.

A History of Commercial Forest Use

The ways in which caboclos and ribereños use their environments to satisfy their daily needs closely resemble the remarkably productive and conservative resource-use techniques of Amazonian native groups. Their knowledge and use of forest plants, their methods of hunting and fishing, and their agricultural techniques all are based on indigenous traditions.

Much of the post-Conquest history of forest use in the Amazon that involved the caboclos reflects the economic needs and changing fashions not of local or regional peoples but of markets half a world away. The search for exportable products in the Amazon started with the arrival of the first explorers; patterns of resource use changed soon afterward. The Europeans were eager to profit from the riches of the vast,

newly discovered territory. The environment, however, did not lend itself to the types of resource use to which they were accustomed. The soils of the uplands did not long produce valuable harvests; the flooding cycles of the large rivers made familiar techniques of agriculture difficult. The sparse population, reduced greatly by European incursions, limited labor supply, and the enormous distances daunted all economic enterprises. Large-scale plantation agriculture succeeded in a very few, limited areas of the Amazon basin. But there were riches to be had in the forest itself, riches that in various periods responded to European needs. Their exploitation wasn't easy either. The enormous diversity of the forest made extraction of dispersed resources a difficult endeavor. A number of forest products were exported in large quantities, bringing enormous riches to a few. The great rubber boom was the most dramatic expression of the extractive mode of commercial forest use in the Amazon basin.

Rubber had been known to Europeans since the eighteenth century mostly as a curiosity: a good "rubber" or eraser, or a good material for waterproofing a mackintosh. With Charles Goodyear's invention of the vulcanization process in 1839, the latex of the *Hevea brasiliensis* tree and a few other species could be made more resistant to temperature change and therefore more useful. Later in the century the need for tires on bicycles and later for cars, as well as the growth of the electrical industries, made rubber a desirable and scarce product. And at that time the Amazon was virtually its only source.

Many caboclos and ribereños tapped rubber, many immigrants and tribal Indians became caboclos and ribereños because of rubber, and many others, particularly in the Peruvian Amazon, died of disease or of the physical abuse and violence associated with the boom. Rubber bred wealth and ostentation: opera houses, elegant tile-covered homes, and fashions imported seasonally from Paris. But the effect of the boom on many caboclo families was vastly different. Rubber gathering was a lonely, tiring, and disease-ridden life for many. Family farms were often abandoned by men gone off to tap rubber or were left to women with many dependent children to tend. Debts were incurred and couldn't be paid off. Although the historian Barbara Weinstein has shown that relations between the rubber tapper and the rubber buyer did not always lead to crushing debt-slavery as has sometimes been stated, abuses were many and the social costs often high. When the production of plantation rubber in Southeast Asia sent the price plummeting, the Amazonian rubber boom was over. Little was left but some buildings, which quickly began to decay, and a large, impoverished, and dispersed caboclo or ribereño population.

Rubber was the most famous forest product exported from the Amazon, but it was far from the only one. Many of the men who once had worked in rubber later participated in a variety of other minor economic booms, all merely faint echoes of the great one at the turn of the century. Among other important exports collected from the forest were animal skins for Europe's coats and shoes, leche caspi (Couma macrocarpa) from which chewing gum was made, vegetable ivory (Phytelephas macrocarpa) used as a predecessor of plastics for making buttons and chess pieces, and rosewood oil (Aniba roseadora) to scent the soaps and perfumes of the rich. Each of these products fetched high prices for a while. But in most cases with the development of synthetic substitutes or of alternative, cheaper sources, the prices fell and the ribereños and caboclos who constituted the workforce for each one of these booms, returned to their farms or drifted to the slums of Amazonian cities.

The swiftness with which the rural folks of the Amazon accommodated themselves to the changes in world markets and prices is remarkable. They were often very quick to seize opportunities and to abandon what was no longer profitable. But the costs of these economic swings were frequently high, involving great geographical displacement and disruption of family and village life. The recent history of the village of San Alejandro and the life histories of some of its older residents show how profoundly the population

and settlement patterns of the upper Amazon have been affected by changing market demands for products of the rain forest.

The present village of San Alejandro has a short history. No one knows who lived on that small hill above the river's flood level before the Spanish invaded and in the first few centuries thereafter. Although the spot itself has obviously not moved, its relation to the ever-changing Ucayali has. Several centuries ago, it was probably well away from the river; now only a few hundred feet of low-lying swamp separate it from the Ucayali's channel. Early European travelers who chronicled their voyages could not see that hill from their canoes, and whoever might have lived there has left us no record.

Today's San Alejandrinos report that during the rubber boom some tappers were living along the nearby Lobillo stream. But the boom was short-lived and so were the settlements. The names of those who worked here are forgotten, and their makeshift dwellings have long since rotted away. Their location can only be surmised from a group of fruit trees at a few sites; these may have been planted or perhaps these groves merely mark the sites of old refuse piles.

All but three or four of the present villagers were born after the boom. Many of them, however, remember well the great fundo, or plantation, called Monte Bello. Once located just upriver from the present San Alejandro, the plantation produced cane liquor and sugar, beef cattle, and barbasco (Lonchocarpus sp.), a woody bush that contains an effective natural insecticide. The plantation had a large work force of Ashaninka (Campa) Indians, brought down from the far upper Ucayali, as well as a few workers from the region.

When the development of DDT and other synthetic insecticides brought down the price of barbasco, and the plantation as a whole ceased to be lucrative, the owner decided to exploit another forest product that was enjoying high prices: the gum-bearing leche caspi tree. Abandoning the estate, he gathered his laborers and a few other men and set off for the distant Putumayo River, where the tree abounded. No wives or children were allowed to come; they remained to manage as best they could tending their own farms.

For two years the workers of Monte Bello cut and bled the leche caspi trees. Then the price of that product too fell, and their patron decided that more profit was to be made planting cane and rice once again. All were transported to another estate, Santa Barbara, along the Amazon.

When the new plantation didn't prosper, the patron's assistant took groups of laborers up many of the Amazon's smaller tributaries to mine the forest for its riches. They brought deer, jaguar, and peccary skins down from the Atacuari River, and they cut precious

Most caboclos and ribereños are, like their native Amazonian forebears, shifting cultivators. Farmers near Iquitos, Peru, fell a tree while standing on a scaffold that allows them to cut above the tree's buttresses.

Annual floods on the Amazon vary greatly in height and may destroy crops and houses. Amazonians readily adapt to such difficulties. Much of the busy Belén section of Iquitos, seen here, is flooded every year. ▷

OPPOSITE BOTTOM: Diverse orchards of fruit trees are planted by both tribal and nontribal Amazonians. Multi-species agroforestry plots, such as this one along the lower Ucayali River, have been hailed as economically and environmentally sound.

hardwoods on the Yavari. After a few years the patron left Santa Barbara and took the group far up another of the Amazon's major tributaries, the Napo. There they went into the forest again to search out and cut the aromatic rosewood for its precious essential oil. Again a two-year stay was all that proved profitable. The patron then decided to leave the area altogether, abandoning his workers hundreds of miles away from their homes. Around 1950 the Monte Bellinos with their former patron's assistant as their new patron at last returned up the Ucayali to the site of the once grand plantation.

But the group that returned was not the same one that had left years before. Some had decided to stay in the widely scattered areas where they had worked, some died, some married. New people had joined the group, and other people had assumed new identities. The Ashaninkas had lost almost all the trappings of their former tribal life; many took spouses from outside their group.

The new community that formed about 1950, located downriver from Monte Bello and named San Alejandro, was composed of people with diverse backgrounds. There were ex-Ashaninkas, ex-Cocamas, mestizos descended from Cocama-European unions, some ex-Quichuas who had joined the group on the upper Napo, several ex-Yagua women from the ill-fated estate on the Amazon. There were and still are several other families whose origins are difficult

to trace. All consider themselves ribereños; their village composition as well as their ethnic identity is very clearly a result of the strange history of forest-production exploitation in the Peruvian Amazon.

Despite all the products of the Amazonian rain forest that proved to be valuable on the world market, despite all the money that has been made in exporting them, the region has seen little economic development, almost no long-term investment. Very few of the ribereños and even fewer Indians who were the tappers, hunters, trappers, and timber cutters that brought those treasures out of the forest have benefitted economically from their labors. Many of those who got rich were not Amazonians, and the few who were took their riches to Lima or São Paulo, to Europe, and more recently to Miami.

In Brazil, Peru, and elsewhere in Amazonia, a surprising number of families still eke out a living collecting forest products for export. Rubber tappers, Brazil nut collectors, and palm heart extractors still live difficult lives often shadowed by unshakable debt to merchants and, more recently, threatened by forest-cutting settlers and cattle ranchers. In Brazil, rubber tappers have recently banded together to form a union. These unlikely union members have grabbed a good deal of attention in the Brazilian media with their demands for "extractive reserves" that would preserve forests rich in natural rubber or Brazil nuts, while allowing extraction of economically valuable products. How successful they will be in protecting the forests that support them is still to be seen.

Regional and Local Use of Forest Products
The societies of Europe and North America continue to find products in the Amazonian rain forest that at first are luxuries and later often become necessities of life in industrial societies. Almost all these resources had been used by Amazonians, although often for purposes other than those to which they were put by Westerners. I have already mentioned the insecticide plant, barbasco, that Amazonians have commonly used as a fish poison. Curare (*Chonodendron tomentosum, Strychnos toxifera,* or others), long an indispensable muscle relaxant employed in cardiac surgery, was used by Amazonian Indians as an arrow poison. Rubber was employed by natives to waterproof materials and leche caspi or chicle to cure stomachaches. The forest products that were exported from the Amazonian forest are many and varied, but many more products are used locally or are traded regionally.

A walk through any Amazonian market will acquaint you with a great variety of bark, leaves, seeds, roots, resins, and flowers that can be used in teas, baths, ointments, plasters, incense, and smoking materials to cure a multitude of ailments of the body and the soul. A whole block of the largest market in the

city of Iquitos is devoted to medicinal plants, many of them already prepared in alcohol. (They raise the spirit while curing the body.) At the other end of the Amazon, in the large modern Brazilian city of Belém with more than a million residents, an ethnobotanist identified more than fifty plants commonly sold in one large marketplace and used to cure; many more could be found for specialized needs. Most of these plants are taken from local forests. Only a few have been adequately evaluated by medical laboratories and exported outside Amazonia's borders.

The range of plants used in rural areas, close to the forest that is the source of many medicinals, is even greater. In San Alejandro, Mejoral, a commercial aspirin and caffeine product, is used for aches, pains, and fevers, but so are many other drugs that grow in peoples' gardens and in the nearby rain forest. The village's foremost curer, Doña Rosario Tapayuri, whose fame attracts patients from nearby towns, uses a large pharmacopoeia of diagnostic, curative, magic, and other useful plants. Medicine in the ribereño village is an amalgam of diverse traditions; perhaps the most important component is the plant-based medicinal knowledge inherited from Amazonian forbears.

Doña Rosario has planted a large garden around her house. At first glance the plants seem to be arranged haphazardly, one species climbing over another. But like a good pharmacist with a crowded store, the sixty-year-old woman knows exactly where each of her medicines can be found. In 1986 I counted and collected seventy-eight different species in Doña Rosario's house garden; all but a few foods and condiments were used for medicinal purposes. Many plants were used for more than one condition, for instance, the shrub called *piñon colorado* is a first-aid kit on a stem. Its milky resin stops children's diarrhea, its seeds kill intestinal worms, and the leaf when heated will keep a boil from becoming infected. The plants that comprise the garden come from a variety of sources, some have been cultivated and used in the region for centuries, others are curiosities that the curer picked up from the Iquitos market or from someone who recently came back from a trip. Many of them, however, are plants brought to the garden from the forest. Doña Rosario transplants many species closer to her house for the sake of convenience. The *curandera,* however, also uses many other forest species. Once she locates them in the forest, Doña Rosario remembers their locations: near Artemio's plantain field, or on the hillock near the stand of *yarina* palms (*Phytelephas macrocarpa*), or along the bend of the Lobillo stream.

The forest also provides food, fiber, and housing for the ribereños of San Alejandro. My neighbor, Don Emilio Maytahuari, has gone off to collect the leaves of the *irapai* palm (*Lepidocaryum tessmannii*) to reroof his house. If he also decides to put a new roof-beam covering, Emilio will probably use the leaves of another palm, yarina, because their shape is better suited for this specialized purpose. Split trunks of two other palms, *huacrapona* (*Iriartea deltoidea*) and *cashapona* (*Socratea exhorriza*), make up the walls and floor of the Maytahuari house. The columns are of *huacapu* (*Minquartia guianensis,* or others), a hard, insect- and rot-resistant wood, and the beams and roof supports of such woods as *espintana* (*Guatteria* spp.), *tortuga caspi* (*G. microcarpa*), or *carahuasca* (*G. elata*) that are flexible and resilient to the wind; secondary supports are made of the arrow cane, *caña brava* (*Gynerium sagittatum*). A vine, *tamshi* (often *Heteropsis jenmanii*) is used to tie the structure together; nails are expensive. The special qualities of each wood, each fiber are known, and the best is used for each particular purpose in the house.

When the river rose far more than usual and the flood reached well into the forest, San Alejandrinos went in numbers to collect another forest product for themselves and to sell in the city. In their canoes they followed a small stream and entered the huge palm swamp that lies behind the river's levee. There, in the brown-stained water stand hundreds of trunks of the aguaje palm. Cutting down these large palms, the men of San Alejandro harvested their fruits for sale in Iquitos. The small scaly fruits are oily and slightly acidic. They make a tasty drink and the best popsicles and ice cream to be had in the city. What is more, buying one's sweetheart a bag of the fruits from the streetcorner vendor each day is said to be a sure way to an Iquiteña's heart. The fruits, Iquitos lore has it, contain female "hormones" and make a suitor irresistible to the woman eating them.

Our other neighbor, Doña Teresa Ríos, made three trips to Iquitos to sell the aguaje fruits last year, each time bringing about sixty hundred-pound sacks of the fruit with her. She could have sold the valuable fruit in San Alejandro itself to any number of traders who travel the river on large boats, looking for the produce of farm and forest to sell in the city's markets. But Doña Teresa decided to try to make a better profit by wholesaling the aguaje herself. She, like several of the village's other women, has spent some time in the city when she was in her teens, working as a domestic, a washerwoman, and as a small market vendor. So Doña Teresa is not to be easily cheated in the bustling market like many of her rural compatriots. She has a sharp tongue, a quick eye, and can do long division in her head with no trouble, although she cannot read.

Gathering aguaje was once an easier task. In front of the village there was once a large *aguajal* (palm swamp), now reduced to only a narrow strip of swamp, with most of the aguajes dead or dying. The river, cutting away at that bank of the river is responsible for the swamp's demise. But before it began to disappear, San Alejandrinos and their neighbors had already degraded it considerably. For decades they had been cutting down the fruiting palms in order to harvest the heavy panicles of fruit. Since only the female aguaje palms produce fruit, the easily accessible aguajal had long been reduced to an almost all-male stand, useless for fruit collecting. It is however, still used for many things. The male trees are felled to make a bridge through the swamp, their leaves are used to weave screens and temporary roofing, the spongy material in the leaf stalk makes a wonderful cork for bottles, and inside the starch-rich trunk are found fat beetle grubs. These grubs, fried, are a great treat by local standards, and a bowl full of grubs will fetch a very good price in any market.

It is understandable that San Alejandrinos choose to cut rather than to climb the palms to harvest the fruit. The trunks are often very tall, eighty feet is not unusual, they are wider around than a man can reach, and their tops, with dozens of dead and drooping leaves, harbor spiders, snakes, wasps, and all manner of creature with which one would not want to share a treetop. However, some alternative manner of harvesting aguajes will have to be found, because many aguajales are being ravaged to satisfy the tastes of Iquitos. Although aguaje is not about to disappear from the Amazon, nor even from the Ucayali River, fruit-laden stands are getting farther and farther from the consuming market centers and the cost of bringing

In 1912, just before the collapse in rubber prices, a river boat brings a cargo of balls of rubber and some tappers down the Amazon to market.

the product in gets higher and higher; many loads of the easily perishable fruit now rot before they get to Iquitos.

Destruction and degradation of a palm forest is, however, not typical of ribereño and caboclo use of natural resources, nor is it a necessary consequence of market exploitation. In the estuary of the Amazon more than two thousand miles downriver from San Alejandro, Brazilian caboclos have developed productive and environmentally conservative methods of managing another kind of palm forest. The *assai* palm (*Euterpe oleracea*) grows in dense stands in the tidally inundated swamps near the large city of Belóm. The palm, like aguaje, is the source of many useful and marketable products. Among these are the fruits, which made into a purplish beverage, are a sine qua non of the caboclo diet. The palm's growing tip also furnishes a highly valued palm heart that is exported to gourmets throughout the world. The roots provide a local remedy for ailments of the liver and kidneys, and the leaves and trunk are used in rural areas for a variety of purposes.

In order to extract a palm heart it is necessary to kill the palm, so the active, export-oriented palm-heart canning industry could easily have destroyed the stands of assai palms, as it had stands of the *jaçara* palm (*Euterpe edulis*) in southeastern Brazil, and as it is threatening to do to native stands of *huasai* (*Euterpe precatoria*) in the Peruvian Amazon. Fortunately the

assai palm, a multi-stemmed species, resprouts more readily than do the other related palms. Fortunately, as well, the caboclos on the Ilha das Oncas and other islands in the estuary near Belém know how to protect and improve the productivity of the palm forests that they rely upon for their livelihood. A group of scientists at Brazil's Museu Paraense Emilio Goeldi, headed by ecologist Anthony Anderson, have found that these caboclo "foresters" selectively thin assai stems and remove other trees that compete with the palms. These local forestry techniques apparently not only produce a good quantity of palm heart but increase fruit production in the remaining stems. The rural folks enjoy both a variety of subsistence products and receive a substantial income from the sale of the fruits and palm hearts in the nearby city.

The management of natural palm forests is but one of an array of caboclo and ribereño resource-use techniques that are difficult to fit into the usual scientific classifications. Most anthropological texts distinguish between hunting-gathering or foraging on one hand, and the more familiar agriculture or horticulture on the other, as traditional ways of making a living. Studying resource use of Amazonians, whether tribal or not, has shown us just how inadequate these classifications are in describing how people use their environments. Between pure gathering of forest resources and pure agriculture, which replaces all forest vegetation with cultivated crops, there is a large, poorly

defined gray area; most caboclos and ribereños engage in such mixed resource use.

Agriculture and Other Ways of Making a Living
Simple classification of these folks by resource-use pattern is difficult. Most ribereños and caboclos do many different things: almost no one is just a rice farmer, palm heart collector, fisherman, or hunter. Diversity and flexibility characterize all aspects of their lives. Exactly what agricultural, plant management, or extractive activities are important in a particular region, village, or household, and how complex the mix of activities is, depends on a variety of factors, among them environmental, economic, historical, geographical, and social variables.

The relationship of the people to the river, and the type of river they live on, are very important in determining how they make a living. Many of the Amazon's major tributaries, like the great river itself, carry heavy loads of silt. Others are brown-stained but clear, and still others are almost crystalline. The silt-laden waterways annually leave fertile deposits along their courses, enriching the soils that the flood covered. Many caboclo and ribereño villages are located in or near such zones of deposition. Their inhabitants use the enriched soil for agricultural production. These areas were once dotted with Indian longhouses and villages; now few tribal groups remain and the fertile floodplains are the domain of caboclos and ribereños.

Above the annually inundated zone on the natural levees are lands that flood only occasionally in years of higher than average floods. There the soils are relatively fertile and flooding, not an annual event, is unpredictable. Behind the levees on the edges of backwater swamps and along the banks of oxbow lakes where water levels rise and fall with the river's rhythm, ribereños also plant their crops.

Higher still are the lands above the flood. Here soils are variable but most are poor in the nutrients that crop plants need for growth. In the large expanses between the major rivers, along small streams and rivers, particularly those like the Rio Negro that carry very little sediment, these are the only lands to be found.

Many ribereño and caboclo farmers use all the varieties of land that the environment offers. Others have only one or two types available to them, or choose to specialize. Given the option, however, most Amazonians decide to diversify their production in several zones. This not only allows them to hedge their bets but also lets them use time and household labor more effectively.

Most folks in the Peruvian village of San Alejandro are fortunate; they have a wide array of options. The settlement site and the lands stretching west for many miles are high, well-drained, and never experience floods. Across the Ucayali River on the left bank lies an immense area of frequently inundated terrain.

While some Amazonian rivers and lakes are gradually being depleted of their most valuable fish species, seasonal fish migrations often bring bountiful catches to village fishermen.

Rice is an important cash crop for the ribereños of the Peruvian Amazon. Unpredictable changes in water level can, however, wipe out a year's potential earnings overnight. This rice along the Ucayali River is about ready to harvest.

It is varied and permits different resource-use patterns; beginning at the river's edge and extending about 150 yards inland lie broad mud flats that appear for several months each year only to disappear when the flood comes again. Following the river edge downstream, the texture of the deposits gradually becomes coarser. At the northernmost extension of this low-lying formation, the river annually uncovers not rich, moisture-laden mud and silt but dry beach sand.

Behind the annually flooded zone, the land rises gently. Known locally as a *restinga,* part of this higher area tends also to flood each year. Just how far inland the water reaches will differ from year to year depending on the severity of the flood. The highest point, a natural levee, only floods in the most unusual years. Behind the levee there again are lower lands laced with a series of oxbow lakes abounding in fish. Another restinga is found south of the village on the right bank where the high ground drops. This is a remnant of a much larger, fertile zone that the river is gradually gnawing away.

All the areas—mud flats, beaches, low and high restingas, flood-free uplands—are used for production of subsistence and cash crops. Not all farmers have access to each kind of field; the floodplain sites, particularly mud flats, are limited. The majority of San Alejandrinos (that is, all but the most recent arrivals) have access to at least two kinds of land. For each type of farm there are suitable crops and specialized techniques. The San Alejandro farmer must make many decisions and choices as he or she plans out the agricultural year.

Our neighbor Don Emilio Maytahuari has within his grasp all the options. He is the son of one of San Alejandro's founders, and his wife was born in the neighboring village. The family has five agricultural plots that require and receive intensive maintenance; in addition they have two other plots that also yield important crops but take less time and effort to maintain. The most important site for cash cropping is a good-sized mud flat where they annually plant about one hectare (two and one-half acres) of rice. They have two pieces of restinga land under cultivation where a combination of plantains, papaya, corn, manioc, vegetables (tomatoes, green peppers, coriander), and watermelon are interplanted. The faster maturing crops are planted in the lower areas where flood danger is greater, the slow crops on higher ground. In addition Emilio and Rosalbina have recently harvested four different varieties of cowpeas from their small plot on the sandy beach.

In the flood-free zone the Maytahuari family also has an intensively managed plot that is mostly planted to manioc, a tuber crop that does reasonably well in poor soils. However, interspersed with the manioc are many other crops, some of which will also yield this year or next, like plantains and pineapple, and others, like fruit-tree seedlings, that will not produce for a while but will then bear for many years. These include the peach palm (*Bactris gasipaes*), the grapelike *uvilla* (*Pourouma cecropaeifolia*), the leguminous *Inga edulis,* and the sweet yellow *caimito* (*Pouteria caimito*).

These fields are created with the techniques known as swiddening or slash-and-burn. An area of forest—often previously used secondary forest—is cut. The wood is allowed to dry, and the slash is then burned.

In the nutrient-rich ashes and around the blackened logs and stumps San Alejandrinos plant their crops. Usually some annual staples are planted immediately after the burn and interplanted with a wide array of secondary annual cultigens. Depending on the availability of seeds, the growing patterns of various crops, the needs and wants of the household, and the configuration of their other fields, any number of tree crops are also often introduced. These larger, taller plants will eventually, of course, shade out the shorter crops. But the poor soils of the uplands, the heavy rains and blistering sun, and the intense competition of weedy grasses and herbs make intensive farming for more than a few years a time-consuming and often unprofitable task. The cultivation of tree crops, which cover the soil, shade out weeds, and may be less demanding of nutrients, can be a successful long-term strategy.

Thus, San Alejandrinos often gradually turn their upland manioc and plantain fields into fruit orchards, but usually these orchards are far more complex than North American and European models. Many of them include not only cultivated species but also forest trees, unplanned and unplanted, but often useful.

When Emilio and Rosalbina clean their old fields, now fruit orchards, they do so selectively. "Good weeds," that is, forest species whose growth and use characteristics make them desirable, are left and even protected; "bad weeds" are cleared out.

As fruit trees pass their prime yielding stage, as some get too tall to harvest easily, and as other, newer orchards begin to yield, less time and management is usually devoted to the field. The orchard soon comes to resemble a young forest more than an agricultural undertaking, but to the knowledgable eye it is obviously not a natural forest. Initial planting and subsequent reseeding as well as years of selective weeding produce a forest that contains a higher than average percentage of plants useful to people. The Maytahuaris own a number of plots in different stages of this abandonment process. One of their oldest forest-orchard plots is still actively maintained, however, almost three decades after its first use. This field, originally cleared and planted by Rosalbina's father, lies astride a path very close to the nucleated village and thus is a convenient source of fruits and other forest products.

These changing fields, a combination of annual crops mixed with trees and cultivated plants interspersed with forest plants, is an obvious development of centuries-old Amazonian traditions. They also incorporate some of the most recent thinking of agronomists and foresters on desirable production systems for the humid tropics. Experts like Wil de Jong, a forester now studying these production patterns on the lower Ucayali, call these agroforestry systems and find that they can be both productive and conservative of the natural resources of soil and forest.

Even this diverse array of agricultural endeavors does not sum up the farming activities of Emilio and Rosalbina. Around and behind the house is the house garden where thirty-two different species of useful plants coexist. Some of these were planted, some are weeds, but useful weeds whose growth is encouraged by clearing around them. Still other plants, mostly trees, are leftovers from other gardens made by earlier residents. A few species were transplanted from the forest.

Rosalbina's garden is not as diverse as Doña Rosario's, but it contains most of what is needed around the house. It is a pantry, a spice shelf, a medicine cabinet, a utility drawer, a flower garden. It also provides a little shade around the house, a windbreak, and a place to keep chickens. Like any pantry it changes constantly. Doña Rosalbina likes plants and will often bring back cuttings when she goes visiting friends and relatives: a plant to bring down fevers, a plant to make your hair shine, or a pretty flower. Even a new variety of a food crop that may be destined for extensive production is first planted experimentally in the house garden on a small scale. Planting and replanting is a constant process, as is the loss of useful plants to pecking chickens, neighbors' marauding pigs, boys chasing balls, and other pests.

Having mentioned forest-product collecting and management, and the many types of agriculture and agroforestry, I have still failed to adequately describe how the Maytahuaris make a living. Emilio spends a good deal of time fishing: he has a few nets including a circular cast net; he also fishes with hook and line, with trotlines, spear, harpoon, and bow and arrow. The last technique he picked up from the ex-Ashaninkas in San Alejandro. Fishing with poisons such as barbasco is forbidden by the government, but it still goes on in more remote areas.

The most profitable place for fishing is usually not the huge, muddy Ucayali, but rather the many ox-bow lakes found behind the natural levees. In these shallow, calmer waters, which are annually replenished with river water during the flood season, many of the desirable fish, such as the giant *paiche* (*Arapaima gigans*) are found. Annual changes in the river's height cause fish and their pursuers to change their locations. At high flood stages, often spectacular fish migrations, called *mijanos,* take place. Enormous mixed schools of fish migrate for miles, often out of lakes or streams and into the main river channel. The passing of a mijano is an exciting time. Fishermen can be choosy in the fish they will bring home; they easily catch more of the desirable species than they can eat. Little food other than fish is eaten for the duration of a mijano.

The people of San Alejandro and of much of the Amazon get a good dietary supplement of fish with moderate effort. Seasons, of course, vary, and so does success in fishing. When the river rises and the waters spill over into the forest, fish are usually much harder to catch. Hunting on the levees during this time is, however, often easier.

All of today's Amazonians detect a gradual diminution in the number of fish they catch and a rise in the number of hours they spend fishing. Several reasons may be cited: destruction of fish habitats when stream-side vegetation is cleared is one, but large-scale commercial fishing and destructive fishing practices have also taken their toll. Refrigerated fishing boats will reach even remote oxbow lakes, taking for the city and for export the fish that were once available to the ribereño and his family. The residents of San Alejandro and hundreds of other villages have no jurisdiction over the lakes close to their house. In their inability to protect the resources that they habitually use to feed their families, the ribereños are even less protected than the tribal groups, whose plight is better known. In some countries, including Peru, some tribal communities have been granted exclusive rights to their hunting and fishing grounds. Often inadequate or violated, these rights give at least some protection. The nontribal, forgotten folks of the Amazon have no way of protecting the natural resources of forest and water that are the basis of their subsistence.

Hunting tends to be far less profitable in the rather thickly settled areas of the main river channels. Higher up the rivers along small tributaries and side channels, however, hunting is an important activity. Here fishing yields much less, and the ribereño family relies for dietary protein on wild animals, especially the two species of piglike peccaries (*Tayassu pecari* and *T. tajacu*), deer (*Mazama americana*), and the many large rodents. The sale of forest animal meat, although prohibited by the government, is very common. Peccary stew and paca (*Cuniculus paca*) steaks are on the menus of the best Iquitos restaurants. The urbanites' taste for exotic delicacies is not only threatening the continued existence of some forest species such as the big river turtles and large forest birds but is also affecting the diet of the ribereño family. The high prices that hunted meat can bring in the market are tempting to cash-poor ribereños; they will frequently deprive their own families of needed protein and sell whatever they have hunted.

The economic life of the ribereño household, which includes farming and tending many agricultural fields as well as gathering, hunting, and fishing, demands that the family constantly make decisions. What and where to plant, how much, what to sell, where and how and when to fish or hunt, are only a few of the almost daily dilemmas. The diversity of subsistence and other economic activities appears confusing and distracting, but it pays off when disaster strikes. An early flood may wipe out a family's entire rice crop, but the subsistence crops along the restinga and upland will carry the household through the year. An exceptionally high flood may destroy almost all the household's production, but then forest products can be gathered for sale, hunting and fishing may help the family survive, and upland crops will be used to their fullest.

Beyond the Villages

Another stopgap measure in times of trouble is temporary migration to the city in search of wage labor. Often ribereños are familiar with the towns, having spent some time there in their youth. Young people are naturally drawn to the larger towns and cities; some go for several years to attend secondary school, many go to work. But the towns these days offer little employment. Young women can find jobs as domestics and washerwomen, but these bring them little freedom and less money with which to sample the pleasures of the city. Young men work as cargo carriers or at other menial jobs. The more enterprising ribereño migrants accumulate a little cash and turn to small-scale retailing and wholesaling to get them through. But wheeling and dealing in Amazonian markets is a very risky and competitive business. All but a very few lucky and astute newcomers lose their shirts within a few months, if not earlier. The unlucky will usually then go back to the farm, often poorer than before.

Several movements back-and-forth between city and village are not uncommon. Ribereños tend to be a very mobile lot; their history has taught them not to sink very deep roots. Permanent moves to the cities are now more frequent as well; these reflect the risks of rural life as well as its lack of economic opportunities. Perhaps an even more important push is the inadequacy, if not nonexistence, of medical, educational, and other services in the countryside. Amazonian towns and cities are now surrounded by sprawling shantytowns, which although they often appear vibrant are usually plagued with malnutrition, under- and unemployment, illiteracy, poor health, and alcoholism—the ills that drove the villager from his poor village.

The move to the city has often betrayed the dreams of the villagers who hope for a brighter future

for themselves and their children. Many ribereños have also concluded that they can expect little help from the state. In the thinly-populated great expanses of rural Amazonia, representatives of most branches of government are rarely seen. Plans for development of Amazonia are usually drawn up by urban dwellers and ultimately serve to benefit urban places. But out of considerable distrust and scepticism on the part of ribereños and caboclos has, in many cases, arisen not despair but rather a determination to act to help themselves. The previously mentioned Brazilian rubber tappers' union is one such response to increasing threats to a caboclo way of life. In the Peruvian Amazon, ribereños are also coming together in attempts to improve their lives. An integral part of the programs of these organizations is the demand for local control of access to local natural resources. The ribereño and caboclo know that although many of their daily needs are met by their farms, without the forest their way of life could not continue.

The participation of Wil de Jong in field research in the Peruvian Amazon and in discussions of ribereño resource use is gratefully acknowledged. Valuable information and criticism was also given by Miguel Pinedo-Vasquez and Mario Hiraoka. The kindness of the residents of several communities along the lower Ucayali River is particularly appreciated. This research was done as part of a cooperative agreement with the Instituto de Investigaciones de la Amazonia Peruana.

◁ Ribereños and caboclos produce for their own subsistence and for the market. A load of plantains has arrived in Iquitos' busy port.

BOTTOM LEFT: Ribereños use many different forest species in making their houses. These palm trunks when split will be used for flooring and walls.

BOTTOM RIGHT: In small riverine villages, families tend to form early and have many children. A young family along the lower Ucayali River.

The ready, although illegal, market for wildlife in Amazonian cities is leading to the depletion of many species and to the impoverishment of the rural diet. A woman brings caimans for sale in the Iquitos market.

THE RIVER PEOPLE
OF MAYNAS

MIGUEL PINEDO-VASQUEZ

In Peru, as in the majority of Amazonian countries, few studies of natural resource use have been done. The works that exist are of varying value. Many do not reflect the situation as it exists; they are based on approximations, generalities, and misconceptions. Most of these reports are written by government functionaries or technical personnel in the public administration who are out of touch with the life and needs of the rural Amazonian. There are other studies of great value that examine not only the state of natural resources but also the risks involved in their misuse. Almost none of this information ever reaches the population that is most concerned, the people of the vast Amazonian expanses. Thus, no matter how accurate and important they are, such scientific works serve largely to further scientific and political debate.

Perhaps the greatest gap in studies of natural resources and their use in the Amazon is the almost total lack of attention paid to the wishes, needs, and plans of the most important users of those resources: the farmers, hunters, fishermen, and gatherers in the thousands of small settlements throughout Amazonia.

On behalf of the members of the Federación Campesina de Maynas (Small Farmers' Federation of Maynas), an organization that represents the rural people of the northeastern Peruvian Amazon, I hope to remedy this situation somewhat by presenting some of the ideas and hopes that our organization has for the future of the forest and its users.

For a very long time Amazonians have used the riches of their environment for their own subsistence and for commerce. In the past commercial use of natural resources was almost completely oriented toward serving the interests of companies tied to foreign (largely British) capital. Forest products were harvested with no thought to their conservation, and exported with little benefit to the collectors. During this era of economic control of the area by outsiders, the population of the lowland Peruvian Amazon changed greatly. The immigration of peoples from outside the area led to much cultural and racial mixing, giving origin to the population of *ribereños,* who now constitute the majority of rural inhabitants of the lowlands and most of the membership of the Federación Campesina.

The Use of Natural Resources by Present-Day Ribereños

Today, the use of natural resources by ribereño villagers still combines subsistence with market participation. Methods of extracting forest products are often destructive; in few cases are natural resources gathered or used in a sustainable fashion. Many important resources have become scarce, while others such as the large Amazonian river turtles and the manatee have been almost extinguished. Hunting these animals is prohibited by the Peruvian government, but government regulations are almost without effect in many areas. The public administration cannot enforce its laws, having neither sufficient funds nor personnel. The population that suffers most from this depradation, the ribereño family, has almost ceased to consume meat since virtually its only source, forest animals, is greatly reduced. The small number of animals that hunters do kill is usually destined for the markets of Iquitos, where demand and prices are high. The ribereño villagers have never experienced such scarcity of resources: animals were always plentiful and fish were caught with little difficulty. The Federación Campesina is taking action to protect the resources that are most important to its members: those products important in the daily diet of the rural family. The Federación Campesina has begun to promote in rural communities a plan for control of natural resources by the villagers themselves. Some communities have already taken an active role in managing the *cochas* (oxbow lakes) in their territories in order to secure better fish production, others are beginning to plan how to manage and protect the timber-rich forests and valuable palm swamp resources located near their homes.

Planning for the Future

The Federación Campesina, together with the majority of other organizations of rural Amazonians (both of tribal natives and ribereños), knows that the only way to protect and ensure proper use of natural resources is through the organized participation of all the sectors of society that are involved in resource exploitation including, of course, the state. The goal is to transform the native and ribereño populations into the protectors and stewards of the forests and waters that they know and use. Each village will have its community or intercommunity reserve so that each local village can control, regulate, and, above all, plan the use of its natural resources. Such reserves are not meant to be inviolate preserves closed to all resource exploitation, but rather managed limited-use forests where villagers will be able to obtain the daily necessities of life: meat, thatch, fruits, and other products. A few such reserves have already been established in the region.

To aid in the establishment of communal reserves, the Federación Campesina helps to get community discussion of problems started. Villagers are sure to have some difficulties maintaining such a reserve. The Federación Campesina engages in educational campaigns to make rural dwellers more aware of the importance of natural resources and their preservation. Since its formation, the Federación has been sending the Peruvian government its proposals for legislation that would more effectively regulate the ownership and use of natural resources.

The Federación has petitioned the government to allow village assemblies to regulate the use of natural resources with the participation of representatives of both state and private institutions that are concerned with resource use. Each village first needs information: how far does its territory extend, what resources are present within that territory and in what state are they found. While villagers themselves know about the specific trees, animals, and fishing spots found in their own territories, other legal and technical information should be furnished by the state.

The Federación Campesina has proposed to the government that oversight committees be formed on the village level. The members of these committees will be the guardians of their reserves and the reporters of any infractions.

There should be periodic evaluations of the state of our natural resources, and all sectors of society, particularly the rural population, should take part in such assessments. Use of natural resources must be planned, and for this the organizations of rural peoples, such as the Federación Campesina, must be consulted. Our members, the ribereños and tribal natives, know those resources. The present patterns of using resources in the Peruvian Amazon are not leading to any true and sustained development in the region. Resources are extracted without any knowledge of or concern for how much has been taken, how much remains, or what the potential value of the product is. In the future any sound use of the resources of the Amazonian forest will depend on the organization and cooperation of the rural population.

Conversations with many farmers of the Iquitos area helped in putting together this brief paper. I would, however, especially like to thank Miguel Siqueda Enocaisa, the General Secretary of the Federacion Campesina de Maynas, for sharing his opinions with me.

9

THE INDONESIAN
TRANSMIGRANTS

GLORIA DAVIS

Indonesia, with 170 million people, is the fifth most populous nation in the world. More than 100 million of these people live on Java, an island with about 7 percent of the nation's land. Between 1980 and 1986 the Indonesian government resettled over two million people from the overcrowded inner islands (mainly Java, Madura, Bali, and Lombok) to the less densely settled outer islands (primarily Kalimantan, Sulawesi, and Irian Jaya). This program, which the Indonesians call *transmigration,* is the largest voluntary, government-supported resettlement program in the world. Settlement of the outer islands was curtailed in 1986 due to budget constraints resulting from declining oil revenues, and virtually all new land clearing was halted. But the transmigration program is not expected to stop completely, and the spontaneous movement of settlers from the inner to the outer islands is not likely to cease.

Since the outer islands of Indonesia are heavily forested, the scale of recent movement has attracted the attention and concern of environmentalists; it has also generated strong views on both ends of the development spectrum. One group claims that settlements on the marginal soils of the outer islands are unsustainable and paints a picture of transmigrants resorting to shifting cultivation, destroying forests and wildlife, and ultimately abandoning their land. Others view transmigration as an absolute necessity in the context of Java's population problems and portray settlers as industrious agriculturalists who, although poor, improve their own welfare and benefit the regions around them. The argument is one of more than academic interest since it will help shape future social and environmental policy in Indonesia. If transmigration settlements cannot be sustained or if there are other ways to produce employment and increase farmer welfare that are not now getting full government support, then settlement could or should cease. If new settlement policies are responsive to pressing social and economic problems, if spontaneous migrants will continue to move with or without government support, and if migrants are only one of many groups placing pressure on the forest, then the strategy for protecting and conserving forested land is not only different but more urgent.

The People

Every migrant has a different story.

Joko and his wife Murni had reason for optimism when they married in Java. Joko had a ninth-grade education and was working as a clerk in a small store, and Murni had a certificate to teach grade school.

A mother from central Java and her children. The need for labor encourages larger families, and the government supports active family-planning programs at all transmigration sites.

Not all of Java is fertile. Many migrants are recruited in critical areas such as this, where soil fertility is low and erosion danger high. Only such undemanding crops as manioc will grow here.

Shortly after they married, however, the store closed, Joko lost his job, and Murni was unable to find a teaching position. They lived for a year in Joko's father's house because Murni's family was too poor to help; but when their first child was born they decided to join the transmigration program sponsored by the Indonesian government. To the outside observer the couple remains poor. Their new house in Sumatra is small and has only a dirt floor, and their incomes are low, but Joko and Murni believe that their lives have improved. Joko farms 1.25 hectares (2 acres) and is able to meet the subsistence needs of his family from his own production. Murni earns a cash income from teaching in the village school. Joko, who as a dependent in his parents' house had no official status in his village in Java, is now a member of the village council and holds a clerical position. Joko and Murni are looking forward to the birth of a second child, and they would like Murni's parents to join them to help raise their family and work the land.

Pak Purni was better off than most in Java. He and his brother farmed slightly more than .5 hectares (1.5 acres) of Java's rich, irrigated rice land, which they inherited from their father. But Purni had four children and his brother had five, and since all children (boys and girls) were entitled to inherit equally, it was evident that this land could not support the next generation. After long discussion, Purni and his family decided to join the transmigration program, while his

brother farmed the land. Purni's family obtains rent from his brother, and with this money Purni has already acquired a house lot for his eldest son from a transmigrant who returned to Java due to ill health. Purni hopes to establish his second son on another lot and turn over his own house to his youngest son. When his children are married and settled, he hopes to retire in Java.

In Sudarto's household it was his wife who chose to move. Yasmin ran a very small store from her home, but despaired of advancing financially because of constant requests from their relatives for goods on credit. She is concerned that her reasons for moving will sound selfish, but she is not sorry she moved. In Sumatra she has already opened a small food stall in her house and is an active trader in the twice-weekly market. Sudarto supplements the family income by repairing bicycles and appliances, and he has recruited a nephew from Java to assist in the cultivation of their land.

Not all migrants are suited to pioneer life. Some miss the bustle of Java's crowded villages, while others miss their families and friends. For others the difficulties of the adjustment period are complicated by infertile soils, sickness, or accident; and some return home. But the vast majority of those who move say that their lives in Indonesia's outer islands are better than they were in Java, and even those who are uncertain are reluctant to return home. When asked why they stay,

A transmigration settlement in Sulawesi, seen from the air.

the reason is almost always the same. They have nothing to go back to in Java, they say, but with land of their own, they have hope.

The Indonesian Transmigration Program

Government-sponsored programs of land settlement began in Indonesia in 1905. In the colonial period (through 1942) most of those who moved were settled on 1 hectare (2.5 acres) or less of irrigated land. This was sufficient to meet the subsistence needs of the original household, but as children grew up and married, their needs placed considerable pressure on the land. The Dutch also experimented with programs to drain coastal swamps for wet rice production, but these efforts remained limited in the colonial period.

Following World War II and the Indonesian struggle for independence from the Netherlands, the Indonesian government resumed resettlement, but because of shortages of funds, irrigation works were often deferred, and migrants were usually dependent on rain-fed (unirrigated) agriculture in the early years. The government developed a program to support rain-fed food crop production in the 1970s and since then most migrants have been settled on rain-fed schemes. Since 1978 the government has also experimented with the development of settlements growing cash crops such as rubber, oil palm, and sugar. In the third five-year plan (1979–84) nearly 80 percent of sponsored migrants were settled on rain-fed schemes, 18 percent

in areas reclaimed from swamps, and 2 percent on cash crop schemes; but in 1984 and 1985, about 20 percent of families were settled with cash crops.

To facilitate transmigration, the Indonesian government identifies land for sponsored settlement and ensures that it is free of alternative claims or negotiates for its release. Although the government does not pay for land, it does pay for the loss of productive trees, and local people must agree to release their land before it can be used for settlement. The reception of local people to transmigration has varied and problems have occurred, but historically most outer island residents have welcomed settlement because it also brought jobs, schools, and clinics; no large-scale movement in recent history has occurred with less communal tension. With the acceleration of the program, however, it has been increasingly difficult to find large areas suitable for settlement and there has been increasing concern in the international community that local people, particularly those who are isolated and unsophisticated, may agree to relinquish land even though it is not in their best interests to do so.

Since 1980 the World Bank has supported the government's efforts to identify land suitable for agriculture and to ensure that this land is free of claims by local people or by the Indonesian Forestry Department. The government has taken steps to strengthen provincial involvement in the selection of sites and to improve forums for the redress of grievances in com-

Map showing destinations of government-sponsored transmigrants, 1950–1984. Percentage of transmigrants relocating in each region is indicated.

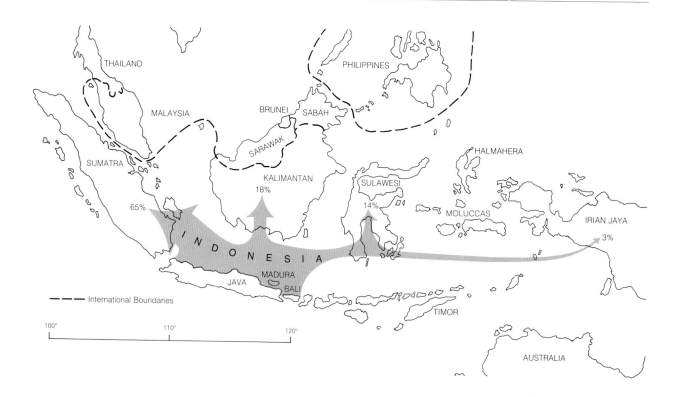

pensating local people for their land. Many sites investigated under the recent World Bank-assisted program have been rejected because of conflicting claims on the land by local people or by the Department of Forestry.

Transmigration officials recruit migrants in critical (overcrowded and environmentally degraded) areas, particularly in Java, but virtually all migrants enlist voluntarily, and in recent years more people have applied for resettlement than could be moved. Applicants for government-sponsored settlement are generally young couples who are landless or near-landless agricultural laborers with few opportunities in their area of origin. These families join the transmigration program to obtain land to meet their subsistence needs and to provide opportunities for their children. It is common for poor families in Java to encourage one or two of their grown children to migrate in order to avoid further land fragmentation and to explore economic opportunities in the outer islands. If these children are successful, other family members follow; if not, some return home.

Each government-sponsored family receives 1 to 1.25 hectares (2.5 to 3 acres) of cleared land, a small wooden house, agricultural inputs (seed, fertilizer) for three years, and reserve land of 1 to 2 hectares (2.5 to 5 acres) for future expansion. Migrants are settled in villages of 150 to 500 families in regional settlements of 2,000 to 10,000 households; schools, clinics, and village facilities are provided. About 10 percent of the sites are reserved for local people. Standards are modest to keep costs low, and the total government investment is about $5,500 per family. Migrants settled with two hectares (five acres) of tree crops, a program that costs about $10,000 per family, are required to repay part of the cost through credit schemes. Most spontaneous migrants move to be near family or friends and do not receive any government assistance.

Between 1905 and 1980 about one million people were resettled through government-sponsored programs. Because oil revenues were growing, the government accelerated the transmigration program in the third five-year plan (1979–84), and during this period about 366,000 families (1.8 million people) were settled; almost double the number moved in all preceding years. Between 1984 and 1986 another 150,000 families (650,000 people) were resettled; after that date the program was slowed. Of those who moved since 1950, about 65 percent have been sent to Sumatra, the largest and best developed of the outer islands, 18 percent to Kalimantan, 14 percent to Sulawesi, and 3 percent to Irian Jaya.

In addition to sponsored settlers, there has long been a spontaneous flow of people moving without government support from the inner to the outer islands. The 1980 census showed that about 7.3 million people in the outer islands spoke an inner-island language as their mother tongue. Some were government officials, members of the armed forces, and other tem-

porary residents, but an estimated six million such people lived and worked in rural areas. Of these six million, about two million were sponsored settlers and their descendants, which suggests that the rate of spontaneous movement to sponsored movement is about two to one.

Transmigration generally refers to the flow of people from the inner to the outer islands, but some outer islands people are also very mobile. For example, the 1980 census showed that over 600,000 Batak and Minang people (Sumatra), 500,000 Bugis (Sulawesi), and 360,000 Banjarese (Kalimantan) were in areas other than their ethnic homeland. While few in relation to the number of Javanese who have moved, this indicates that about 13 percent of all people speaking these outer-island languages have moved in comparison to about 7 percent of all Javanese. Bugis from densely populated South Sulawesi are particularly active in land settlement, especially in tidal swamps. Bugis settlements in Kalimantan are described by Andrew Vayda later in this chapter.

Why Does the Indonesian Government Support Transmigration?

One need only visit Java and see farmers working small plots in upper watersheds to understand the emotional basis and practical need for land settlement. Java has twelve million families who derive their main source of income from agriculture, and it has only 7 million hectares (17.5 million acres) of agricultural land. Nearly two-thirds of agricultural households own less than .5 hectare (1.25 acres) of land, the size of a large suburban yard, and only 4 percent of Java's farmers own 2 hectares (5 acres) or more of land. In contrast, the average farm in the United States is about 182 hectares (450 acres) in size. This pressure on the land has caused poor families in Java to move onto increasingly steep slopes, which causes erosion and premature siltation of the dams and irrigation canals upon which Java's economy depends. In 1984 average incomes in Java were about $700 per family per year, and about 40 percent of the population fell below a poverty line estimated at about $540 per family per year.

The outer islands have poorer soils on average than Java and Bali and have supported smaller populations in the past. As a result, they have 93 percent of Indonesia's land and about 36 percent of her population (34 people/km² versus 685 people/km² on the inner islands). The outer islands also have the major portion of Indonesia's natural resources such as oil, coal, and timber. As a consequence, land holdings in the provinces to which most transmigration is taking place (Sumatra, Sulawesi, and Kalimantan) are larger and household incomes are somewhat higher than in Java, averaging about $1,000 per family per year. In such

resource-rich provinces as Riau and East Kalimantan, which have large oil and timber reserves, average household incomes are higher still.

Because nearly two million workers enter the labor force each year, Indonesia's key development objectives are the creation of jobs and alleviation of poverty. The country has tackled this problem in a number of ways. It has an active and well-financed family planning program and has made a major thrust to improve education. The government has strongly supported smallholder agriculture through investments in irrigation, fertilizer production, agricultural research, and smallholder tree crop development. The mechanization of agriculture has been discouraged because it means a reduction of jobs. The Indonesian government has also encouraged the growth of small-scale industries, which have kept pace with domestic consumer demand, although the growth of export industries has lagged.

Most programs are successful. Population growth in Java has fallen to about 1.8 percent per year, a very low rate for a country at Indonesia's level of development, and universal primary education has been virtually achieved in the last decade. Agricultural production grew at an average rate of 4.1 percent per year between 1976 and 1985, and Indonesia was able to move from the world's largest importer of rice in 1980 to a position of self-sufficiency in 1985. Rural incomes have also increased largely as the result of growth in

Migrants in heavily forested areas cut timber from their reserve land to add to their incomes.

CENTER: This farm shows a typical, diversified approach. Suitable, low-lying areas are planted to rice, other sites to perennial crops.

BOTTOM: Local people and spontaneous immigrants moving in along a new road clear land to plant both annual food crops and perennials.

A farmer at a transmigration site holds some black soil ▷ in his hand.

agriculture. Manufacturing is believed to have grown by about 10 percent per year over the same period, and the government has recently taken steps to deregulate some aspects of trade and industry in order to improve export trade.

Even with these initiatives, however, the number of job seekers has outstripped employment opportunities, and resettlement has been seen as a measure to provide employment, reduce poverty, and prevent unmanageable urbanization. In the third five-year plan, the government's stated objectives for transmigration were to reduce population pressure in the inner islands, to raise the living standards of migrants, and to promote regional development. Recent programs have also emphasized the need to increase agricultural production and reduce environmental degradation in the inner islands.

How Successful Has Transmigration Been?

The fact that people move voluntarily on government programs and that large numbers of people move spontaneously provides some evidence that economic opportunities are better for migrants in the outer islands. Just how much better is a matter of dispute, and a number of recent studies have made an effort to evaluate the transmigration program.

On the positive side, recent World Bank studies indicate that transmigration in the third five-year plan created at least five hundred thousand permanent jobs, mainly in agriculture, at a cost of about $3,000 per job. Although higher than the cost of employment creation in services, this is lower than the cost of creating a permanent job in industry (estimated at about $10,000 per job). Much temporary work was generated by the settlement process, and it is estimated that nearly one-quarter of a million households benefitted from jobs created by land development alone. Of public investment programs, only temporary rural works programs and tree crop development programs generated more jobs in the plan period. Although sponsored migration in the third five-year plan moved only 1.5 percent of the inner island population, it relocated almost 15 percent of those moving into the labor force for the first time.

The evidence also suggests that the lives of most migrants have improved. While virtually all migrants were below the poverty level while in Java, a recent study by the Indonesian Central Bureau of Statistics indicates that about half of all settlers in the sample were above the poverty line. Less encouraging is the fact that agricultural incomes were lower than planned and about half of all income, regardless of type of site, was from off-farm work. The income study also indicated that most migrants met their nutritional requirements and were as well off, nutritionally, as either inner or outer island residents. Needless to say, large-

scale transmigration has also had a major impact on the regions to which migrants have been sent, increasing labor, infrastructure (roads, schools, hospitals), and agricultural production.

These achievements have not been realized without difficulties and significant problems with the program. Chief among these are the increasing difficulties of finding suitable unclaimed land, low incomes from agriculture, and low rates of return for some types of sites. There is also concern about the large-scale movement of spontaneous migrants and about the impact of the program on local people, forests, and wildlife. A number of administrative problems have also been identified. To reduce these problems, recent studies have recommended that new settlement be slowed and that priority be given to the consolidation of existing sites to promote self-sustainable growth and to raise family incomes. These studies have also suggested that more be done to channel spontaneous migrants into areas suited for agriculture and that more attention be given to social and environmental concerns.

In response to budget constraints and evidence that incomes were heavily dependent on off-farm work, the Indonesian government began to reduce the scale of the program in 1986. For the 1987–88 budget year, some families will be settled in areas where land has already been cleared or where tree crops have been established, but no new land clearing is scheduled. Instead, the government will use available funds to consolidate and upgrade settlements and to improve existing production systems. The government is reviewing the possibilities in the future of using transmigration to complemen' industrial and regional development and of reducing large-scale settlement, particularly in forested areas.

Are Transmigration Settlements Sustainable?

A central question in evaluating transmigration is whether or not sites on marginal soils can be sustained. Several chapters in this book describe the reasons for the low fertility of tropical soils (heavy rains, leaching of organic materials, and so on) and the resulting changes in the tropical forest and the adjustments its human inhabitants have made. Traditional cultivators, for example, have typically relied on shifting cultivation to meet their subsistence needs. They clear the land and burn trees to provide nutrients for the soil; after a year or two the area is no longer cultivated for food crops. At that point farmers either establish tree crops (fruit trees or rubber) or permit secondary regrowth of the original forest. A family may need fifteen to twenty hectares (thirty-five to fifty acres) of land to sustain itself on this basis.

Critics of transmigration often argue that transmigrants will not be able to sustain food crop production on one or two hectares (two to five acres) of marginal land and suggest as a corollary that migrants must eventually engage in widespread shifting cultivation, which is destructive to the environment, or abandon their sites. Unsuccessful land settlements in Brazil have reinforced this view. Javanese and Balinese migrants, however, have little access to additional land. This history and a combination of cultural, technical, and economic factors encourages sedentary rather than shifting agriculture.

It is difficult for migrants to buy or rent previously cultivated land in the outer islands because land use is generally under traditional systems of community control. Outsiders who have permission to use community land may be subject to ongoing requests from different local people for compensation, or they may have their land reclaimed if its value improves. For this reason many poor people from the inner islands are reluctant to move unless land is identified by the government and security of tenure is guaranteed, and sponsored migrants do not generally use land outside the official settlement area. Even if land is available for sale, most migrants are too poor to purchase it or are unable to negotiate complicated land registration procedures. Because finding unclaimed land is difficult, spontaneous settlers often encroach on forest or conservation areas and in the aggregate clear large areas of forest, although they seldom use the land for extensive shifting cultivation.

Traditional shifting cultivators in Indonesia do not generally plow or hoe the land. Once they have burned the forest litter and have established a clear surface, they poke holes in the soil and drop seeds into them. When weeds intrude and soil fertility declines, they find it easier and more profitable to clear new land than to try to eradicate weeds and establish their crops. In contrast, Javanese and Balinese, who have a tradition of labor-intensive wet rice cultivation, prepare the land using hand hoes and plows. By turning the soil on small plots of land they are able to prevent the regrowth of shrubs and trees and suppress, although not entirely eradicate, invasive weeds and grasses. The work is backbreaking and the rewards are meager, but cultural tradition, discipline, and necessity often permit subsistence-level cultivation on parcels of land that are only marginally suited to food crop production.

The crop yields and incomes of farmers cultivating low-fertility fields have benefitted from agricultural research, new varieties of seeds, and the availability of inorganic fertilizers, although the effect of these innovations should not be overstated. Today, the standard farming system used by migrants involves planting corn at wide intervals with the first rain, interplanting rice as the corn matures, and establishing manioc in or around the field as the rainy season advances. Manioc, a tuberous plant, is left in the field through the dry season providing a carbohydrate bank when rice supplies are short. Beans, peanuts, taro, fruit trees, and poultry occupy the houselot. Agricultural researchers have identified better varieties of upland rice for distribution, and they encourage the use of inorganic fertilizers, which became widely available in the outer islands in the 1980s; however, farmers use these expensive inputs sparingly.

In some areas where soil fertility is particularly low, farmers imitate the strategy of the local population and convert their food crop land to tree crops within the first three to five years. On smallholdings of one hectare (less than three acres) farmers mainly plant trees producing edible fruits such as jackfruit, durian, and coconut, but on larger holdings they introduce such cash crops as coffee and cloves. Government programs to assist smallholders to plant two hectares (five acres) of rubber and coconut, with credit for planting materials and fertilizers, have recently been extended to transmigration areas.

The scale of migration development has also helped sustain recent settlements. Prior to the mid-1970s, most settlements were small (one hundred to five hundred families); agricultural yields were low; and marketing surpluses was difficult. Farmers were isolated and had only limited access to off-farm work. That these communities persisted is a tribute to the migrants and a testimony to the conditions they left; but many farmers were very poor. Recent settlements show a different pattern of development. Nearly half of family income in the larger (two thousand to ten thousand families) communities is derived from off-farm work, and this money raises migrant incomes above subsistence levels. High levels of non-agricultural income are due to the larger size of the communities, which permits internal differentiation; to wage work associated with site development and the establishment of plantation crops; and to new roads, which permit migrants to move considerable distances to find work. Whereas traditional cultivators, and even settlers in the early 1950s, were largely dependent on their own crops for survival, migrants today are part of the larger cash economy.

There are still many outstanding questions about the level at which settlements can be sustained. In particular, the concern exists that reductions in the government's development budget may reduce off-farm employment, increase the number of subsistence-level settlements, and lead migrants to return to Java. This prospect has provided a strong argument for further development of existing sites. The evidence to date however, lends little support to those who claim that settlements cannot be sustained. There have been settlements on marginal soils in the outer islands since the 1950s. The rate of departure in the first five years is estimated at about 10 percent, which is low for movement on this scale; virtually all migrants who leave are replaced by spontaneous migrants, and there is little evidence of large-scale abandonment of settled sites. Migrants have been moved from, or left, some infertile areas, particularly in swamplands. Unlike Brazilian cultivators, who were often provided with 110 hectares (250 acres) of land or more and lacked the labor, capital, or managerial capacity to bring this land into production, Indonesian transmigrants are meeting their subsistence needs from small plots of land and sedentary cultivation.

Critics of the transmigration program have recently linked destruction caused by shifting cultivation to the nomadic practices of spontaneous migrants. The evidence presented here suggests that this is incorrect, particularly in Sumatra where nearly two-thirds of migrants have been sent. Indonesian migrants seldom engage in shifting cultivation over a large area because they have limited access to land. They do encroach upon forested land, occupying one to two hectares (two to five acres) per family, and sometimes the area occupied by spontaneous migrants is so infertile that it is abandoned. It would be wrong, however, to characterize most new forest settlement as shifting cultivation. Immigrants do not ordinarily put land under production on a temporary basis. This is not an argument for complacency because both new settlement and traditional shifting cultivation do seriously threaten Indonesia's forested land.

Impact on Indonesia's Forests

Indonesia covers about 190 million hectares (475 million acres) and is about one-fifth the size of the United States. Of this area, an estimated 75 percent is under shrubs and trees and 60 percent is under closed canopy forest. (Some observers feel that encroachment has significantly reduced the land under forest cover; these figures are now under review by the Indonesian government.) Indonesia is believed to possess about 10 percent of the world's remaining tropical rain forest and about half of that remaining in Asia. The area is one of remarkable biological diversity and includes some five hundred species of mammals, fifteen hundred species of birds, and more than ten thousand types of trees. For these reasons Indonesia's forests and wildlife have been a focus of international interest, and serious concern has been expressed about the impact of transmigration and other forms of agricultural development upon Indonesia's forest reserves.

Since 1980 the government has cleared some 650,000 to 750,000 hectares (1.6 to 1.9 million acres) of land for sponsored transmigrants, and an additional 500,000 hectares (1.2 million acres) have been allocated to migrants and included within the boundaries of settlements, although not yet cleared. Land-clearing costs indicate that the type of vegetation on this land was roughly equally divided between grasslands, scrub and

Soon after arriving at a transmigration site, a farmer begins the task of clearing around his new home.

High population pressure on land in Java means that even the steepest land is cultivated.

secondary regrowth, and logged-over primary forest. This means that about 400,000 hectares (one million acres) of primary forest and an additional 400,000 hectares of scrub and secondary forest came under the command of sponsored migrants in the 1980s. This is somewhat less than 1 percent of the outer-island forest areas. If spontaneous migrants brought an equal area into production, perhaps 1.5 percent of forested land in the outer islands has come under the control of settlers since 1980. New plantation development since 1980 has converted perhaps 100,000 hectares (250,000 acres) of primary forest and 200,000 hectares (500,000 acres) of secondary forest and stands of low-quality rubber. Thus, even though development programs have slowed, nearly two million hectares (five million acres) or 2 percent of the forested area in the outer islands could potentially be converted to agriculture by transmigration and plantation crop development in this decade. Of this, somewhat more than half would be in secondary forest, somewhat less would be in primary forest. Although lower than many critics allege, this is nevertheless a very large number.

While transmigration and other forms of development have resulted in as much as two million hectares (five million acres) of forest lost since 1980, the area under shifting cultivation by local people in the outer islands is much larger. Recent data indicate that the area under cultivation in Kalimantan, for example, is on the order of eleven million hectares (twenty-seven

million acres), about 22 percent of the area. About 2.5 million hectares of raw land has come under shifting cultivation in Kalimantan alone since 1980. In contrast, transmigrants to Kalimantan since 1980 have been allocated about 200,000 hectares (500,000 acres) of which only a portion has been cleared. These figures suggest that heavily forested areas in Indonesia are under pressure mainly from local people and secondarily from transmigration and other types of development.

What Can Be Done?

The sources of environmental degradation in Indonesia are poverty and underdevelopment. Poor families in both the inner and outer islands who do not have social security or pensions of any type need three or four children to ensure family welfare (the labor of children is valuable in an agrarian economy). Industry and manufacturing, beginning from a relatively small base, cannot grow at a pace sufficient to absorb two million new workers into the labor force each year, and service sectors are already overcrowded. Traditional cultivators can be expected to expand the area under shifting cultivation, and there will be continuing pressure from inner island residents to find new land to meet their subsistence needs.

Under the circumstances, what can be done? First, the government must continue to address the root causes of poverty with support from developed countries. As we have seen, Indonesia is making a broad effort on this front. Second, the production systems of indigenous smallholders must be upgraded to the extent possible and appropriate through the introduction of more productive crops (rubber, palm oil, coffee, or coconut). This would reduce pressure on the intact forests from shifting cultivation. Agroforestry (mixed tree and crop systems) may also have an important role in upgrading production. Third, since land hunger on the part of local people and spontaneous migrants to the outer islands is likely to continue, underused but previously cultivated land should be identified and made available to both local cultivators and transmigrants. To do this, the government must find ways to permit smallholders to buy underused land from people who wish to sell; provide adequate credit for land purchase; and simplify land-registration procedures. Fourth, and perhaps most painful to environmentalists, some areas suited for agriculture must be earmarked for clearing whether forested or not. Finally, those areas not suited to agriculture and not already under shifting cultivation must be rigorously and rapidly protected.

Mapping carried out recently in association with the transmigration program has significantly improved our knowledge of those areas in the outer islands that are suited to agriculture. Some of those areas should be earmarked for settlement by local smallholders and spontaneous migrants from both the inner and outer islands, people who would otherwise encroach on areas that should be preserved under forest cover. At the same time, a major effort is needed to demarcate areas that should be saved for watershed protection, timber production, and conservation purposes. Indonesia, a poor country, cannot be expected to bear on its own the cost of preserving ecosystems of value to the world. A major international effort is needed to identify high-priority areas for watershed protection and for the conservation of wildlife and to provide the funds to set aside and protect them. To argue that all forest should be preserved and that all agricultural expansion cease is to place a burden on less-developed countries that could not be sustained in developed ones. Instead, to recognize the need for development is to identify the strongest possible argument for parallel programs for environmental protection.

Research for this paper was carried out in cooperation with the Indonesian Ministry of Transmigration, the Central Bureau of Statistics (BPS), and the National Coordinating Body for Surveys and Mapping (Bakosurtanal). The help and assistance of Indonesian colleagues and officials is gratefully acknowledged.

BUGIS MIGRATION TO KALIMANTAN FORESTS

ANDREW P. VAYDA

The Bugis people, whose homelands are in the southwestern part of the Indonesian island of Sulawesi (Celebes), have sailed and traded throughout maritime Southeast Asia since the early sixteenth century. This has gained them a widespread reputation as roving adventurers. Many Bugis, however, remained at home to lead the settled lives of farmers. The trading and sailing are noteworthy not because they show any general love of movement among the Bugis, but rather because these activities established networks along which information about opportunities in other lands could flow back to potential migrants among the Bugis in Sulawesi.

As part of a project to identify and evaluate factors contributing to deforestation in the Indonesian province of East Kalimantan on the island of Borneo, a U.S.-Indonesian research team studied migrant Bugis farmers in East Kalimantan's Loa Janan district. In a twenty-year period these migrants converted 1,170 hectares (473 acres) of lowland tropical forest to plantations of pepper (*Piper nigrum*). What had brought them to the forests of Loa Janan?

The pioneer Bugis pepper farmers of the district had previously cleared forests and grown pepper near the East Kalimantan coastal town of Muara Badak. They had moved to Muara Badak in the early 1950s to escape disturbances caused by a rebellion in South Sulawesi. In the early 1960s the rebellion was still going on in the Bugis homelands, and the plantations at Muara Badak were becoming unprofitable because of declining pepper yields. At the same time construction had begun in Loa Janan on East Kalimantan's main road. Thus the Bugis found conditions propitious and practical for moving to Loa Janan.

The rebellion ended in 1965 and it became safe for Loa Janan pepper farmers to visit their relatives in

South Sulawesi. Just emerging from years of privation, these relatives and other friends were attracted by the wealth the migrants displayed, the gifts they brought, and the stories they told of opportunities at Loa Janan. Many Bugis who had suffered through the rebellion now lacked the capital and equipment to restore their neglected rice fields to full production and decided it was worth seeking a better life in East Kalimantan. As a consequence, a new wave of migrations occurred, impelled this time by prospects of social and economic advantage or advancement rather than by the fear and insecurity that had driven earlier migrants to Muara Badak. The cost of the trip was relatively low, so starting a new life at Loa Janan not only held the promise of greater rewards but, for some, could also be cheaper and easier than reconstruction at home.

Developments in the 1970s enhanced the attractiveness of Loa Janan, even when the effects of the rebellion were no longer being felt in South Sulawesi. As the numbers of Bugis in Loa Janan increased, they built more schools and mosques; new migrants could thus find comfort in a community life similar to the one they had left in South Sulawesi. Converting forest to pepper plantations became easier when timber companies began their operations in Loa Janan in 1969. Later migrants could use logging roads to reach the forest, and they found the forest easier to clear because the logging companies had already removed some of the biggest trees. In 1976 transport was also eased by the long-delayed completion of the main East Kalimantan road. Thereafter at least twenty Bugis settlers arrived each month. By 1980 Loa Janan had about eight hundred pepper-farming Bugis families comprising a total of approximately three thousand people.

The Bugis farmers in Loa Janan cleared forest areas by slashing underbrush with bush knives and felling the larger trees with axes or chainsaws. They kept some timber for use as house-building materials, firewood, and support stakes for pepper vines, but they left most of the cleared vegetation to dry in the sun and then burned it. The resulting ash provided nutrients critical for farming in the otherwise poor soils of Loa Janan.

To plant rice, the men made holes in the ash-covered ground with long dibbling sticks, and the women sowed the seed. A few farmers planted corn, but most, regarding rice as their staple, made that their first crop. Rice was used for their own subsistence as well as for sale.

After a single harvest, farmers converted most of the area planted in rice to pepper plantations. Sometimes they planted a small portion in rice for a second year of subsistence while waiting for income from the pepper, which takes about three years to develop a substantial yield.

Some migrants also planted fruit trees such as jackfruit, durian, rambutan, and mango. Although planting these trees might be regarded as establishing a claim for permanent rights to the land, the Bugis migrants to Loa Janan apparently were not concerned with owning land in the migration area. Interviews with local government officials and the pepper farmers themselves revealed that few Bugis intended to apply for government certificates of land ownership. The slowness and expense of the certification process and the fear of having to pay taxes discouraged the farmers. The substantial erosion and depletion of soil nutrients caused by their farming also suggest that the migrants cared little about long-term ownership of the land. These farmers must not be confused with other peasant farmers who, being dependent on local resources and having little opportunity to move on, try hard to avoid destroying those resources.

The Bugis migrants in East Kalimantan have always had access to either suitable primary or logged-over forest when old plantations were to be abandoned. But some said that if suitable lands for development of new pepper plantations were to become difficult to obtain, they would move to newly opening frontiers in Central and Southeast Sulawesi to plant cloves, cashews, or oil palm, rather than find ways to reuse old land.

Our findings on Bugis migration and land use have implications for forest-protection programs and future road building in areas like Loa Janan. Since these programs are likely to be more successful if they are directed toward controlling rather than completely stopping forest clearance and settlement, Bugis migrants might have a role as developers of buffer zones along the roads; that is, they could cultivate strictly delimited bands of land along the roads and thus keep illicit timber cutters and other destructive elements out of the forests. Recommending Bugis migrants for this role are the rapidity with which they can move to new areas and their ability to transform them into plantations and settlements at no expense to the government. On the negative side is their limited concern with land conservation, but this could be counteracted by government incentives to promote erosion control by the farmers.

I gratefully acknowledge the participation of Ahmad Sahur of Hasanuddin University in the East Kalimantan research. This report incorporates material from two articles that provide additional details: Vayda, A. P., and Ahmad Sahur, 1985, "Forest Clearing and Pepper Farming by Bugis Migrants in East Kalimantan: Antecedents and Impact," *Indonesia* 39: 93–110 and Vayda, A. P., 1987, "Self-Managed Land Colonization in Indonesia" in *Community Management: Asian Experience and Perspectives,* D. C. Korten, ed., West Hartford, CT: Kumarian Press.

IO

FOLLOWING
THE AMAZONIAN
HIGHWAYS

EMILIO F. MORAN

The great Amazonian forests, unknown, unmapped, and roadless, offered some safety to indigenous people for much of the post-Columbian era. They couldn't protect most groups from devastation by Western diseases—first in the sixteenth century and again in the past two decades—but most Europeans didn't venture much beyond the major rivers.

That era has ended. The forests are no longer beyond the reach of national policy and the desire for land of modern Brazilians, Peruvians, Bolivians, Ecuadorians, Colombians, and Venezuelans. As one flies over the vast Amazon basin, there is increasing evidence of human settlement. The communities one sees are rarely inhabited only by native Amazonians. Increasingly they are planned and spontaneous resettlement schemes promoted by ministries of rural development, agriculture, and planning. Unlike native villages, which seemed to blend with the forest and the river, the new settlements stand out dramatically against the lush greenness around them. The new settlers remove all vegetation and push the forest back from their homes as if it were an enemy. They put their houses along highways built by national governments intent on reaching the vast interior and linking this last frontier to the rest of the nation. Of all the countries in South America, Brazil has been most notable for the scale of its resettlement schemes and its success in building highways crisscrossing the Amazon basin.

Massive immigration into the Amazon had previously occurred but had not been sustained. During a short period of the rubber boom in the late nineteenth century, when the lust for wealth led many adventurers to seek Indian labor in the search for rubber trees growing wild in the forest, perhaps three hundred thousand Brazilians came into the great forests.

Peruvians, Brazilians, Bolivians, Ecuadorians, Venezuelans, and Colombians were lured into the Amazon during that era. Some remained to form the fascinating regional cultures of the Amazon, combining indigenous methods of subsistence and resource use with elements of European culture. These regional groups, referred to as *ribereños* in Peru and as *caboclos* in Brazil, have been little studied.

Following the discovery of oil in the Ecuadorian Amazon and the efforts of many countries after World War II to develop their natural and human resources, governments began to build roads into the Amazon in an effort to gain access to the presumed riches of the mythical El Dorado. This process began in Peru with the construction of the Peripheral Jungle Highway (*Carretera Marginal de La Selva*). Because of the steepness of the terrain east of the Andes, progress was slow. As these roads were built, concern rose over the potential economic and military role each nation might

The construction of a network of highways in the Brazilian Amazon has attracted new settlers into the region. A road crew pushes through a Brazilian rain forest.

Upon arrival, new settlers, like this family in the Brazilian state of Rondonia, put up temporary shelters using local materials. Many settlers come from distant regions such as southern Brazil and are second or third generation immigrants from Germany or Italy.

EMILIO F. MORAN

In the last two decades, highways have largely replaced rivers as the avenues of access for settlers in the Amazon forest. Along the new roads, new peoples, technologies, and diseases have streamed into the Amazon basin.

preference, selection criteria gave overwhelming preference to applicants with large families, assuming that most of these would come from the northeast, since that area is overpopulated relative to the rest of the country. Using household size to determine selection, rather than region of origin, resulted in a much smaller representation (only about 30 percent) of northeasterners than was projected.

Nor did the group resemble most spontaneous migrants. These are predominantly young families with slightly higher literacy rates than the general population. They usually visit the area in advance of the migration and send males ahead of the rest of the household. Because the government was intent on bringing as many as one hundred thousand families in the first five years, it undertook the task of flying families into the Amazon, bypassing the fundamental process of self-selection. Thus, the final composition of the population included many families that in more normal circumstances may have never undertaken such a risky, long-distance move. It included many people with little agricultural background and large families with older heads of households. And it included an unplanned 30 percent group of Amazonian peasants—descendants of rubber boom and World War II waves of migrants who moved from riverine locations to claim land along the new highways. The government ignored their presence but permitted their claims to land.

The migrants that came to occupy the government-built communities along with Brazilian Transamazon Highway represented a diverse group with respect to experience as well as homeland. Forty percent had either owned or managed the land they worked before coming to the Amazon, whereas the other 60 percent had worked for others as carpenters, electricians, masons, drivers, plumbers, teachers, soap makers, rice farmers, cowboys, irrigation farmers, and any combination of these occupations. On average, families had moved more than five times before coming to this new area and some households had moved as often as twenty times, a common phenomenon in inflation-ridden and territorially ever-expanding Brazil.

To 70 percent of the newcomers, the land was unfamiliar. The 30 percent from the northeast were most aware of the contrast between their arid land and the lush evergreen forest. Those from arid areas seemed satisfied to know that there was plenty of water in the Amazon and asked few other questions. Consequently some of them presumed that the tall forests and abundant water meant that all the soils were rich. The 25 percent from southern Brazil noticed differences between the relatively homogeneous pine forests of Paraná, planted since the 1950s in coffee plantations, and the heterogeneous tropical forest. They assumed

play in the region. Each nation grew restless about the efforts of the others to gain access to these lands of promise and mystery.

The military-controlled presidency of Brazil announced in 1970 that Brazil would undertake a Program of National Integration (PIN). Such a program would be begun with a network of highways going east-west and north-south across the vast Amazon forests. It would be accompanied by settlement projects promoted by the federal government with considerable investment in developing infrastructure and services for the newcomers.

That the roads were indeed built, that people were resettled, and that the region stopped being totally unfamiliar to national citizens surprised observers of the Latin American scene. Although the unrealistic government resettlement goals were not achieved, there has been a steady inflow of settlers hoping to make the necessary adjustments to life in the rain forests.

Who Were the Settlers?

The settlers who came to the Transamazon Resettlement Scheme were neither the ones the government plans envisioned nor the ones that usually characterize spontaneous migrations. The government intended to attract 75 percent of settlers from the drought-stricken northeastern section of Brazil. To achieve this regional

Rainforest highways of the Brazilian Amazon.

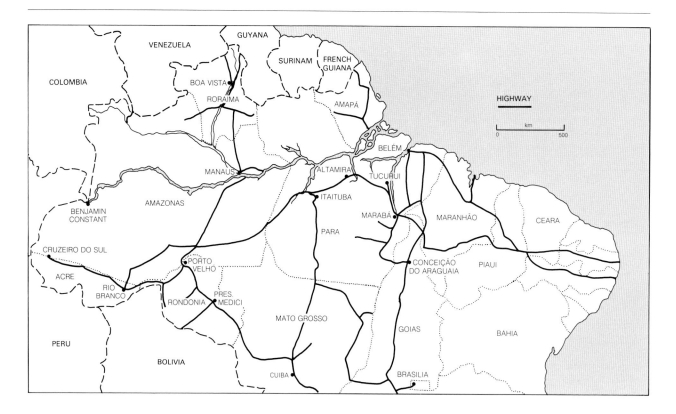

forests of Altamira giant buttressed trees were associated with poor, rather than fertile, soils. The 15 percent from the savannas of central Brazil found the Amazon attractive because they assumed their cattle would suffer less from seasonal drought. Fewer errors in soil selection were made by this group since the soils of central Brazil were similar to those of the Amazon.

The newcomers did not recognize the trees, the soils, or even the animals they found in their new land, but they were slow to ask advice from their Amazonian neighbors. At first, local Amazonians were branded as poor farmers, more concerned with hunting and foraging from the forest than with cultivating their land. This simplistic view was slow to die until repeated superior harvests by the Amazonians led to interactions, mutual respect, and eventually intermarriage. The local Amazonian caboclos used the vegetation to identify less acid soils with high levels of phosphorus, potassium, and organic matter in an area dominated by acidic, low-nutrient soils. In the early years, crop yields per acre and per hour of labor were higher on the farms of Amazonians than on those of most newcomers. Amazonians were also more open to new technology than their neighbors from other areas, particularly in the use of chainsaws to clear forest. Amazonians cleared less forest per year than newcomers, but they cultivated more of the land that they cleared. It was not uncommon for new immi-

grants to clear ten hectares (twenty-five acres) but plant only four to five hectares (ten to twelve acres) because the land had not adequately burned or because the labor of weeding large fields had been underestimated. In part such practice was a result of credit policies, which favored felling forest for agriculture and discouraged other farm investments (farm buildings, processing equipment, tools, fencing, draught animals) and longer-term land use. Gradually, newcomers have learned to clear smaller fields, to manage them intensively, to rely more on manioc and bananas and less on corn and beans. They have learned to hunt near fruiting trees and to use more forest resources for food and fiber.

The Policy Environment of New Land Settlement

The bureaucratic structures that promoted Amazon settlement proved incapable of responding to the needs of the migrant population. Because Brazilian bureaucracy is characteristically centralized, planning was far removed from, and unresponsive to, the realities of the new settlers. Local-level managers were unable to adjust programs in response to unexpected problems. Thus, when one local manager found soils that were too poor to cultivate and that did not match his preliminary map, he requested that the rate at which migrants arrived be reduced. This would have given him time to adjust the settlement of farmers to the patterns of initial soil fertility. Central planners ignored his request; the high pace of immigration forced him to place farmers on any available piece of land picked from the map without regard for soil quality or other environmental problems.

As a result, many farmers took out substantial bank loans but were unable to produce on the sometimes infertile soils. When the bank refused to cancel their debts, the farmers were unable to farm and unable to move for lack of credit at the bank. Many of the problems farmers faced in the Amazon forest were due to institutional malfunction. In fact, the farmers who largely ignored government directives and who relied upon their own or local expertise did far better. The Transamazon Resettlement Scheme, like most other tropical rain-forest development projects, was undertaken without the benefit of feasibility studies, ecological surveys, or other preliminary studies that would have permitted timely policy changes. It was administered without enough bureaucratic flexibility to permit adjustment or abandonment of plans if field experience proved them flawed.

Strategies that Worked

The most successful newcomers to the Amazon rain forest were those who sought advice from local caboclos. These were the newcomers with management experience who recognized that they did not know what worked in the new area and who recognized that the technical personnel appointed to help them were as inexperienced in farming the rain forest as they were.

Whereas the government agencies promoted (and gave credit for) the production of rice, corn, and beans, the better managers diversified their production by planting manioc, peanuts, and tobacco, and converted their corn into pork and chicken, which were scarce in the local markets. Those who didn't, suffered. Since the majority of the newcomers responded to the government incentives, there was a harvest-time oversupply of rice and corn and subsequent low prices. Bean production was extremely low in all years due to plant diseases. But manioc, the traditional Amazonian crop, could be made into flour, thereby providing a steady cash flow. Since it was relatively scarce, it fetched a prime price. Tobacco production required considerable expertise but was a crop that had a cash value that far exceeded those of the three promoted crops and could be produced on relatively small areas of land. Diversified subsistence production was common among the more successful households during the early frontier period since cash requirements were thereby reduced.

Many successful newcomers also took wage-paying jobs. Frontiers everywhere have a scarcity of labor, particularly skilled labor, so wages tend to be high. Since the government often is prepared to spend money building offices, schools, and other infrastructure, even poorly trained carpenters, electricians, plumbers, and others can earn top dollar in a frontier area. Hardly any frontier immigrant does well in the early years without this inflow of cash. Nonfarm jobs may also buy time for settlers to learn about the new environment and farming practices. Migrants to the Transamazon Resettlement Scheme helped build roads, schools, and houses for government-planned settlements. They drove ambulances and built fences for those with some initial capital. The children of many farm households worked at experimental stations as office personnel and even as teachers in local primary schools. A household without at least one wage earner generally did not persist in the area for more than one or two years. Most households had two or more members who worked a substantial portion of the year for others.

A third strategy that worked well was to adjust the work load to the amount of available household labor, rather than rely on bank credit and hired hands. Thus, households with few able-bodied workers were more successful raising cattle, whereas larger households could pursue labor-intensive activities like tobacco curing, horticulture, and service activities like general stores and transportation.

A fourth survival strategy was marriage. Early successful households were joined by marriage to other successful families. In the new town or *agrovila* that I studied in 1972–74, the more productive households established bonds of godparenthood and marriage and maintained these ties by frequent visits. This, as it were, solidified the accomplishments of the families and assured continuity in their control of important resources. Poor households, by contrast, intermarried with other poor households and were rarely able to make an advantageous marriage.

Marriage is an especially important event in agrarian societies since land is inherited and family ties are powerful mechanisms for social mobility and stability. Where marriage involved a government civil servant and a farmer's daughter, the bride's family acquired a stable salary, education for the children, and even an escape from the hard life of the farm. Depending on the level of the bureaucratic position, it might provide preferential access to government resources. In other cases, the marriage of an Amazonian caboclo to a newcomer joined environmental familiarity with experience in urban bureaucratic institutions, often a successful combination in a developing agrarian setting.

The Amazon Frontier in the 1980s

Returning a decade later to this Transamazonian Highway frontier was eye-opening. The town I had known well and that served the colonization area had grown

This recent settler in Rondonia, like most migrants, looks to the future with hope, anticipating economic and social advancements for herself and her children.

in population from fifteen hundred to ten thousand between 1970 and 1974. By 1984 the town had fifty thousand inhabitants and boasted a modern airport that rivaled larger communities in the U.S. Well over 70 percent of the original population was still in the area, although not necessarily on the land. After eight to ten years, many migrants had sold their land at a substantial profit, bought houses in town, and returned to working for wages as they had done before coming to the frontier. They were satisfied with their wages and new lives, even if they expressed some regret at having sold their land. Others had moved from government-built communities that had marked the early years of settlement to their own land and self-built homes. They were happier with their new homes since they were more conveniently located near crops and animals.

The better farmers continued the practices discussed earlier, although activities shifted as children married and left home. Some had developed beautiful and successful cocoa plantations of twenty hectares (fifty acres), with their own fermentation vats and drying systems. Others had acquired mechanical equipment so that they could offer threshing services. Those who had encouraged their children to work for wages and to study at night could now see their children working in town in the government civil service.

There are also the tales of sorrow of any human population. The favorite son of one promising farmer experienced a devastating, paralysing accident, which drained the family resources and eventually meant abandoning the farm to place the now paraplegic son closer to medical facilities and comfort. Another farmer had built up a beautiful farm and orchard only to be shot in the back by another farmer. The widow and daughters were left bitter and alone in a frontier that they had not wanted to come to and in which they stayed now in memory of the husband and father who had died trying to conquer it.

The frontier is full of similar heartrending stories of individuals seeking opportunity in an environment filled with danger. At any one time over 20 percent of the settler population had malaria. Although it killed mostly infants, in low-lying areas it debilitated the population and sapped their ability to work. High rates of infant and child mortality were caused primarily by gastro-intestinal diseases leading to dehydration. Stingrays affected fewer people but their stings could lead to festering wounds that took months to heal. Venomous snakes, giant stinging ants, and disease-carrying black flies (*Simulium*) made agricultural work unpleasant and often dangerous. But all of these dangers paled in comparison to the danger that man represented. The biggest cause of noninfant death was accidental trauma, primarily automobile crashes and falling trees during land clearing.

Other Experiences in the South American Forests

The focus of attention in Brazilian resettlement for the past decade has been the formidable migrations into Rondônia, and more recently into Acre. Rondônia has some sizable patches of good soils, although these are intermixed with even larger infertile areas. Because of its good resources for agriculture, the area received early attention and is already a significant producer of cocoa, coffee, and especially timber. Unlike the Transamazon Resettlement Scheme, less emphasis was placed on fixed settlement programs, although the state did determine the configuration of lots, which, like those in the Transamazon, were often drawn without regard for the suitability of the land for agriculture. More emphasis was placed on road construction and maintenance. World Bank loans were obtained to pave a major highway across the central plateau of Brazil, Rondonia's heartland, and another road extended it to the second largest city in the Amazon, Manaus. Clearly, lessons were learned in the Transamazon Resettlement Scheme, but many assumptions and errors persist as well. Presumptions about the superiority of southern Brazilian farmers continue to be used in promoting resettlement and in offering credit. The failure to incorporate local knowledge of resource use persists. The presence of good soils has not compensated for the low yields on acidic, low-nutrient areas; whole settlements, like the Sidney Girão Project, failed when planners presumed that all soils in Rondônia had equally high agricultural potential. Deforestation is proceeding at a devastating rate. As recently as two years ago 3 percent of the state had been cleared of its forest for timber and for the temporary fields of migrant shifting cultivators. More recent figures put deforestation at 15 percent of the state.

The Brazilian experience is mirrored in other nations with Amazonian territories. In the Andean countries, migration has been from the highlands into the *selva alta*, or mid-elevation rain forest. These populations also follow the agricultural methods learned in their homelands rather than adopt local practices, and

Building a road through the rain forest frequently attracts spontaneous settlers and leads to extensive and unplanned deforestation. Shifting cultivators have cleared their fields along a road in eastern Brazil.

CENTER: Communities of government-sponsored migrants, unlike villages of native Amazonians, stand out, rather than blend with their surroundings. An early community "Agrovila Abraham Lincoln" along the Transamazon Highway in Brazil.

BOTTOM: The planned communities along the Transamazon Highway, known as *agrovilas,* were built to a standard configuration. Equal rows of sixteen flat-roofed houses are arranged in a U-shape around a square cleared of vegetation.

stereotyping of local Amazonians, common in Brazil, has had its equivalents in the Andean nations. In contrast to Brazilians, migrants from the highlands more commonly retain small land parcels in their homelands and continue to work both areas. In both the Andean countries and Brazil, government policies have exploited the rain forests to solve foreign exchange problems rather than develop the areas according to their own particular natural and human resources. For example, prices rarely favor producers, credit is not made available in timely fashion, and development projects are based on faulty data. As a result, settlers' efforts in both production and marketing often go unrewarded.

Agriculture, even major commercial production, need not be a failure in Amazonia. Lowland Amazonian rice production has made both Bolivia and Peru self-sufficient in this crop in less than a decade. Surplus production is now supporting rice-based beer industries that provide new forms of employment to rural Amazonians. In Brazil, Japanese immigrants have been successful in producing black pepper, and this profitable experience has been borrowed elsewhere although with mixed success. Both coffee and black pepper offer a solution to one of the most serious disadvantages of lowland Amazonian agriculture—the high cost of transportation. By marketing low-volume and low-weight crops of high market value, producers are more likely to be competitive.

Groups such as the Japanese in Brazil and the Mennonites in Bolivia are living proof that farming the rain forests does not always result in disappointment and poverty. These two groups have been successful because they combined initial capital, technical expertise, community organization for production and marketing, and a nurturing attitude towards the land. The Japanese intensively manage crops that do not require continual clearing of forest but instead thrive in well-tended small fields. The Mennonites have operated on a larger scale but have chosen relatively flat areas of the Amazon with considerable initial soil fertility. A substantial initial capital investment has allowed them to effectively deal with constraints. Their community organization and attitude to production has made them major regional suppliers within a brief period of time.

Since they emphasize national goals, development plans rarely address the need for producers to meet regional demand for a broad array of products that could serve as the basis for seasonal, labor-intensive, regional industries. Without such development the region will not develop and its people will continue to experience the winds and fortunes of unpredictable external markets. For example, the Amazon is capable of producing soybeans, corn, molasses, sorghum, and manioc chips—the major components of animal feeds. Regional production of animal feeds would reduce the costs of importing these items, increase meat yield and quality, and provide needed employment. Harvest of diverse Amazonian fruits could provide a high-value cottage industry in canning, drying, juice concentrates, or preserves, and the development of new markets.

Why are these regional industries slow to develop? In part, lack of appreciation of many forest products in urban centers means that demand must be developed. In addition, neither the traditional nor newly settling populations have the skills or the knowledge necessary to establish the industries. Interest and enthusiasm for marketing local products in regional, national, and even international markets abound among local producers. What is lacking is the knowledge of how to make the connection, how to market these new products. Amazonian farmers are all too aware of the efforts of others to exploit their labor and to lead them along lines of production that assure only continuous poverty and dependency.

What is needed, then, is enlightened leadership, one that believes that the resources of the rain forest should first benefit the people who have chosen to live there and only secondarily those outside. Such a philosophy, which apparently runs contrary to the organization of highly stratified societies, would be the surest guarantee that the people of the rain forest would benefit from their labor and that the rest of us will benefit as well from their enterprise and knowledge.

The route taken will depend upon the choices made in each country and by the international banks. It is at this level that decisions lead either to the development of local products and industries, to regional diversification, and to the creation of new markets based on now unfamiliar products or to the production of crops that assure the impoverishment of the region and its people. The story of the resettled people of the Amazonian rain forest is so far the story of development decisions of the latter sort. The success stories are the result of the ingenuity of settlers, not of government assistance. Their abilities to find formulas to accommodate to life in the rain forests were learned from local Amazonians. It is time for leaders to see that the impoverishment of their vast rain forests in both socioeconomic and environmental terms is a cost that benefits only the unenlightened elite. The people of the rain forest wait for better roads to markets, for credit to produce locally advantageous crops, for investment policies that favor local industrial production, and for creativity in marketing their unique products.

The support received from Social Science Research Council and Tinker Fellowships, Fulbright and National Institutes of Mental Health grants, and sabbatical-year support from Indiana University are acknowledged. None of these institutions should be held responsible for the views stated herein.

BIG BUSINESS
IN THE
AMAZON

MARIANNE SCHMINK

Outsiders to the Amazon are inclined to see the lowland tropical forest as a vast storehouse of riches awaiting discovery. For centuries the image of the region as a cornucopia attracted visionaries and adventurers of all nationalities who sought to profit from its natural resources. Such grandiose schemes as those promoted by Henry Ford in the 1920s and the more recent Jari project financed by Daniel Ludwig became known throughout the world for the ambitiousness of their design as well as the drama of their failure. More typical of the region are the small trading companies, sawmills, farms and ranches, food-processing plants, and numerous extractive industries such as hunting, fishing, rubber tapping, and gathering Brazil nuts and other forest products.

Over the centuries extractive activities have depleted the stock of such highly prized species as manatees, turtles, and jaguars, yet none of the traditional business ventures caused the wholesale environmental disruption that we are beginning to see today. In the last two decades in Brazil newly constructed roads, government-sponsored colonization projects, and large-scale investments in mining and hydroelectric plants have proved highly destructive to the natural environment. These ventures and others subsidized by tax incentives and lenient credit policies, such as cattle ranches, could not be profitable without market interventions by the state. It is expected that the frontier will continue to expand into Amazonia in the years to come as people from across the country migrate to the region in search of land and livelihood. The challenge is to meet the needs of a growing population while promoting forms of production adapted to Amazonia's unique environmental conditions.

The Foreigners' Dream: Fordlandia and Jari

Two visionary Americans made history with their bold schemes in Brazil's Amazon basin. Henry Ford and Daniel Ludwig, two of the world's most successful and innovative entrepreneurs, both dreamed of installing plantations in the Amazon rain forest to produce commodities needed on the world market. Both invested millions in projects that would never yield a profit to them. Problems with soil degradation and disease beset their plantations, and labor shortages and other social problems spoiled their initially friendly relations with the Brazilian government. In the end, both were forced to sell their properties and abandon their jungle empires. They found the risks of failure to be proportionate to their grandiose ambitions.

Henry Ford's rubber plantation scheme was first encouraged by Herbert Hoover, then Secretary of Commerce, who wanted to increase U.S. rubber production when Great Britain's Stevenson Plan of 1922

In tropical Latin America the principal cause of forest conversion is cattle production. Yet, unless properly managed, cattle ranching is one of the worst alternative uses for tropical lands.

BOTTOM LEFT: This pulp mill and power plant on the Jari River were towed on two barges from Japan. The mill depends on local timber for fuel.

Hardwood logs are pulled in a raft to a mill on the Amazon. Of several hundred commercially usable species only about twenty are well known on the international market. ▷

BOTTOM RIGHT: Pine (*Pinus caribaea*) plantations in four stages of growth in the Brazilian Amazon. Pest problems have plagued experiments in plantation forestry.

reduced the supply of rubber from British colonies and raised its price. After Hoover sent a team of technicians to explore the Amazon, Ford decided to try plantation rubber there. It was a logical response to the growing demand for tires for his expanding automobile industry. The government of the state of Pará was enthusiastic enough about the proposal to grant the newly created Ford Industrial Company of Brazil a free concession of 1,000,000 hectares (2,471,000 acres) of land along the Tapajós River. Ford's company was exempt from state and municipal taxes for fifty years, but after twelve years of operation the enterprise would begin to share its profits with the state and the municipality.

The project began in 1926. By December 1932 there were four thousand people living in the community of Fordlandia, the harbor site on the 120-kilometer (75-mile) waterfront of Ford's property. The town boasted a school and well-equipped hospital as well as costly houses complete with screens on the windows. The plantation itself consisted of 485,000 rubber trees planted on 2,770 hectares (6,843 acres). There was also a nursery for the seedlings, a functioning sawmill, and eight kilometers (five miles) of railroad. Tropical hardwoods were sawn and shipped to the United States, and the first rubber trees were to be ready for tapping in 1936.

Technical problems began almost immediately. Ford's property was so hilly that after clearing the tropical rains quickly eroded the soils and flooded the bottoms of valleys and ravines. Many parts of the property were rocky, and avoiding these problem areas led to irregular planting patterns that were inefficient to harvest. Exportable timber was rapidly depleted, and the sawmill closed down after only two years. Most of the young rubber trees were killed by an invasion of the South American leaf blight. At the same time world rubber prices were dropping.

A few years later Ford moved his operation to a new 285,000-hectare (700,000-acre) site, called Belterra, farther down the Tapajós River. Well-drained soils on a flat plateau surface there permitted the installation of a regular rectangular pattern of sixteen-hectare (forty-acre) plots. Some of the technical and infrastructural problems were avoided in the new location. The company began a double bud-grafting program using Malaysian seedlings to produce high-yielding, disease-resistant trees with healthy native roots. By 1941 Ford had planted three million trees, two million of which had been grafted with the Malaysian stock.

By this time the project suffered from a shortage of labor. Workers did not respond well to Ford's social philosophy, which included housing and menus

Planting rubber tree seeds at Fordlandia, Brazil, 1930.

imported from Detroit and such unfamiliar leisure activities as square dancing. Amazonian natives were accustomed to the unregimented life of free-lance rubber tappers, while the growing prosperity in Brazil during this period made it difficult to attract workers from other regions to the remote jungle outpost. By 1941 Ford had 2,723 employees at both plantations, but 11,000 rubber tappers would be needed for the project to reach its production goals.

The persistent threat of leaf blight and the high cost of grafting combined with labor shortages and the expense of providing housing and services to workers conspired to doom the Fordlandia-Belterra project. These unanticipated problems made Ford's original goal of planting 162 hectares (400 acres) per year remote and unrealistic. When Henry Ford II became president of the Ford Motor Company in 1945, he sold the plantation to the Brazilian government for 500 thousand dollars as a cost-cutting measure. By this time Ford had invested more than nine million dollars without marketing any commercial rubber.

Jari

Ford's lost investment was nothing compared to that of shipping magnate Daniel Ludwig decades later. One of the wealthiest men in the world, Ludwig would sink approximately 750 million dollars of his fortune in the largest tropical forestry project in the world. The Jari project began in 1967 after Ludwig purchased 1,200,000 hectares (3,000,000 acres) in the northern part of the state of Pará in Brazil's Amazon region. Its primary activity, a massive plantation forestry and pulp-processing facility, was intended to respond to a projected future world shortage of wood fiber. Ludwig chose *Gmelina arborea,* a fast-growing East Indian tree, to be planted on his 100,000-hectare (250,000-acre) plantation. Secondary activities were to include mining, livestock, and the world's largest rice plantation, 14,000 hectares (35,000 acres) of irrigated land where aerial sowing and spraying were to produce two annual harvests. Like Ford's, Ludwig's vision of the tropical enterprise included high technology and well-equipped planned communities for workers. He built airports and landing strips, over four thousand kilometers (twenty-five hundred miles) of roads, and eighty kilometers (fifty miles) of railroad tracks.

Like Fordlandia, Jari suffered technical setbacks from the very beginning. Ignoring his foresters' advice, Mr. Ludwig used expensive bulldozers to clear the natural forest for planting. Only after planting the first *Gmelina* did he learn that the machines scraped off most of the thin tropical topsoil and so compressed the remainder that most of the seedlings perished. The company was forced to turn to manual forest clearing and hired some two thousand workers through contractors. The shift to manual labor for forest clearing raised new problems. Hundreds of thousands of dollars spent on the bulldozers were lost, and new costs in wages, housing, and other services were added to the operation. Scandals related to treatment and payment of workers by the notorious Amazonian work-crew contractors created bad publicity for the project. A spontaneous settlement called Beiradao grew up on the riverbank opposite the planned company town of Monte Dourado. The demand for services surpassed the project's capabilities. Labor turnover was as high as 200 to 300 percent per year.

By the mid-1970s rising world market prices created favorable conditions for the beginning of Jari's pulp operation. Ludwig commissioned a $270 million pulp mill and wood-fired power plant to be built in Japan and financed primarily by a $240 million loan from the Japanese Export-Import Bank. The Brazilian military government generously agreed to guarantee the loan through its National Economic Development Bank, thus taking responsibility for the project's future success. After the plant was built Ludwig towed it on two barges around Southeast Asia, across the Indian Ocean, past the Cape of Good Hope, across the Atlantic Ocean, up the Amazon River, and, finally, up the Jari River to the port of Munguba where it was installed in its permanent home.

By this time Ludwig faced serious difficulties. While costs had doubled, planting and growth targets for the plantation were far behind schedule. Less than one-fourth of the projected acreage had been planted; yields were 30 to 50 percent below projections. As a result there was a shortage of timber for the pulp mill. The *Gmelina* trees did not perform as well in the Amazonian environment as they had been observed to do in other sites. They did especially poorly on sandy soils, where they eventually had to be replaced by a Caribbean pine (*Pinus caribaea,* var. *hondurense*) that did not grow as rapidly as the *Gmelina*. Experimentation was also intensified with *Eucalyptus deglupta* which produces a lower-quality pulp. The cost of stopping the pulp mill operation, even briefly, was prohibitively expensive. The plantation's pulp was therefore produced by mixing the high-quality *Gmelina* with about 20 percent from over eighty species of native trees such as *imbauba* (trumpetwood) and *parapara*. Native timber was also used for construction purposes and as a fuel for the pulp mill.

Ludwig's dreams for Jari were thwarted by technical problems and mistakes, labor shortages and turnover, and rising costs, which together undermined the viability of his ambitious growth targets. Like the forestry division, other aspects of the project had to be scaled down or abandoned. The capital-intensive rice operation proved to be too costly. The only profitable part of the enterprise was mining a kaolin (white clay) deposit serendipitously located on the property.

To complicate matters further, the company was unable to secure clear title to the whole of its territorial claim and by the early 1980s could no longer count on the special favors and steadfast support that had been offered by a succession of military presidents. As Brazil began a transition to a democratic system, the vast and secretive multinational operation became a political liability. After Ludwig demanded and was refused government intervention to clarify his land title and to guarantee a loan for a second pulp mill to be brought from Japan, the entrepreneur announced that he would abandon his Jari operation. Backed by the government, a consortium of twenty-seven Brazilian companies finally purchased the forestry project, the kaolin operation, and the livestock ranch (including some three thousand head of cattle and seven thousand water buffalo) for a total of $280 million in 1982, and Mr. Ludwig retired from his Amazonian adventure. The project is still operating at a more modest scale.

The fates of Fordlandia and of Jari are a cautionary tale. The potential for sustained-yield plantation forestry in the Amazon has only begun to be tested. Its contribution to the regional economy or to the creation of stable employment has yet to be proven. Monocultural plantation forestry is seldom possible in the patchy Amazonian soils, which may require more diversified cropping. Plantations should emulate the forest's natural biological diversity, which helps to check the spread of pests. The lush vastness of the tropical environment is misleading enough to create unrealistic visions of rapid growth and sustained production that have not, however, been achieved even by the great minds and fortunes of the world. The foreigners' dreams turned out to have little to do with the realities of the Amazonian rain forest.

Business as Usual: Ranchers, Loggers, and Miners

While Fordlandia and Jari have received attention because of their size and international visibility, most business ventures in Amazonian forests are controlled not by foreign but by domestic investors. Their activities and those of multinationals are often actively encouraged, if not subsidized, by governments and by international lending agencies. Commercial ranching, logging, and mining are the most prevalent business ventures in today's Amazon basin.

In tropical Latin America, unlike other parts of the world, the principal force behind forest conversion is clearing pasture for cattle ranches. Cattle were introduced to the New World following the Spanish conquest, and raising cattle continues to symbolize gentlemanly prestige. Ranching is also profitable: it is a relatively inexpensive way of expanding culti-

The new town of Serra Pelada, Brazil, sprang up almost overnight following the discovery of gold nearby.

BOTTOM: Gold mining with high-pressure hoses leaves devastation in its wake in Camaru, Brazil. The seas of mud provide excellent breeding grounds for mosquitoes.

vated areas and rights to land, requires little labor after the initial forest clearing, and produces a commodity (beef) that is in increasing demand. In Central America alone, probably more than two-thirds of the arable land is used for livestock production.

During the 1960s and 1970s Brazil's military government actively promoted the expansion of ranching in the Amazon region as a means of attracting investments by multinational businesses and by those based in southern Brazil. Starting in 1966 a program called Operation Amazonia provided generous tax credits, holidays, and exemption from import and export duties to corporate entities that were seeking to diversify their investment portfolios and to gain access to land as a hedge against inflation. Over the next decade and a half investments of well over a billion dollars were approved for Amazonian cattle ranching, and the largest share of the direct tax credits under the new program went to the livestock sector. The clearing of forest areas for pasture may have accounted for most forest alteration in the Brazilian Amazon region during this period, although hard figures are lacking.

Cattle ranching was said by its proponents to be the logical vocation for the Amazon region. There was a history of ranching on the natural grasslands of Marajó Island, and improved technologies could be adapted from other parts of the world. Corporate ranchers would underwrite the costs of frontier development and thereby save government revenues while increasing exports and creating employment. The cattle lobby argued that whereas agricultural colonists used ecologically predatory practices of slash-and-burn cultivation, studies had shown pasture to be an environmentally sound alternative that actually nutrified the soil.

Hindsight reveals these claims to be overly optimistic. More detailed studies of Amazonian pastures have shown that the initial enrichment of the soil (from cutting and burning of trees and other plants) is at the expense of total available nutrient stocks in the ecosystem that gradually decline in subsequent years. Lacking the defenses of the diverse natural system many pastures were invaded within a few years by pests and weeds, some of them highly toxic to cattle. These problems led to overgrazing and in some areas to the abandonment of degraded pastures after just a few years. The costs of fertilizing and weeding were often so prohibitive that clearing new forest was more profitable than investing in pasture recuperation. These conditions acted as a disincentive for investments in such long-term resource-management strategies as selective clearing in accordance with topography, preservation of forest corridors along watercourses and between cleared areas, and rotation of pastures.

Nor did an international market materialize for Brazilian beef, which is subject to diseases that do not exist among cattle raised in Central America and Argentina. Amazonian cattle ranching did not succeed in contributing to Brazil's export earnings, but then productivity of the ranching enterprise itself was not the crucial factor in determining the profitability of Amazonian ranching investments. Rising inflation rates, fiscal incentives, tax holidays, and government-sponsored road-building programs made Amazonian land values increase rapidly—even if productivity declined. Conditions for investors were so attractive that the profits to be made bore little relationship to productivity, much less to long-term sustainability. The productive capacity of land was secondary to its potential for resale and as a means of obtaining access to federal subsidies and such other forms of wealth as forest resources and minerals.

Although Brazil terminated its generous subsidy program for new cattle enterprises in tropical forest areas several years ago, credit for livestock operations is still available, and investment continues in already established projects and in the majority of Amazonian ranches that have been installed without subsidies. Clearing for pasture is still the best way to acquire large areas of land. Despite its prevalence, many now argue that cattle ranching is one of the worst alternative land uses for the tropics. The conversion of large blocks of natural forest to pasture and its subsequent rapid deterioration may remove vast areas from use at least until methods for recuperating degraded pastures can be improved.

The conversion of diverse natural forests for beef production is, in any case, ecologically inefficient. One calculation found that the production of enough ground beef for one hamburger requires the destruction of approximately seventy-five kilograms (two hundred pounds) of living matter, including some of twenty to thirty different plant species, perhaps one hundred insect species, and dozens of bird, mammal, and reptile species.

This calculation dramatizes the dilemma of Amazonian economics. While one hamburger has an easily measurable market value, the one-tenth ton of forest required to produce it does not. Natural forests are not recognized as being productive. Under Brazilian law access to land (and to fiscal incentives) is contingent upon demonstrating that it is being used, so clearing the land of forest is the first step toward establishing ownership or access rights. The clearing itself is a legally defined improvement, which increases the value of the land. Investors may clear land for resale using public resources to cover most of their costs and, on a similar scale, colonists who receive subsidized plots in official settlement projects may also clear and resell. With so much money to be made it is not surprising that a vast army of so-called *grileiros* (land grabbers) devote their energies to finding illegal ways to make

a profit on buying and selling land. The most direct threat to Amazonian forests emerges from the struggle for control over land not from the debate over appropriate forms of production in the region.

The chaos and greed that reign in land transactions frequently bring different social groups into direct confrontation. Rights to government lands occupied by indigenous groups may be guaranteed in law, but their uncertain boundaries invite incursion by loggers, miners, migrants, and would-be ranchers. Migrants who establish farms on public lands often find that someone else holds a piece of paper, of unknown validity, claiming the same land. These competing claims accelerate pressures to clear more forest land. In some areas they also lead to violence. The land wars raging in southern Pará for the past decade between ranchers, colonists, and native groups have claimed over three hundred lives. Far from creating sources of local employment, the expansion of cattle ranching in Amazonia has tended to concentrate landholdings and substitute a relatively few hired workers on land that could support dozens of smallholders.

Cattle ranching is an established activity in some parts of the Amazon region and is an appropriate land use in natural grasslands or thinly forested areas. Proper pasture management, including soil conservation measures and appropriate inputs, can sustain existing pastures, and such strategies to recuperate degraded pastures as the use of nitrogen-fixing leguminous trees and shrubs need to be tested. Experiments are now underway to integrate livestock raising with lumbering and such plantation crops as oil palm. A stable cattle industry can play an important role in supplying the growing regional population's demand for beef, milk, and other products—especially as traditional protein sources (from hunting and fishing) are depleted. The national market for beef is also good. Cattle ranching thus has an important role to play in Amazonian development, if based on good management practices with an emphasis on sustained productivity and if not installed at the expense of tropical forest areas or of other, more intensive forms of land use.

Logging

The Amazon basin is an enormous warehouse of tropical timber: it contains over 600 million hectares (1,500 million acres) of forest. The 260 million hectares (650 million acres) located in Brazil comprise some fifty billion cubic meters of standing wood, of which about fifteen million cubic meters are currently marketable. Many have argued that forestry development is the Amazon region's true calling.

The Brazilian government's fiscal incentives program has also favored the producers of industrial wood. Livestock and logging firms together captured

At the peak of the gold rush, some fifty thousand miners
worked over three thousand small claims in Serra Pelada,
Brazil. The mine has been operating since 1980.

Land is cleared for new forest plantations at Jari by burning off the natural forest.

most of the subsidies. Wood producers also benefited from separate measures designed to promote exports. The combination of the subsidies programs and the government-financed road system in the Amazon stimulated a massive shift in logging investment from southern Brazil, where stands of the Paraná pine (*Araucaria angustifolia*) had been depleted by clear cutting. In the state of Pará, the region's largest wood producer, production grew over 4,000 percent during the 1970s.

Brazilian law prohibits the export of unprocessed logs, a measure that protects smaller companies and keeps the price of logs low for use in domestic wood-processing industries. This prohibition, however, also reduces the incentive to extract carefully higher-priced whole logs that could be exported for use in the making veneer. Instead, loggers typically concentrate only on the better parts of the log and discard the rest. Of several hundred commercially usable species, only about twenty are well known on the international market for sawn lumber. Industrial wood producers in Brazil responded to foreign demand by an increasing specialization in a relatively small number of species such as *Virola,* cedar, and mahogany. Trading companies that dominated the market were interested only in rough lumber and actively discouraged diversification of production oriented to local market consumables and to secondary wood products for national markets. As a result, many other potentially valuable trees of lesser-known timber species were simply burned in the process of forest clearing for agriculture or ranching.

As with the livestock sector, tax and export incentives have vastly exceeded private investment in industrial wood production in the Amazon. Ironically, the depletion of lumber resources in southern Brazil probably would have provided sufficient inducement to wood producers to invest in Amazonia even without the generous subsidies. Even worse, funds intended to promote exports were sometimes diverted from productive uses to speculation in lucrative, short-term capital markets. As in the case of ranching, subsidies to industrial wood production ultimately served to stimulate disinvestment in productive activities while creating attractive profits for a small group of high-volume lumber producers and exporters.

Wood resources also play a role in the struggle for control of land. Land-grabbers often sell off the valuable tree species from properties first, then sell the land itself. Alternatively, ranchers whose holdings have passed through a cycle of agricultural crops and then degraded pasture may finally exploit the timber from remaining forest patches. Conflicts also arise between sawmills competing for access to increasingly distant sources of valuable woods, and penetration into forest or indigenous reserves may lead to confrontations with native groups or with authorities.

Because selective logging does not require forest

conversion (as does clearing for pasture) it presents a far less dramatic threat to the rain-forest environment. But the indirect impact of logging operations should not be overlooked. Some 400,000 hectares (1,000,000 acres) of native forest are affected each year by the operations required to extract twenty cubic meters of commercial species. Logging roads that open access to new areas for the first time often promote new settlements and spearhead new forest clearing. The interaction of selective tree harvesting and burning for pasture can open corridors by which fire can more easily penetrate into adjacent forests.

Industrial wood production creates more stable jobs and better working conditions than do most other Amazonian businesses. The relatively skilled employment in logging is generally reserved for trained outsiders imported by the company, but some opportunities for manual work are also created. Sawmills often play a pioneering role in establishing frontier communities, building roads and settlement sites, which sometimes last only as long as do the accessible valuable trees and other times survive to become more diversified towns. A fledgling wood-processing industry, primarily oriented to the regional and national market, is beginning to emerge in some Amazonian communities. Veneer plants and furniture factories provide new sources of employment and a stimulus for the local market.

With greater control and management, there is a potential for sustainable forestry management and wood processing in Amazonia. Already, two-thirds of Brazil's exported sawn wood comes from the Amazon, and both domestic and international markets for wood products and derivatives are good. A new emphasis on sustained-yield tropical forestry, forest management, and agroforestry is emerging as a priority in Amazonian development. Much has already been learned from the Fordlandia and Jari experiences, and it is hoped that new policy initiatives will encourage future learning.

Mining

One of the Amazon basin's greatest sources of potential wealth is its deposits of aluminum, tin, copper, tungsten, manganese, uranium, iron, gold, diamonds, and other minerals. While small-scale mining has historically occupied Amazonian inhabitants, multinational mining companies began work in Amazonia during the 1960s, and Brazilian companies, especially state enterprises, intervened by the 1970s. Like cattle ranching and logging, government policies have been important in determining business patterns in the mining sector. The government controlled the principal mineral discoveries in the 1970s and 1980s, and the state also managed the conflicts between state and private mining companies and small-scale miners known as *garimpeiros*.

The discovery in 1967 of massive iron ore deposits in the Serra dos Carajas drew attention to the Amazon's mineral resources. That same year a state geologist also discovered gold in the state of Pará, but the find was kept in secret until 1977. Small-scale prospectors began to extract gold nearby, which then led to the discovery of Serra Pelada and to a latter-day gold rush in 1980. Serra Pelada is an exceptionally concentrated gold deposit inside a hill initially dubbed "Babylon" that is now a pit 100 meters (270 feet) deep and more than 1,200 meters (3,000 feet) across. The pit was dug by teeming, mud-drenched masses of workers who have received extensive international media attention. Five months after its discovery, when the military government intervened in Serra Pelada, there were thirty thousand garimpeiros working there, and a ton of gold had already been extracted. As the pits sunk deeper and deeper, the miners had to carry their sacks of extracted dirt up an elaborate and precarious network of rustic ladders. Collapses of ladders and the walls of the pits led to fatal accidents during the following years. Yet the garimpeiros have refused to stop their work, even in defiance of a presidential decree and despite the fact that the pit reached down to the water table and could only be worked using numerous water pumps.

Serra Pelada is only one, if by far the most concentrated, of the gold deposits in southern Pará and other Amazonian states. Some quarter million garimpeiros spread out over the vast Amazon region were responsible for over 85 percent of Brazil's gold production in the 1980s. In Serra Pelada alone by 1986 garimpeiros had produced over thirty million kilograms (thirty-three thousand tons) of gold. Manual gold mining is the Amazon's largest business measured in terms of either employment or production. These mining operations, usually linked to mineral buyers or phantom mining companies, also benefit local businesses who capture the garimpeiros' earnings.

Yet the presence of the garimpeiros in Amazonia is controversial, and they are often in competition with mechanized mining enterprises for the same minerals. Government mining agencies and the mining companies argue that small-scale mining is inefficient, unsafe, and inequitable. The gold is often sold clandestinely, so the government does not receive its tax benefits. While most garimpeiros suffer from terrible work conditions, the returns from their work tend to be monopolized by a few investors. The companies that are subject to legal regulations cannot compete with the wildcat garimpeiros, who counter that their practice of recleaning gold recuperates most of the ore lost in the manual process. Unsafe work conditions and tax evasion could be addressed by repairs and by better supervision. The mining areas provide employment and a stimulus to the local economy and do not depend on costly loans from overseas banks. This unresolved debate took on political importance with the transition to a civilian government that is still struggling to find the answers to the garimpeiro dilemma.

In the past manual mining did not have lasting environmental effects because the methods used were rudimentary and operations tended to be small in scale. But beginning in the 1970s a technological revolution began in Brazil's placer mines, and semimechanized techniques using hydraulic units to dig pits and extract ore have gradually transformed the landscape in gold mining areas. The abundance of water turns the mines into seas of mud that provide excellent breeding grounds for mosquitoes; rates of malaria infection are highest near the mining areas. Runoff of the water also affects the local rivers, introducing a new load of sediment that contains both human wastes and mercury, which is used in the agglutination and amalgamation of gold. There are no federal regulations concerning mercury, which is routinely used by both manual and mechanized miners. Although its conversion to highly toxic methylmercury in the waterways could pose a serious threat to human health, the impact of mercury on Amazonia's rivers has not been monitored. More directly affected are the garimpeiros themselves, who handle the mercury with their bare hands and, worse yet, regularly breathe the toxic mercury vapors released when the gold and mercury mixture is burned to remove impurities.

Mechanized mining operations potentially offer high economic returns per unit of land, and with precautions they can minimize such negative environmental effects as pollution of air and water. The bauxite facility run by Mineração Rio do Norte on the Trombetas River is a good example. Before bauxite extraction began, the company commissioned botanical, zoological, archaeological, and forestry inventories of the area to be affected and removed the commercial lumber for use in local construction. Exploitation of reserves of more than 450,000 kilograms (500 tons) of high-grade aluminum ore affects only small areas of forest every year. Measures have been taken to prevent soil erosion and air and water pollution, and the landscape is reconstructed in each site after available ore is exhausted. Since the enterprise is located in a remote area where few jobs are available, its environmental and social impact has been limited compared to other kinds of businesses in Amazonia.

Probably the best example of a successful big business project in Brazilian Amazonia is the ICOMI (Indústria e Comércio de Minerais) manganese mine in the territory of Amapá, operated since 1954 by a partnership between Bethlehem Steel and CAEMI (Companhia Auxiliar de Empresas de Mineração), a Bra-

zilian holding company controlled by entrepreneur Augusto Antunes. The high returns realized from the sale of the strategic mineral have allowed the company to finance needed infrastructural and service investments, to pay for labor costs, and still to experiment with a wide variety of potential investments in Amapá. After attempts with cattle ranching and sugarcane and fruit plantations in forested areas, by the 1970s the company had established some 121,500 hectares (300,000 acres) of pine plantations as well as large area of oil palms on scrub savanna areas where productivity was found to be higher. The manganese deposits will be depleted within the next ten to twelve years, but the development of wood and oil palm industries may provide future employment and income for the territory.

More recently the Carajas Iron Ore Project, operated by the state-controlled Companhia Vale do Rio Doce (CVRD) and partially financed by the World Bank, has implemented an exemplary program of mining development with environmental protection.

Future of Business in the Amazon

Brazil and other Amazonian countries have conceived different, sometimes conflicting roles for Amazonia in national development. The region has been seen as a producer of cheap food for urban workers, a safety valve for excess population, or a resource frontier for export products. Brazil's road building and fiscal incentive policies, rapid migration, and volatile markets for land and Amazonian commodities have unleashed a process of environmental and social change the magnitude of which exceeds that anticipated by government bureaucrats or private entrepreneurs.

The environmental and social costs of economic change in the Brazilian Amazon region have been high. If lessons from the past are heeded, these costs can be reduced in future Amazonian development. In Brazil the end of the economic miracle in the mid-1970s and the transition to a democratic political system in the 1980s have encouraged more serious attention to conservation and equity issues. A Special Environmental Secretariat was created, and in 1981 a comprehensive National Environmental Policy led to the establishment of parks and reserves and to environmental monitoring of major development projects like Carajás.

The plans for developing the Amazon region elaborated by Brazil's new civilian government explicitly recognize the mistakes of past policies and seek rational resource uses maximizing benefits to the local and regional economy. Instead of viewing forest resources as transitory to agriculture and livestock operations, proposed changes for both forestry and land regulations will remove the incentives for forest clearing. Local research agencies are increasing their emphasis on forestry and agroforestry systems. Management and enrichment of natural forest products, sustained-yield forest extraction and reforestation, and introduction of perennial crops, especially trees, are new priorities for both industrial and small-scale development.

The failures of many ambitious, large-scale schemes (that might seem appropriate to the vastness of Amazonian tropical forests) provide valuable lessons. The experiences suggest caution and selectivity in supporting big business enterprises in the tropical forest, an environment better able to recover from human disturbances that are relatively small scale and selective. When large areas of forest are destroyed much of the diverse, natural richness of Amazonia is lost.

The presumption that simplified, man-made systems of production are better than the natural forest remains to be proven. The large-scale, high-technology schemes attempted in the past have been beset by technical problems. The technologies developed in temperate regions are less appropriate in the tropics. Since biological diversity and environmental heterogeneity underlie the rain forest's regenerative cycle, attempts to introduce large-scale monoculture have suffered from problems with pests, erosion, and rapid depletion of soil nutrients. Initial success stories of high productivity have typically foundered in later years. The cost of necessary inputs to counter these problems is prohibitive.

Even when large agribusiness ventures in the Amazon are productive, their success does not necessarily benefit the regional economy or the local population. Historically, extraction of Amazonian forest resources was controlled by foreign businesses or allied traders who were able to appropriate most of the gains. The profits made from the export of such products as rubber, Brazil nuts, spices, and lumber primarily enriched the trading companies and agents who controlled the chain of supply and trade that eventually reached the individual forest-dwelling rubber tappers, most of whom lived in poverty and perpetual debt. As a result, in countries like Brazil, foreign presence in Amazonia is politically controversial.

The people of the remote Amazon forest can benefit from economic development that brings jobs, road transportation, electricity, schools, and health care. Private sector businesses and the government policies that support these enterprises help to bring improvements. Ultimately, even sustained economic performance will depend on minimizing damage to the environment and broadening the distribution of economic benefits like jobs, resources, and income.

The author thanks Clarence Boonstra, Susanna Hecht, John Browder, and Charles H. Wood for helpful suggestions about this paper, but they are not responsible for the point of view it expresses.

CARAJÁS

ROGER D. STONE

Pilots flying north or south over the eastern edge of the Amazon basin had long noted compass fluctuations while crossing the Carajás mountain range in Pará state. But until the mid-1960s the mineral wealth of the region, then surrounded by dense tropical forest and only lightly populated, remained unknown. In 1967 a helicopter carrying the Brazilian geologist Breno Augusto dos Santos, on a U.S. Steel Corporation assignment to look for manganese, was forced down onto a rocky Carajás outcrop. Under the scrubby vegetation he discovered rich iron ore. Thus, inadvertently, began the boldest economic development effort ever attempted in a tropical-forest setting.

What had come to light, it was soon found, was no less than the world's largest deposit (eighteen billion metric tons) of high-grade, high-quality iron ore with characteristics well-suited for the world market. Subsequent discoveries of other minerals nearby—copper, bauxite, manganese, gold—quickened the pulses of Brazilian planners and patriots. For decades they had sought a way to transform the mostly agrarian economy that, despite earlier industrialization efforts, still characterized their "land of tomorrow" and bring about long-awaited modern prosperity. Carajás could be brought into production quickly. The political timing was good: in 1964 the military had thrown out an inept leftist regime and now, several years later, the generals remained firmly in charge. With confidence restored in international financial circles, Brazil's access to foreign capital was vastly increased.

By the mid-1970s plans had been drawn up for the Grande Carajás program to bring about the crash development of more than 10 percent of the entire country—895,000 square kilometers (345,560 square miles) encompassing large portions of the states of Pará, Maranhão, and Goiás. In addition to mining ac-

Part of the Carajás mining project in the foreground, with the mine construction camp in the back, and the Carajás settlement barely visible in the distant left. The large expanse of forest surrounding the site testifies to the project planners' attempt to minimize wanton deforestation.

BOTTOM: The Ponte de Madeira marine terminal where ore from the Carajás mines is loaded onto supercarrier ships.

project proceeded smoothly toward the inauguration of ore shipments in 1985 and the achievement, by 1988, of peak capacity of 35 million metric tons loaded per year.

From previous operations CVRD had learned the wisdom of applying high air and water pollution standards at and near its mines, and it was no surprise that these should reappear at Little Carajás. Less predictable was the considerable attention that the company soon began to pay to environmental concerns everywhere in the region under its control including the railroad right-of-way and the port facility in São Luís.

As an initial step, the company established tight security around the periphery of its own territory. Thus, sometimes harshly, CVRD prevented the kinds of penetration into the forest—for hunting, subsistence agriculture, gold-panning along streams, and exploitation of resources such as hardwoods—that usually accompany the opening-up of an untouched section of Amazonia. Forest clearing was tightly controlled: of more than 400,000 hectares (a million acres) within the mining concession, only 3,500 hectares (8,500 acres) were deforested for any reason. Great care was taken with the landscaping design at the site of the mine.

In an effort to provide amenities for those settlers at the edge of the mining reserve who could not be accommodated within it, the company built a small town called Parauapebas and equipped it with housing, a hospital, and a school. CVRD's agreement with FUNAI (Fundáçao National do Indio), the government's sometimes controversial Indian-protection agency, provides land protection and health services for thirteen thousand Indians in twenty-one communities whose lives were disrupted by the construction of the railway and other aspects of the project. Biologists, some from the respected, well-established Emílio Goeldi Museum in Belém, were hired to conduct baseline inventories leading to the establishment of conservation strategies for the mine region and for the biologically rich bay of São Luís.

Results of CVRD's direct efforts are not uniformly impressive. By 1987 $6 million had already been misspent on an ill-considered and poorly designed zoo near the mine. The FUNAI agreements have not prevented many of the Indian groups—one discovered only in 1982 as a direct consequence of CVRD activity—from the tragic slide toward disease and extinction that usually accompanies the imposition of external pressures on their traditional lands. The three hundred members of the hunting-gathering Guajá group, extremely isolated until the 1980s, currently face grievous losses of range and habitat as a result of the iron-ore project as well as other regional development activities. Parauapebas fell into near-chaos when it was engulfed by sixfold the anticipated population.

Still, the overall success rate is high. Almost ev-

tivities, the scheme called for major investments in minerals processing, hydroelectric power, cattle ranching, agribusiness, and infrastructure. In return for total capital input of about $70 billion, the ambitious project would generate 1.5 million jobs and, by 1990, $15 billion in export earnings (sevenfold Brazil's total exports in 1964). The region's population would more than double.

During the late 1970s Brazilian representatives for the project pitched it hard in Europe, Japan, the United States, and the Middle East. The world, still largely unaware of the environmental hazards involved, was impressed. "In spite of all Government of Brazil rhetoric and publicity," said the U.S. Embassy in Brasília in a 1981 message to Washington, "Carajás is a serious undertaking offering an immense spectrum of business opportunities to U.S. suppliers and contractors."

Forming the program's core was the $5 billion "Little Carajás" iron-ore project. The Brazilian government assigned its development to Companhia Vale do Rio Doce (CVRD), a mixed-enterprise corporation that had already proven its mettle in the successful management of large-scale mining activities in south-central Brazil. After studies, CVRD decided to build a 890-kilometer (550-mile) railway—in part through untouched rain forest—from the mine north and east to the coastal port of São Luís. There the ore would be loaded aboard ships for transport to Japanese and European buyers. Financing was arranged, and the erywhere within the region controlled by CVRD is evidence of environmental concern. The figures are impressive. By the end of 1986 the company had spent more than $66 million on conservation and Indian-protection measures for Carajás. This sum, however, represents only a fraction of the $140 million it cost CVRD to cure early environmental problems at its older mines in south-central Brazil.

In areas beyond the less than 6 percent of Grande Carajás that CVRD controls directly, the story—economically as well as environmentally—is far different. The mining ventures and the big, four million kilowatt hydroelectric power plant at Tucuruí proceeded more or less on schedule. But the capital shortage accompanying Brazil's debt crisis, which has persisted since the early 1980s, held up many secondary industrial projects. Moreover, the agriculture, cattle-raising, and colonization portions of the Grande Carajás scheme have largely failed for the usual reasons of ecological fragility and disregard for environmental impact as well as because of mismanagement by corrupt public and private agencies. There was, for example, the infamous CAPEMI (Caixa de Peculio dos Militares) a group of military pension-fund managers who haplessly found themselves trying to log the land to be inundated by the Tucuruí dam and predictably botched the job.

Except for a lucky few, those who rushed into Grande Carajás in search of the Brazilian dream are no better off than they were elsewhere in Brazil. Despite a current agrarian reform effort, most remain landless. Squatters face the constant threat of attack by large landowners' hired gunmen. Jobs are scarce now that the labor-intensive construction phase at most of the projects has ended. Although thousands work there, the famous gold mine at Serra Pelada near the Serra dos Carajás provides a living for only a few. The prime tropical forests of Grande Carajás, whose loss has been extensive, have been replaced by a patchwork largely composed of degraded and burnt-over lands and highly disorganized, mushrooming towns where human misery, vice, and sordid violence prevail.

Though CVRD can hardly be assigned a major share of the blame for this shocking outcome, the company is not blameless either. It was, after all, CVRD's opening-up of the area that led to everything else. And if its overall environmental record has been good, the company has been less concerned about other regional issues. For example, the sociologist Stephen G. Bunker of Johns Hopkins University reports that CVRD, among others, advocated the construction in towns along the railway of pig-iron plants as a means of creating jobs and adding value to raw ore before it is shipped abroad. These make unsustainable use of fuelwood from the natural forest. Smoke from the plants, moreover, is said to be threatening the region's traditional Brazil nut economy by driving away the bees that pollinate the trees and weakening the trees themselves.

CVRD is nevertheless aware of its need to exercise regional leadership in environmental protection and the highly creative activities backing up these allegations of responsibility. Among the studies the company has supported (together with World Wildlife Fund) are several of fundamental areawide importance. In one, alternative techniques of forest regeneration in a badly mauled tract near the Serra dos Carajás have been assessed. In another, conducted in partnership with Brazil's agricultural-research agency, researchers are examining multicrop models (involving trees as well as smaller plants) in areas with high population pressures. CVRD is also developing new information about the value of greenbelt zones around farmlands in the region and conducting a well-rounded investigation of the very industry that it is accused of damaging: Brazil nuts.

Whatever the shortcomings of CVRD's environmental-protection program within and beyond the range of its direct influence, the Carajás iron mine is an important attempt at economic and ecological balance in rain-forest development. The danger is that, despite the company's best efforts, its own elaborately protected area might soon, for reasons the company cannot hope to control, become a green island surrounded by unproductive semidesert.

12

THE LOGGING INDUSTRY
IN TROPICAL ASIA

MALCOLM GILLIS

In the mid-1980s tropical Asian countries contained only 23 percent of the world's productive, close-canopied rain forest but accounted for 83 percent of the volume of world exports of tropical hardwood products. Three Southeast Asian countries have dominated world trade in this market in the last quarter century: Indonesia, Malaysia, and the Philippines. In 1982 Malaysia and Indonesia each exported more tropical hardwood products than all Latin America and African countries combined. These large-scale logging activities have had a dramatic impact on the forests of these three Southeast Asian nations.

The natural forests of Indonesia, Malaysia, and the Philippines are dominated by the family Dipterocarpaceae, which contains ten genera and over 350 species of trees. Logs from the short-fiber trees in this family are valued for use in veneer and joinery. Such logs are called *lauan* in the Philippines and *meranti* in Indonesia and are known in the United States as Philippine mahogony. The richest and most homogenous stands of dipterocarps were originally found in the Philippines and in the East Malaysian state of Sabah on the northwest tip of the island of Borneo. Both Peninsular Malaysia and the Indonesian province of East Kalimantan on Borneo also contain extensive tracts of dipterocarp trees that even today allow commercial yields per hectare four to five times those of the rain forests of West Africa and Latin America, where concentrations of commercial species are much less dense than in Southeast Asia.

The early exploitation of the region's tropical moist forest, however, centered not on the dipterocarp family but on teak and such premium-quality decorative hardwoods as ebony.

As late as 1940, except in the Philippines, the natural forests in the region remained relatively untouched by logging activities; even in the Philippines large-scale logging was rare. Very large segments of the natural forests of Peninsular Malaysia, however, vanished a half-century ago; from 1910 to 1930 forest cover shrank from three-quarters to two-thirds of the total land area of Peninsular Malaysia primarily because of land clearing to accommodate rubber plantations. Neither logging nor land-clearing for plantations were significant in the East Malaysian states of Sabah or Sarawak before 1945. In Indonesia the Dutch colonial administration cleared very large tracts of forest for rubber plantations in Sumatra and for tea and teak plantations in Java. Virtually all of Indonesia's log exports arose from Dutch-owned teak plantations in Java. The great dipterocarp forests of Kalimantan, covering over four-fifths of the region's area, were largely unaffected by commercial activity of any kind.

The early years after the Second World War brought major changes in ownership of property rights to virgin forests, but few immediate changes in

Unmechanized logging in the peat swamps of Sarawak. Logs are pulled out of the swamps over greased rails.

Loading logs in Sabah. The use of heavy machinery ex- ▷ tracts a heavy toll in erosion and damage to the remaining timber and seedlings.

patterns of forest use. The constitutions of the newly independent Philippine and Indonesian nations vested all ownership rights in virgin forests in the central governments. The twelve states of West Malaysia and the East Malaysian states of Sabah and Sarawak formally gained title to all virgin forest resources within their boundaries only after independence was gained from Britain. The fact that natural forest lands in Malaysia are owned by the state governments, not the national government, has meant that each state has almost complete autonomy in matters relating to the use of the forest.

Large-scale logging in the region first emerged in the Philippines in the early 1950s. With the subsequent rapid depletion of the islands' virgin dipterocarp stands, logging activity shifted southward to Peninsular Malaysia, then to the previously inaccessible timber provinces of East Malaysia, and in 1967 to the newly opened forests of Kalimantan and Sumatra in Indonesia.

The combination of logging, an aggressive policy of forest clearing for plantation agriculture in Peninsular Malaysia, and shifting cultivation in the Philippines, East Malaysia, and Indonesia produced dramatic consequences. From 1950 through 1985 forest and woodland cover in Peninsular Malaysia shrank from 66 percent of land area to 48 percent. At recent rates of deforestation, the peninsula's productive forest resources will be all but exhausted before 1995. In the

East Malaysian state of Sabah, all the productive close-canopied forest had been committed to exploitation (but not totally cut) before 1985, while in nearby Sarawak much of the hill forest and virtually all the once-rich swamp forests have been under logging license. By 1982 the virgin dipterocarp forests of the Philippines had shrunk to less than one-third of what they had been in the 1940s; the remainder is to be logged by the mid-1990s. All timber demands will then have to be met from second-growth forests, themselves under unremitting pressure from shifting cultivators, known in the Philippines as *kaingineros*.

By 1985 Indonesia still contained the most valuable and one of the largest tropical forests in the world, constituting three-fifths of the productive forests of all of Southeast Asia. Even so, the total reduction in the nation's forest area between 1950 and 1985 has been estimated at some 39 million hectares (97.5 million acres), an area greater than the total land area of East and West Malaysia combined. As in the Philippines and Sabah, virtually all of Indonesia's productive forest had been committed to logging concessionaires before 1985.

The Wood-Products Industry in Southeast Asia
The role of logging in the postwar deforestation in the Philippines, Malaysia, and Indonesia is best understood in the context of the evolution of the wood

products industry in the region. Changes in the nationalities of logging firms and in policies governing forest use have given rise to demands on the natural forests that are entirely different than those prevailing as recently as two decades ago. The implications for the virgin forest are more ominous than ever.

The evolution of the wood-products industry has followed a strikingly similar development in all three nations, although the phases have become compressed as the industry moved southward from the Philippines. In the Philippines, the cycle began in the early 1950s, reached Peninsular Malaysia in the late 1950s, Sabah in the early 1960s, and Sarawak and Indonesia not until the late 1960s.

The process begins with a logging boom. In the Philippines this stage lasted nearly two decades but in Indonesia less than a decade. In this phase virtually all logging activity is carried out by multinational forest-product enterprises on concession areas as large as 250,000 hectares (620,000 acres). In the Philippines these were primarily American-based firms and in Malaysia principally British multinationals. The nationalities of logging firms were more diverse in Indonesia: there were large and medium-size American, British, Philippine, Korean, and Malaysian firms as well as smaller enterprises backed by capital from Japanese trading companies.

In the logging boom, the first phase of the cycle, the government, as owner of property rights to the natural forest and sovereign taxing power, typically receives not only low stumpage fees (royalties) for logs harvested but also offers generous incentives for foreign investment in logging, including income tax exemption for five to seven years.

In the second stage the government begins to curtail the availability of incentives for foreign investment in logging and at the same time undertakes active encouragement of domestic investment. Almost all timber concessions, as well as tax incentives, are awarded to domestic citizens.

The third and final stage of the process involves a gradual shift from the export of logs to an outright ban on the export of wood in log form. This is done to force much greater domestic processing of tropical hardwoods into sawtimber, molding, and plywood.

By 1987 the wood-products industry in the region bore little resemblance to that of the earlier logging booms. Aside from a few logging licenses near expiration in Sabah and Sarawak, virtually all logging concessions were in the hands of domestic firms in all three nations. Large multinational firms in the wood-products industry were either entirely absent, as in Indonesia since 1981, or limited to minority participation in timber-processing operations (the Philippines and Malaysia). Small firms from neighboring developing countries operating under contracts with domestic holders of concessions have displaced large American-based multinationals in logging.

The Philippines, the world's leading exporter of tropical hardwood products in the 1950s, had long since been surpassed both by Malaysia and Indonesia. By 1986 Peninsular Malaysia was the foremost source of sawtimber from tropical logs, Sabah the world's leading log exporter, and Indonesia the world's largest exporter of plywood.

The Role of Logging in Deforestation

In contrast to Latin America, cattle ranching has not yet become a significant source of deforestation in Southeast Asia; unlike tropical Africa, fuelwood gathering is not now a major cause of forest destruction in the region. Conversion of rain-forest land to plantations, a major reason for deforestation in Malaysia in decades past, has been slowed by the decreased demand for palm oil and rubber on the world market. What, then, has been primarily responsible for the receding of natural forests in the region in recent years?

Logging itself is often not the major source of deforestation in Southeast Asia, particularly within Malaysia and Indonesia. In Sarawak deforestation directly attributable to logging has been clearly less than that arising from shifting cultivation in the poverty-stricken rural areas of this state. It is likely that in the near future logging in Sarawak will lead to less direct deforestation than that which will occur as a result of such government projects as the large hydroelectric power complex that will soon flood vast areas of forest south of the provincial capital of Kuching. In Peninsular Malaysia it is certainly true that logging over the next few years will result in much less deforestation than the scheduled clearing, for security reasons, of a 900-square-kilometer (350 square miles) swath of land along the Penang-Kuta Baru road. In the Philippines fishponds have recently come to occupy 100,000 hectares (250,000 acres) of what were once mangrove forests. Finally, the Indonesian government's transmigration program has and will continue to be responsible for four to five times as much annual deforestation as that directly attributable to logging.

In any case, logging as currently practiced in the Philippines, Malaysia, and Indonesia rarely results in the complete clearing of the land. Although the Indonesian government allows clear-cutting, it is confined to very small tracts in Malaysia and has been relatively rare in the Philippines. Instead, virtually all logging is carried out under some variant of a selective cutting system in which loggers extract only desirable trees above a certain minimum diameter. In the past Malaysia has prescribed a uniform cutting system under which only desirable trees were removed and all others above a specified diameter were either cut or poisoned to provide growing space for saplings of some fast-growing species. Neither selective nor uniform cutting systems necessarily result in total deforestation, although selective systems usually result in serious degradation of the forest since high-quality timber is removed with little concern for its regeneration. As many as half the immature trees in the stands are damaged or destroyed in the process.

The most important source of deforestation in the region is shifting cultivation, although in Indonesia land clearing for the transmigration program has recently assumed an equivalent importance. But for all three countries the roles of both shifting cultivation and logging in deforestation must be cited together. It is the interaction of logging, rural poverty, and laws providing open access to the forest that result in the high rates of forest clearing by shifting cultivators. Skidding tracks and logging roads open up previously inaccessible forest. Thus, the fires of shifting cultivators merely administer the coup de grace to logged-over forest.

Shifting cultivation is thus not at the root of most deforestation in the region. Except in Peninsular Malaysia, rapid rates of shrinkage in the natural forests are the outcome of the pernicious combination of persistent rural poverty and government policies allowing excessive and needlessly destructive logging. While the role of rural poverty in deforestation is readily apparent, the part played by policies is much less so.

Government Policies and Deforestation

Both forestry and nonforestry policies have encouraged excessive rates of deforestation in the region, both by design and by accident. In all three nations policies governing logging and nonforestry government programs such as transmigration that affect forest use have maximized log and crop production from forest soils. All governments in the region have largely overlooked important nonwood products such as fruits, herbs, oils, nonwood fibers, chemicals, and meat that may be harvested by local people without removing trees.

The forest policy dilemma, then, is not simply that of resolving a clash between narrow economic values and broader, unquantifiable social values that flow from the protection provided by the forest to soils, watersheds, plant and animal species, and climate. The more immediate problem is resolving the conflict between single-minded pursuit of profits from wood and agricultural production on the one hand and, on the other, the maintenance of both nonwood-product industries and the protective services furnished by the natural forest. The conflict has been consistently resolved in favor of the former: the forest has been viewed predominantly as an asset to be liquidated for the available wood or for its limited agricultural potential.

Throughout the region, but in particular in the Philippines and Indonesia, the philosophy of government officials in agencies overseeing forest use has had profound effects upon forest conservation. In the Philippines and Indonesia the national governments equated rapid growth in harvests with more forest tax revenues and foreign exchange earnings. This prevailing outlook helps to explain the virtual absence of any effective reforestation policies and programs in these three nations and the setting of forest fees and taxes at levels well below the economic value of timber harvested.

Recently, however, other policies affecting forest use have emerged with implications for the rain forest that are no less portentous than the failed forestry policies of the past. The first of these has been the emphatic shift toward domestic processing of logs into sawtimber, plywood, molding, and chipboard. The second is the establishment of population resettlement programs ranging from relatively small ones, as in Sarawak and Sabah; to medium-size programs, as in the Philippines; to truly large resettlements as in Indonesia's transmigration program.

Proponents of the shift to domestic processing rather than export of logs sought much greater benefits to the domestic economy in the form of wages paid to employees in processing activity and profits received by local owners of sawmills and plymills. Because as much as one-half the weight of a tropical log is lost in processing, freight savings on exported processed products are considerable. In addition the conventional wisdom that domestic processing of tropical timber cannot fail to confer economic benefits upon countries with timber endowments is heard in ministries of industry throughout the region. While the catchphrase "a cubic meter of plywood fetches two and one-half times the price of a cubic meter of log exports" has sometimes been true in periods of high world demand for plywood, the statement is extremely misleading. It ignores the fact that as much as 2.3 cubic meters (1.8 cubic yards) of logs are required to make a cubic meter of plywood. Up to now forest-based industrialization policies have often resulted in sizable net costs to nations pursuing them.

Economic costs and benefits aside, these policies have ominous implications for deforestation. The Indonesian case furnishes a particularly telling example. Incentives for investment in log processing resulted in the construction of more than one hundred plywood mills between 1977 and 1986. By 1998 the natural forest is expected to provide 45 million cubic meters (176 million cubic feet) of logs or about three and one-half times the 1982 harvest. Log production at these levels will require logging 8 million new hectares (20 million acres) between 1988 and 1998, resulting in the creation of no more than 150,000 jobs. That is, each new job would require the use of resources contained on 53 hectares (133 acres) of forest.

Vigorous pursuit of such policies can yield new jobs but at some significant costs to forest resources. The sawmills and plywood mills that have been constructed in response to these policies also introduce a new element of inflexibility in policies governing log harvests. Prior to the shift to domestic log processing, harvests of logs fluctuated according to shifts in world markets; during periods of slack demand and low prices harvests were lower. Once a large number of new local processing facilities are in place, however, they have a claim on Indonesian (or Malaysian or Philippine) logs that no foreign mill could ever exercise. Domestic mills do not need to curtail or suspend operations in periods of slack world demand because they are indirectly but heavily subsidized by government policy. Moreover, they will be unable to reduce or suspend operations. Having fostered the creation of thousands of new industrial jobs in wood processing, governments may force the mills to continue production even at large losses rather than cope with the political problems that would arise from jobless workers. In Indonesia nearly 500,000 workers were employed in the forest-based sector in 1984, in Malaysia about 130,000. To safeguard these jobs, logs have and will continue to be harvested for these mills even in periods of depressed wood-product prices.

Benefits from Large-Scale Projects and Programs

It might be expected that over a quarter-century of large-scale forest use has generated considerable national benefits for the Philippines, Malaysia, and Indonesia. Such benefits include jobs in the wood-products industry, government tax revenues, and foreign exchange earnings from timber product exports. These benefits, however, have been secured at costs well in excess of those anticipated by the regional governments. Indeed, it is not at all clear that the benefits have been large enough to compensate citizens for the steady shrinkage in the economic value of their national forests and for the environmental and other social costs of forest destruction. These costs include silting of rivers, damage to watersheds, changes in climatic patterns, and even disastrous fires. They also include irreversible loss of nonwood forest products for the Dayaks of Indonesia, the Kenyah and Iban of Sarawak, and the nearly six million people belonging to Philippine cultural minorities in addition to losses in animal habitat and the decline of plant species diversity.

Further government incentives to promote forest-based industrialization have been costly not only in foregone tax revenues but also in foreign exchange earnings and resource misallocation. For example, in the early 1980s, the government of Indonesia gave up $2.20 in export taxes on logs for every additional dollar

An area of lowland species-rich Dipterocarp rain forest in the Kutai National Park of East Kalimantan, Indonesia. The photograph on the left was taken four years before the major drought and forest fire of 1983, the photograph on the right, four months after. It is estimated that the drought and fire killed approximately 50 percent of all canopy trees, 90 percent of woody climbers, and all seedlings and saplings.

of domestic value-added gained in plywood exports. This startling result was due to two factors. First, plywood exports are exempt from the 20 percent export tax that applies to logs. Second, the Indonesian mills, being heavily protected from competition, were less efficient than mills in Japan, Korea, or even Gabon, leading to more wastage of logs in plywood manufacture. For similar reasons, the government of Sabah sacrificed $1.78 in export taxes on logs for every additional dollar of value-added gained by exporting sawn wood rather than logs.

Also in Indonesia over one billion dollars of investments in plywood mills made possible by government incentives policies caused a net drain on the nation's resources amounting to $950 million. Partly because of the plywood glut created by government policies, plywood was exported at prices below costs of production. Under such policies, the sought-for benefits of domestic processing of timber are actually costs, exactly the opposite of the intention of the policy.

Southeast Asian governments do not have much to show from decades of imposing taxes on logging and processing. The governments collect stumpage fees on timber harvests in their capabilities as owners of the timber resources; they collect taxes on timber operations in their capacities as sovereign fiscal authorities. In the first capacity, governments in all three nations, with the exception of Sabah after 1978, sold

their resources too cheaply. In the second capacity, governments have foregone substantial amounts of tax revenue by providing early income-tax exemptions for logging firms and later by providing export tax incentives for domestic investors in the wood-processing industries.

Economists suggest that governments in this region, and in Africa as well, have collected less than half the feasible forest fees and taxes on forest-based operations. Governments have consistently sold timber resources too cheaply for the benefit of stockholders in large overseas timber enterprises, overseas consumers of hardwood products, and domestic investors in the wood-processing industries.

Conclusion

Southeast Asia has little to show for allowing decades of accelerating deforestation. The most prosperous of the three nations, Malaysia, had the most to show for the process by 1987. Eight decades of land-clearing for plantations in Peninsular Malaysia have left the country with a fairly diversified agricultural structure in which permanent tree crops such as rubber and palm oil have replaced the once-extensive natural forest. Indeed, Peninsular Malaysia may be far wealthier than East Malaysia, the Philippines, and Indonesia partly for this reason. And while Peninsular Malaysia has on occasion paid the price of floods and siltation arising from destruction of natural forests, the cover provided

by tree crops planted in cleared forest has at least prevented ecological catastrophe.

East Malaysia, still in a relatively early stage of forest exploitation, has gained less in the way of permanent assets, but Sabah at least has been more aggressive in collecting forest fees and taxes. In both Sabah and Sarawak logging opens up new areas to shifting cultivators each week, and Sabah, like Indonesia, has suffered catastrophic losses from fires in logged-over forest in 1983.

The Philippines has 40,500 hectares (100,000 acres) of fishponds as consolation for consumption of its most valuable forests, but not much else. The Philippines has been foremost among those governments who have sold their forests too cheaply.

Commercial activity in the Indonesian rain forest has left that country with very little benefit from two decades of extensive exploitation. Only between 1978 and 1982 did the government capture any significant tax benefits from logging. By 1983 Indonesia had found that its single-minded policies for promoting forest-based industrialization had brought the country little more than the dubious benefit of producing an excess of plywood in its numerous inefficient plymills. The controversial transmigration program has now become the chief threat to the future of the natural forest; its benefits to the nation have yet to materialize if in fact they ever arrive.

The record of national benefits from logging is therefore checkered at the very best. But the social and environmental costs of forest despoilation are becoming more apparent with each passing year. These include the familiar costs involved in erosion, siltation, damage to carrying capacity of watersheds, decline in species diversity among plants, loss of habitat for wildlife, and loss of wildlife species.

These risks from large-scale use of natural rain forests have been known, if not heeded, for years. Another risk has recently emerged unforeseen and unheralded, but with stunning impact: disastrous forest fires in East Kalimantan and Sabah between December 1982 and June 1983 consumed over 3.5 million hectares (8.8 million acres) of forest in Indonesia (an area the size of Taiwan) and perhaps half that in Sabah.

Fires set by shifting cultivators were the precipitating factors in the calamity, but shifting cultivation was not the underlying cause. Drought contributed to the fires, but reliable records on droughts in the moist forest area extend well back into the late 1800s with no contemporaneous history of disastrous fires. The underlying cause of the fires was commercial activity in the forest over the past two decades: selective logging predisposed the forest to disastrous fire damage. Before the onset of large-scale logging in East Kalimantan and Sabah, those fires that occurred burned at low temperature in the undergrowth because the forest in its natural state leaves little fuel on the ground for very long.

The fires raged in Indonesia and Sabah for four months over thirty-five thousand square kilometers (thirteen thousand square miles). The unlogged primary forest suffered only very light fire damage. The logged-over forest, in the words of one observer, "went up like a torch." Timber resources equivalent to four years of exports were destroyed along with tens of millions of dollars of renewable nonwood forest products vital to local residents. Populations of at least two species of hornbills and uncountable species of plants and insects native only to the burned sections of the forest were also decimated in these fires.

It remains to be seen whether the fires of 1983 portend future disasters on a similar scale. The pace of forest use in low-income Indonesia, East Malaysia, and the Philippines is not likely to slacken substantially since hundreds of locally owned processing mills now have a strong stake in continuing high rates of timber harvest. Until the forest is valued as much for its protective function and its nonwood products as for its timber and the agricultural potential of the land, the natural forests will remain a hostage to the poverty of the nations owning them. Until then, conservation of dwindling natural forest resources will depend critically upon whether wealthier countries recognize their stake in the process and upon their commitment to defray large proportions of conservation costs, particularly by subsidizing reforestation and through contributions to acquiring parks in the tropics. Grounds for optimism on both points are difficult to find.

Several people have helped to ignite and sustain my interests in tropical forest issues. They include Peter Ashton of Harvard, Robert Repetto of the World Resources Institute, and a vibrant group of Duke colleagues in Botany, Zoology, Forestry, and the Primate Center.

13

A QUESTION
OF SUSTAINABLE USE

PETER S. ASHTON

Those who heed the pessimistic forecasts of naturalists and conservation managers concerning the future of tropical rain forests and the astounding biological diversity that is contained in them should recall the ancient and brilliant civilization of Bali, a tiny, densely populated island where humans developed one of the happiest places on earth for themselves yet still preserved the rain forest. To be sure, overpopulation has in recent years led to deforestation, erosion, and pollution in Bali too, but does that mean that we practical, action-minded Westerners have nothing to learn from the gentle but very tough-minded Balinese? The problems we face are indeed mainly of our creation but if we can acquire the humility to learn from the Balinese and others who have triumphed in the tropics, we can solve our human problems and save the forests too.

The solution is to be found by pooling the resources of peoples with very different perceptions of nature and of their place in the universe: people like ourselves whose ancestors had to win a living from a capricious god of nature and who have applied their ingenuity to technological solutions; and people like the Balinese to whom nature was bountiful provided she was respected and cherished, and who therefore made a treaty, kept to it, and devoted their ingenuity to life and to art. Bring the two together and we shall succeed. But only if we regard each other as equals and share respect and humility. Can we do it? We have to.

Worldwide, the pattern of forest use changes in relation to the demands put on it. In agrarian economies of the tropics these demands have changed principally in accordance with increases in population density. This chapter describes the history of forestry in two Asian countries chosen on account of their contrasting population density. One, India, has been densely populated for centuries and remains overridingly an agricultural civilization. The other, Malaysia, was mainly settled along its coasts until this century and is even now densely populated only in restricted regions inland; but Malaysia has been experiencing rapid industrialization (particularly if the adjacent but politically independent island of Singapore is considered).

Both India and Malaysia experienced a period of European colonial domination, but both outgrew it. In both, the original inhabitants have now reinherited the land, but Western values, including inappropriate Western perceptions of the natural world, have left an indelible mark and dominate the minds of those who make government policy. The unfortunate consequences of these inappropriate perceptions, borne of an alien, cool, and unforgiving climate, are daily becoming more manifest.

Plantation of rubber trees on Langkawi Island, Malaysia.
Years of tapping for rubber-yielding latex have left
blackened scars on the lower trunks.

The arrival of colonial governments in the tropics signaled for many countries a dramatic increase in the exploitation of native forests. Tree camphor had been traded from the forests of Sumatra and Malaya to the Middle East and, ultimately, Europe since at least the twelfth century; scented eagle wood and sandalwood were likely traded from South Asia and the Far East just as early. But the impact of such exploitation appears to have been local and not destructive and at an altogether different scale from that which followed the establishment of government in the tropics by the agents of the European powers. Though European control of the forested hinterland occurred first in the neotropics, this control was exerted principally by settlers rather than by government, and the primary commercial interest was in minerals rather than forests. Greater documentation of the history of this control and its consequences for biological resources exists in the Old World tropics and particularly in Asia.

The history of forest use has differed from one continent to another. The economic potential and requirements for sustainable management of forests is highly specific to site, climate, soil, and available flora and fauna. But the history of use also has been determined in substantial part by the ownership of forested land. In Asia, with the exception of the Philippines, forests have generally been owned by the ruler or, in the colonial period, by the central government—a policy that has both advantages and disadvantages.

But differences in the history of human invasion and settlement and in the nature of the land and its biological resources have also been important.

India

The Indian subcontinent is without doubt the world center of human cultural diversity. The earliest Dravidian inhabitants still dominate the southern states. The north was colonized by Aryan invaders from South Central Asia some four thousand years ago. Their culture and religion are thought to have gradually absorbed the ancient animistic religions of the Dravidians to form Hinduism, the predominant religion of the citizens of the modern Republic of India.

When the first European traders arrived in the sixteenth century, India had for several centuries been experiencing invasions by Moslem armies from central Asia, Afghanistan, and Persia. Northern India, from Baluchistan to Bengal, had come firmly under the control of the Moguls, whose emperors were the first to consolidate the many existing cultures into a single political entity. Farther south, though, much of the country was still ruled by Hindu princes of an earlier order.

This history is important because the different traditions embody dramatically different attitudes to the natural world and continue to influence the fate of the forest.

The Hindus have inherited perceptions of a people

Seeds and seedlings of sal (*Shorea robusta*), one of India's most important commercially exploited species. (Drawing from R. S. Troup, *The Silviculture of Indian Trees,* vol. 1, 1921.)

who have lived since ancient times in a humid climate particularly favorable for forest life. Settled people, they see themselves as one with the natural world, as both custodians and dependents. The people of India continue to harvest an astonishing diversity of products from the forest. Forests of the mountains and watersheds have traditionally been sacred; springs and the natural landscape in their vicinity have attracted special veneration. The Hindus learned, from their predecessors millennia ago, a mythology, sociology, and technology of irrigation that has enabled the most intensive yet sustainable agriculture humanity has so far devised.

By the eighteenth century forest land use in India had become very diverse. Throughout the mainly Hindu and animist rain-forest regions of India there existed, and in a few places still exist, sacred groves of aboriginal forest usually owned by a temple, a member of the religious elite, or by rulers who traditionally have embodied religious values. Some forests were only a few acres, others covered a whole watershed. In such forests as the Devara Kadus of Coorg or some of the sacred tribal forests of the Garo and Khasi hills of Assam only products for the temple could be harvested; not so much as a twig was—and is even now—permitted to be removed by the villagers. The *kans,* or woodlands, which are typical of Sarab in the moist parts of western Mysore, were prototypes of a technique currently being promoted as a new approach to forestry: agroforestry. In a region dominated by deciduous forests that were annually burned, the *kans* stood out as belts, often miles long, of evergreen forest along the moist scarps of the western Ghat hills. Assiduously protected by the villagers, these once natural forests had been enriched by the inhabitants through interplanting of such useful crop species as jackfruits, sago and sugar palms, pepper vine, and even coffee, an exotic. Agroforestry is a new and unfamiliar technique, still resisted by foresters of Western training, but on a deeper level it represents a very different perception of the forest and our interdependence with it. The concerns of our time for productive yet sustainable management of forest lands and the solutions we now seek were already discussed and enacted in India over one century ago.

The early British colonial period in India witnessed increased devastation in the short term; the introduction of new approaches for forest administration; and new values, whose long-term effects are still with us and are a very mixed blessing.

By the mid-eighteenth century, Britain was overwhelmingly a timber-importing nation, satisfying her needs from her American colonies while her own forests were converted for sport and other recreation. The American Revolution caused major disruption in supplies, particularly for the navy, and the British

turned to India for such resources. *Gurjun (Dipterocarpus)* and other oils from the rain forests of India replaced pitch from the pitch pine, while teak replaced white pine and oak. Already in the great peninsular state of Hyderabad, the Nizam, a Muslim ruler over a largely Hindu population, was permitting his dependent chiefs to meet their tribute through overexploitation of the dry deciduous forests; deforestation had proceeded to such an extent that the mighty Godavari River, navigable for many miles inland since ancient times, had already become silted by the eighteenth century. His neighbor, Tippoo Sahib, Sultan of Mysore, claimed exploitation of timber from the moist and evergreen forests of his state as a royal privilege and arbitrarily commandeered it from private lands under his dominion.

Using Tippoo Sahib's precedent as an excuse, the agents of the East India Company extended the requisitioning of private timber in the southwest, incurring much ill will. When Ajmere-Merwara were ceded to Britain in 1850, the dry, less-valued forests taken over from the previous Hindu rulers and heretofore protected were turned over to the villagers as common land in a well-intended but misguided gesture of liberalism. By the time of the drought of 1867–68 the trees had been cut and sold for charcoal and the hills were denuded. Cattle perished and the villagers starved while next door, in the still-independent princely states under the suzerainty of the Maharajah of Udaipur, no

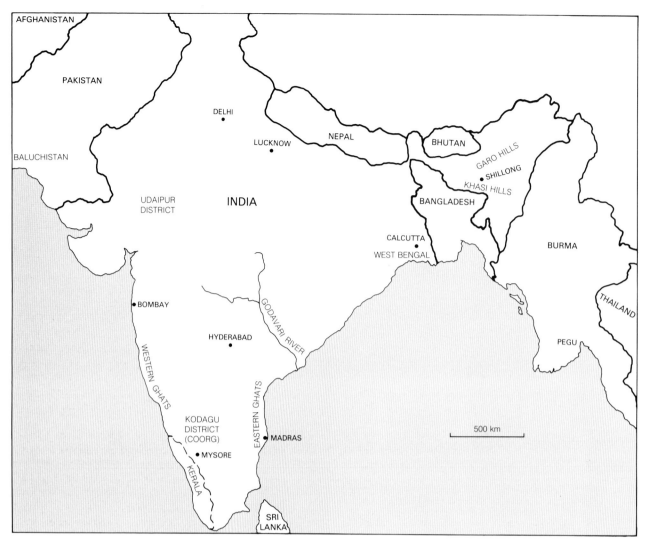

tree had been felled in the royal forests. The Thalar of Bednor, a feudatory of the Maharajah, had resisted the generous contracts offered by merchants in the adjacent British territory; he was able to provide hay and forage for his people to whom the great drought brought little suffering.

But by far the most profound and permanent impact brought by the introduction of Western culture was the onslaught, albeit unintentional, on the ancient Hindu perception of forests as belonging to God, with the ruler acting as the deity's custodian. No corps of secular foresters or police however dedicated can receive the respect and obedience due to the Maker.

Early in the nineteenth century a few courageous and farsighted individuals spoke out against the destruction. Sir Thomas Munro, governor of Madras, in 1822 stated of teak requisition that "the people now submit reluctantly to our monopoly, but we should recollect that no paltry profit in timber can compensate for the loss of goodwill." He placed the policy of timber requisition in abeyance but also failed to enact forest protection! By 1844 teak supplies had become so reduced that Mr. Conolly, an administrator in Malabar (now Kerala), negotiated the purchase of land for what was the first timber plantation in the tropical world. It is a reflection of the spirit of India that this remarkable initiative, which resulted in a magnificent stand of giant teak, has been recognized by its permanent protection as a national monument and preserve.

Above all, however, colonial policies were inconsistent, being at the whim of successive administrators and the political pressure brought to bear on them. Even the best were far less effective than the gentle and steady restraints of ancient and venerated custom. The situation was so serious that in 1850 the British Association for the Advancement of Science appointed a special committee to review the economic and physical consequences of deforestation in the tropics and particularly in India.

The recommendations made by this committee to the British government led to the establishment of the Indian Forest Service, whose proud tradition and unrivaled reputation continues to this day. The initiative was a difficult one for Britain to implement. Forestry did not exist as a profession in Britain. In the nineteenth and early twentieth centuries Britain, the wealthiest country in the world, imported her timber from Scandinavia and Germany where labor was cheaper and, of course, from India. Her forests were still principally used for sport and recreation. When the First World War cut off timber supplies, the British Forestry Commission was at last founded, sixty years later than in India. It can truly be said that British forestry was acquired from India.

The 1850s was an exciting time in the history of Indian forestry and wildlife management. In 1853 the Bombay Natural History Society was founded, "by some gentlemen interested in natural history, who propose to meet monthly, exhibit interesting speci-

Natives of Peninsular Malaysia during colonial times, extracting dammar, a particularly valuable forest product.

mens, and otherwise encourage one another." They immediately began publishing a journal, the contents of which, besides including an encouraging number of excellent studies, reflected the sensibilities of the time: "On conjugal infidelity among birds" (a note on the disgraceful conduct of a tame pigeon), and "Freak in a *Zinnia parviflora* exhibited by Mr. Frank Rose, Public Works Department." This society continues to lead the movement for wildlife conservation in India.

Germany was the home of scientific forestry, already well-established in the eighteenth century. During the nineteenth century, forestry in Germany and France, in contrast to Britain, had developed and intensified to meet the increasing domestic demands put on forests by industrialization and population expansion. In 1855 the government of India hired one of the outstanding German foresters of all time, Dietrich Brandis.

Lower Burma had just been ceded to British India, and the mighty teak forests of Pegu, until then a royal prerogative, came under government administration. Brandis repaired at once to the governor general with a plan to "protect and, as far as possible, to improve the forests; to arrange the cuttings so as to keep well within their productive powers, in order to ensure a permanent and sustained yield; to make the inhabitants of the forests and the people in the vicinity my friends and allies; . . . [and] as soon as possible to produce an annual revenue surplus." Brandis succeeded triumphantly in every respect, though it must be said that the population density of Pegu was low at that time. The forested hills of Pegu were cultivated by slash-and-burn methods, known there as *taungya*. Brandis arranged to have the farmers paid to interplant their crops with teak trees. Thus, the taungya system of agroforestry, in which annual food and timber crops are grown on the same land, was brought into existence and is now widely advocated in the tropics. With the aid of Brandis's working plan for the forest, implemented well before any working plan for any forest in England or North America, the teak forests of Pegu continued to increase in yield and profitability into recent times.

Brandis was appointed first Inspector-General of Forests for India. He set at once to drawing up a system of forest law appropriate to India for that time, and in 1868 the Indian Forest Service was inaugurated. In the early years Brandis hired further German foresters. One of these, William Schlich, later founded the first forestry school in a British university. His classic *Manual of Forestry,* published between 1889–98, laid the groundwork for forestry both in Britain and in the empire. Brandis consistently urged that "ultimately it is hoped, that a large proportion of native forest officers for the higher appointments may be available." Through his efforts, by 1878 the Forest School (later

The temple at the sacred forest of Sanggi, Bali, Indonesia. This relict of the primeval forest has been preserved for centuries and is surrounded by irrigated rice lands.

Indian swiddeners illegally farming within a forest reserve. A cash crop of cannabis has been planted between the rice.

the Indian Forest College) was established, although many decades passed before Indians filled a significant number of senior appointments.

It is fascinating to look back after more than a century at Brandis's priorities. He emphasized that as the population grows, so the needs of the home market for forest products must increasingly take precedence over the forest export industry. He recognized that forest conservation rests ultimately with the will of neighboring villagers, who view forests not as stands of timber but as sources of various goods and services, including litter for fuel, honey, fruit, drugs, forage, and in dry regions, hay. The question of whether the villagers collected forest products by right or as a privilege was central to the forest plan. The tradition of the princely states was that it was given by the rulers as a privilege, so this permission could be taken away. This principle that permission for grazing, for example, could be temporarily withheld was recognized by Brandis as essential for forest management.

> There has been much thoughtless talk, as if the natives of India, in burning the forests and destroying them by their erratic clearings, were committing some grave offence. If the matter is carefully analyzed, they will be found to have the same sort of prescription, which justifies the Commoner in the New Forest (in England) to exercise his right of pasture, mast and turbary. Such rights, when the public benefit requires it, must be extinguished; but the wild tribes of India have the

same claim as the holder of prescriptive forest rights in Europe, to demand that provision be made for their reasonable wants and requirements.

Brandis emphasized the multiple values of forests. He promoted hay cutting in forest reserves and stall feeding of cattle rather than grazing and browsing, which destroyed regeneration and reduced the soil's capacity to store water. He was able to see the benefits of this policy when, in the great drought of 1896, cattle were allowed into the protected forests following ancient tradition in famine years, bringing vital relief to the populace without lasting detriment to the forests. He promoted the management of particular forests for tannin, India rubber (*Ficus*), and for charcoal. But he also recognized that the harvesting of forest produce by villagers for commercial gain, as distinct from domestic need, was neither a privilege nor a right and subject to the licensing laws of the land. The breakdown of enforcement of this principle is perhaps the single greatest cause of deforestation in India today.

Brandis wrote at length on the merits of managing forests to maintain tree species in mixture, giving examples of disastrous epidemics of disease and insect pests that had ensued in European forests where this principle had been ignored. He was not only responsible for the enactment of the first forest legal code but also in 1906 completed the first popular manual of Indian trees, which includes all indigenous species then

In many areas of India, as well as in other tropical regions, firewood and other nontimber forest products have great commercial value and their sale is important to rural villagers. A woman in central India carries firewood to market.

known as well as commonly cultivated exotics, and all shrubs, vines, bamboos, and palms. The book remains a classic to this day. He also wrote the first monograph on the Dipterocarpaceae, preeminent hardwood family of the Asian tropics.

It is extraordinary to discover that the principles advocated today for the management and conservation of tropical forests were already recognized and promoted in the nineteenth century. It is extraordinary, too, and disheartening that Brandis faced many problems, which today are still unresolved. Between 1881 and 1891 India's population, already high, increased by 2 million each year to 218 million. Already, 1 million square kilometers (390,000 square miles) of wastelands existed. Brandis promoted tree plantations on these wastelands to take pressure off the protected forests, but this suggestion was often difficult to enact due to complex customary land tenure laws that prevailed. Nevertheless, by the time Brandis retired, a forest policy had been established and written into the law and protected state forests had been constituted, often through liberal compensation of hereditary landlords. Most of what has followed has been due to the exertions of Brandis, one man who seized the extraordinary opportunities of a remarkable moment in Indian history.

Teak (*Tectona grandis*) and sal (*Shorea robusta*) are the two leading tropical hardwoods of India, and both occur over a wide range of seasonal climates. They were subjected to exhaustive, nationwide research aimed at managing natural stands for maximum timber production on a sustained basis. Both trees occur as single species stands in nature, and methods to encourage this tendency were sought. In so doing, much was learned of the ecology of these species, and of the importance of fire and cattle browsing in the regeneration of tropical forests of seasonal climates. Successful prescriptions were eventually devised for both species and for most of the diverse site conditions under which they occurred. But, as Brandis had predicted, pest and disease problems were intensified by this quest for monoculture. The fungus *Polyporus shoreae* increasingly attacked the roots of sal, the beetle *Hoplocerambyx spinicornis* the trunk.

The low priority accorded to forest products important to the village economy was revealed by their official designation, "minor forest products." It was implied that community forests would provide such resources, leaving the state forests for state and national timber needs. But community forests were not adequately managed and suffered the "tragedy of the commons" of medieval rangeland, which became degraded in the absence of anyone personally responsible for them. Villagers whose nearby forests were protected for timber production felt betrayed when the plants that provided their forest resources disappeared un-

An officer of the Forest Department in colonial Malaya surveys the effects of the invasion of *Eugeissona tristis,* an undesirable palm, in the forest.

der management practices that favored timber species. Matters were made worse following independence: the princely states were dissolved and forests that were once protected by traditional fiat came under a government administration pressured by its citizens to allow greater access to resources hitherto unavailable to them. Even now, the reserved forests all over India shrink in area as the understory and the tree seedlings are browsed by cattle, cleared for cultivation of shade-loving cardamom, or cut for fuel.

Rain forests were not extensive in India (even as it was formerly defined) being confined to the southwest and northeast, and in coastal and northern regions of Burma. In fact, attention was concentrated on a very small number of species, in particular the faster growing dipterocarps of the genera *Dipterocarpus* (in the northeast) and *Hopea* (in the south) and some other genera of tall-growing, early colonizers of openings and light hardwoods. The extensive montane forests were abandoned for timber production and increasingly converted to plantations.

Thus, the failure to reconcile commercial and community demands on forest resources and, in some cases, to devise appropriate management practices opened the way to increased abuse of the natural forest resource, adding to intense pressure from the burgeoning rural population. In spite of all this, it must never be forgotten that India to this day possesses a forest service second to none in the tropical world, with well-trained staff of great dedication. And it is truly extraordinary how many forests and nature preserves still persist, encroached on but, in many instances, still with extensive well-managed tracts.

The solution that India has increasingly sought to these problems has been the planting of fast-growing exotic species. Eucalypts, and, in the drier regions, mesquite (*Prosopis*) had been introduced long ago. Following the Second World War, eucalypts in particular have been planted on a grand scale in the tropical regions at all altitudes. Forests of eucalypts have largely replaced the southern montane rain forests. As exotics they have been relatively free of disease; as sources of timber they have exceeded expectations when well managed. But eucalypts have met increasing resistance from rural communities and have become the symbol of increasing hostility between villagers and the forest service. This should not have been difficult to foresee. The arrival of the inedible eucalypts has signified the final demise of such forest goods as oil fruits, forage, and hay, which are so essential to the villager. High wood production requires the transpiration of much soil water, and eucalypts have adversely affected irrigation and well water. In the mountains, unlike the moss-laden trees of the old montane-evergreen forests, the geometry of eucalyptus crowns has proven inefficient at raking precipitation from passing clouds.

Since water condensation onto foliage had been a major contributor to annual precipitation in the headwaters of many of India's rivers, water has become a limited resource. Inadvertently the governmental decision-making process has transferred care of an essential commodity—water—from agriculture and the villager to forestry and the government. The decision will now have to be reconsidered openly in the political forum.

Now, at last, the urgency of the villagers' needs is fully recognized. These needs are being met through the introduction of fast-growing nitrifying exotics, which can be regenerated without soil disturbance through stump shoots. Such trees as *Leucaena* and *Glyricidia* can be harvested on a short rotation, provide fuelwood and forage, and at the same time enrich the soil with nitrogen and lessen the danger of erosion. These plants do provide the optimal solution for restoration of the wastelands, which now cover 5,700,000 square kilometers (2,200,000 square miles) in India, and should alleviate the pressure on the residual native forests. Can it really be said that they can represent a restoration of the quality of life that the aboriginal forests provided? Is it prudent to assume that no adventurous bug will invade or evolve to become the primary, if transitory, beneficiary? In fact, an insect is already wiping out *Leucaena* plantations in Melanesia and the Philippines and is currently spreading west through Indonesia.

One imaginative program for diversification of tree crops at village levels is being sponsored in the poor, infertile province of Bihar by the Tata Rural Development Society. Here, beside multipurpose fuel and forage crops, trees are grown for tussore silk weaving, for honey, *bidi* (a native tobacco), and fruit under the auspices village enterprises. Still lacking, though, are effective channels for implementing results of the outstanding research on strengthening the rural economy, which has been conducted by many distinguished Indian institutions. The Botanical Survey is a particularly telling example of good research that is underutilized. The Botanical Gardens in Calcutta were founded in 1775 as a station for the introduction of and experimentation with new crops. The survey of the Indian flora proceeded rapidly: the first technical account of the Indian flora was published there in 1822–26, and by the 1870s a more comprehensive version appeared, which is still in use today. Currently, the Botanical Survey of India conducts a major program for the identification and, where possible, conservation of rare and endangered species. The National Botanical Research Institute and the Central Institute of Medicinal and Aromatic Plants at Lucknow are active in research into indigenous flora with economic promise. But are these promising new plants coming into village cultivation? To what extent is international exchange of useful genetic varieties, which was the spark that lit colonial agriculture, being fostered by such institutes? And with whom can India exchange such material? Until the potential of the native flora to yield new crops is recognized, the diverse resources of the remaining native forests will increasingly be exploited beyond their capacity to sustain themselves.

Peninsular Malaysia
The history of forestry in Peninsular Malaysia over the last century tells a very different story. Although the population, starting from small beginnings, continues to increase at 2.8 percent and the Malaysian government is unique in the developing world because it, almost unbelievably, has an official policy of promoting large families, the national total is still only 14.4 million or 1.12 people per hectare (2.7 per acre), of which fully 11.1 million, or 2.19 per hectare (5.4 per acre) are confined to the peninsula. India, for comparison, has an average of 5.59 people per hectare (13.8 per acre). In this important respect Peninsular Malaysia gives insight to what, in certain respects, must have happened in the early history of India. The lowland climate typical of all Malaysia is unknown in India. In Malaysia, on average, there is more rainfall than expected evaporation every month of the year. Occasional droughts do occur, though, at unpredictable intervals.

Malaysia is not, by internationally accepted standards, any longer a developing country but rather a middle-income nation. Those who bemoan the felling of the Amazonian forests should realize that Peninsular Malaysia's remarkable history of successful development and high standard of living has been overwhelmingly due to the wise management of her generally poor soils, which are no better than those prevailing in the Amazon basin. This has entailed converting the original rain forest to highly profitable artificial forests of exotic commodity crop plants: first coffee, then rubber, and later oil palm.

Until the colonial period the sparse population of the peninsula (then known as Malaya) was concentrated along the coasts, and the economy was based on harvesting the wealth coming down the unruly and turbid rivers. The politically dominant coastal Malays traded jungle produce with scattered inland tribes. Clay and silt brought down by the river was deposited in great alluvial fans supporting mangrove swamps, the spawning ground of a bountiful inshore fishery. Except in the immediate vicinity of the rivers where they reached the lowlands, most of the forest almost certainly had never been cultivated.

By the nineteenth century alluvium of some rivers in the western peninsular states of Perak and Selangor had been found to contain tin, and inland settlements of Chinese tin panners sprang up. The modern capital, appropriately named Kuala Lumpur, which means "mouth of the muddy river," started as one such settlement.

The British, first of the western colonial powers to gain influence in the hinterland of the peninsula, early set about investigating the potential of the indigenous forest resources in international trade and as plantation crops. The botanical garden at their trading center of Singapore was established in 1875 to investigate promising native species and to introduce exotics for trial. In fact, until early this century agriculture and forestry came under the director of the botanical garden. A Forest Department was established under the superintendent of the garden in 1883.

The first indigenous forests reserved for sustained timber production were established as early as 1888 in the heavily agricultural state of Malacca and on the island of Penang. Forests adjacent to villages were lightly harvested for their scattered, naturally durable heavy hardwoods for boat and house building. Inland tribes explored farther afield for game, medicinals, and the equally scattered jelutong (*Dyera*) and gutta-percha (*Palaquium*) latex-bearing trees. Jelutong was a source of chewing gum, while gutta-percha was the preferred source of rubber before *Hevea* was introduced and still has specialized uses on account of its extraordinary elasticity. In the nineteenth century gutta-percha was important in the Malayan export economy.

In 1877 the *Hevea* rubber tree was introduced from Brazil, free from its natural pests and thus amenable to cultivation in single-species plantations. At that time coffee and coconut were the principal commodities grown on plantations, both on a small scale. Although rubber did not become a significant crop until the early twentieth century, the event was to be of cardinal importance in the future of Malaysian forests.

H. N. Ridley, director of the botanical garden while at the same time responsible for agriculture and forestry, was instrumental in the development of both. He became the father of the Asian rubber industry through his policies and innovative research, as well as the father of forest conservation in Malaya. When the autonomous government departments of forestry and agriculture were eventually established, the rubber plantations became the responsibility of agriculture. Thus was instituted a divisive rivalry over land development, which exists to this day. Forestry has never won, though Ridley's reserves still exist.

It was difficult to establish seedlings of the durable hardwoods and gutta-percha trees, both of which are slow growing and shade loving. A successful plantation of gutta-percha was, however, established. In 1900 a senior member of the Indian Forest Service, H. C. Hill, was sent to Malaya to advise on both forest administration and the management of the rain forests for sustainable production of timber. He noticed two important differences between these Malayan forests, which experience virtually no seasons, and the seasonal rain forests of India. The first was that Malayan forests, unlike their lowland tropical Indian counterparts, were well stocked with seedlings and saplings. Reproduction of logged trees could thus be assured if these seedlings were given sufficient space to grow by thinning the small trees and undergrowth. The second difference was that the trees of commercial value were widely scattered among many hundreds of others of unknown value. There are, in fact, sixteen hundred native tree species in Peninsular Malaysia whose trunks exceed twelve inches in diamèter at maturity, and perhaps twenty-five hundred additional, smaller species. The peninsula is one-hundredth the area of the United States, which contains less than one-tenth that number of tree species. Compared even with the seasonal tropics, this number is astounding. In contrast, Brandis recognized only twenty-four hundred tree species of all sizes in the whole seasonal region to the north of the peninsula in Asia, including Pakistan, India, Burma, and Bangladesh.

By 1915 expansion of tin mining and establishment of rubber plantations fueled rapid colonization of the hinterland. Cities like Kuala Lumpur and Ipoh created a demand for firewood, which could be conveniently met by the commercial sale of the small noncommercial trees cut to reduce competition with the hardwood seedlings. Until that time this practice had not been economically practical. By the 1920s the fuelwood thinnings were proving more profitable than the hardwoods themselves.

This process early demonstrated both the benefit and a flaw in management of rain forests for commercial production. High species diversity gives flexibility in the ways in which the forests can be exploited to meet changing demands. The flaw is that changes in demand are unpredictable and take place more quickly than the time it takes to grow a forest tree.

From the 1920s more intensive research into the regeneration of managed natural rain forests was carried out in Malaya than anywhere else in the tropics. By the 1930s mechanization became commonplace. Tractors started replacing bullock-drawn sleds in the forests, while the hand-operated sawpits rapidly gave way to sawmills. At about the same time timber preservatives, derived from the growing petroleum industry and impregnated under pressure, came onto the market. Cheap kerosene, however, had by then largely replaced the demand for fuelwood. Forest researchers introduced inexpensive techniques for girdling and poisoning unwanted trees in regenerating stands. Together, these innovations stimulated more intensive forest exploitation and the beginnings of an export industry. Eventually, research defined uses for the timber of 80 percent of the species reaching merchantable size in the forests of Malaya. Once again, the market had taken a fundamental turn.

Once again though, the change in market was a blessing to forest management. With the introduction of preservatives, a market was found for the light hardwoods of the dipterocarp family—the red *lauans,* Philippine mahoganies, or *merantis.* Unlike the shade-tolerant hardwoods, these species regenerate well in the large openings that mechanized logging causes. Following World War II, foresters found to their pleasant surprise that forests, which had been illegally logged during the war, were well stocked with seedlings of the light hardwoods, which were then favored.

Meanwhile, a half century of experience in the field, strengthened by three decades of careful research, led to the now classical method of managing rain forest for timber known as the Malayan Uniform System, formulated in 1949. This method maximizes the harvest of timber-sized trees. It takes advantage of the fact that plentiful seedlings persist on the ground in the understory. The growth of these seedlings is encouraged by poisoning trees remaining after logging. These established seedlings then grow into an even-aged stand of the most favored species.

Were it not for the vicissitudes of the Second World War and the ensuing civil war (1948–59), this period would have marked the heyday of Malayan forestry. Instead, much of the forest remained inaccessible throughout this period, and the successful methods developed by some forty years of research and experience only brought results on a limited scale. Unfortunately, the Forest Department did not successfully incorporate these procedures and plans for a permanent forest estate based on management of natural rain forests into an official national forest policy. According to Malayan law land was technically under the jurisdiction of the governments of the eleven princely states and former colonies; these provincial governments tenaciously resisted attempts to restrict their freedom of action. Nor were the powerful agricultural interests in central government distinguished by their support for enactment of a national policy.

Malaya became independent, as part of Malaysia, in 1957. The major priority of the new government was to provide work for the landless, a policy that continues to the present day. It was realized that industrialization would not provide a solution to unemployment for many years to come. To provide employment in the interim, the entire lowland forest (except for some national parks and nature preserves) was designated for conversion to commodity plantations, mainly oil palm and rubber, before the end of this century. The forests, before conversion, were hurriedly logged for the most profitable timber. In addition to small areas of mangrove, peat swamp forest and plantation, the forest estate is now reduced to the high-

lands and steep lands of the interior, for which an effective management system has not yet been devised. At the same time use of heavy machinery, inadequate supervision of workers, and steep terrain now play havoc with the established seedlings upon which natural methods of regeneration must depend.

Those of us who are concerned about the future of tropical forests may decry this most recent change in market conditions, which has been disastrous for the old rain-forest resource. But it must also be recognized that the conversion of rain forests to commodity tree crops has allowed Malaysia to become a middle-income nation, bringing unprecedented prosperity to her people and capital for rapid industrialization. Further, the Malayan Uniform System would not have conserved the original biological diversity of the forest. Zoologists have found that the abundant fruits of many strangling fig attract birds and primates from great distances. The fig crops may even determine the number of animals that a forest can support because they provide a food source during long periods when few other species are in fruit. These great strangling figs, on which so many species of wildlife depend, are unfortunately anathema to foresters, because they grow in the crowns of timber trees and eventually strangle their hosts. Vines, too, have often been poisoned and cut out of such managed natural forest because they impede the growth and distort the form of the timber trees. Slow-growing tree species, of which there are many, would also have been eliminated by the Malayan Uniform System because they failed to reproduce within the length of a felling cycle.

If the ameliorative effects of forests on climate and soils are the sole concern, then a well-managed rubber or oil palm estate is not substantially inferior to a natural forest. Its canopy, like that of a rain forest, will remain cool during the day as it evaporates almost as much water as a lake. Its leaves will fix carbon from the atmosphere, which will be converted to wood, latex, or oil. If the central concern is a social one, biological versatility should be maintained in Malaysia and throughout the tropics. The forester and the tree agriculturalist can then continue to respond to changing market trends as they have in the past.

Malaysia is currently experiencing the next major market change in tree crops, which may be the most radical to date. The response, so far, has been at best confused and at worst a misguided expectation that the change is only temporary. All over the humid, tropical world, massive schemes are underway to clear forests for the same commodity crops in which Malaysia has excelled. Malaysia was the first to succeed on the grand scale and has reaped the rewards. But now estate wages in Peninsular Malaysia are up to five times those in Sumatra, only fifty miles to the west across the Straits of Malacca. Capital is moving out of the Malaysian plantation industry in favor of the Indonesian. Increasingly Malaysian smallholders are giving up and moving to the towns. Illegal immigrant labor is being employed on Malaysian plantations. This has happened during an unprecedented slump in commodity prices, which recently caused the first year in which the rate of growth of the Malaysian economy has declined during the postwar period.

There is every indication that relatively low commodity prices will persist. Over the next thirty years, the population of the industrialized consumer nations will not increase much more than 10 percent, whereas that of the producers will double. Where will the market be for the products of all this new labor? The most promising opportunities for market expansion are undoubtedly within the tropical regions, but such expansion will depend on maintaining the hard-won improvements in the standard of living gained to date. Lower transportation costs and greater familiarity of consumers with products within the regions provide enormous opportunities for crop diversification. These new crops will come from innovative research in which modern technology is applied to traditional crops and from the promising species surviving in natural rain forests.

Conservation of the genetic diversity in carefully selected and representative natural forest preserves must be an integral part of future land development. In fact, Peninsular Malaysia has already gone some way toward conserving the lowland forest—by far the richest in species of all ecosystems—although it is still inadequately represented in preserves. Government agencies, urged on by an increasingly informed and articulate public, are creating new preserves and strengthening legislation protecting the old with active assistance from the biological community.

The relative cost of pesticides will increase once the fossil fuels from which they are synthesized become scarce and as poor soils, whose low productivity can only be profitable if maintenance costs are kept low, are brought into plantation. Evidence is growing that populations of contagious diseases and pests can be better controlled in diverse mixtures of tree species than in monocultures. The application of this principle to the scientific design of plantations has yet to begin, although its utility has been proven by the ancient practice of mixed species home gardens and orchards. The final twist in this Malaysian tale is that a relatively low population, combined with a well-managed economy, has kept illegal public incursion into natural forests at a low level. In fact, public demand for goods and services originating from the natural forest should now be stimulated, so that in the future demand for nontimber products, water, soil conservation, and recreation rather than for timber will determine management policy.

I have chosen as examples two tropical countries whose track record for forest management, though far from perfect, are clearly among the best in the developing world. In India, the diverse traditional uses of the forest, though assailed, remained an important and recognized part of the forest economy, while the timber industry, which grew in response to international demand early in the colonial period, subsequently became dominated by the national market. In Malaysia, successful economic development, in which forestry contributed, was export-based and traditional uses of the forest became subordinate. But in recent years the home timber market has grown in importance as the population and prosperity have increased there. In both cases, it was difficult to justify maintenance of natural forest for timber production alone, but the importance of this resource in the long-term development of the rural economy has become increasingly apparent. Even with excellent management, it is difficult to develop a viable land-use policy that conserves the biological diversity of tropical forests. But our success in doing so will determine the quality of life in the tropics. Success is certainly possible.

This essay owes much to the inspiration and writings of Sir Dietrich Brandis, founder of the Indian Forest Service, and John Wyatt-Smith, to whom we owe the final definition of the Malayan Uniform System, which remains the only proven successful method of managing tropical rain forest for timber production through natural regeneration.

14

PERSPECTIVE
ON CONSERVATION
IN INDONESIA

SETIJATI SASTRAPRADJA

Southeast Asia is a large and diverse region. It comprises the area lying between India to the west and the Pacific Islands to the east, China to the north and Australia to the south. It covers countries situated on the Asian mainland, such as Thailand, Peninsular Malaysia, and Vietnam, as well as countries that have national territories composed of many islands and miles of ocean. The insular countries include Indonesia, the Philippines, and Papua New Guinea.

The natural resources of the region, and in particular its tropical forest resources, have attracted world attention. Many animal species are endemic to insular Southeast Asia, that is, they occur nowhere else on earth, and the same holds true for plants found in the area. The tropical forests of the region are home to many plant and animal species of commercial importance, and forests have played and continue to play a central role in the development of this region.

Like the rest of tropical Asia, the Southeast Asian countries are, in general, densely populated, and it is expected that within the next thirty years the population of the area will double. Governments have found it hard to meet the needs of the ever-growing population. Rapid national development and in particular economic development have been largely based on the exploitation of natural resources, which is one of the quickest ways to earn the foreign exchange needed to support development. Natural resource exploitation, however, has not always been based on sound scientific data and planning. The impact of such exploitation on the environment and the resulting degradation of forest resources have aroused the concern of conservationists.

Opinions on how to use forest resources wisely as well as how to plan and implement their conservation have been discussed at many national, regional, and international meetings. Actions that would put these ideas into practice, particularly at the national level, have not been pursued as vigorously and successfully as they should be. No matter how excellent the discussions and formulations have been, without national implementation they are condemned to remain only interesting academic topics.

Keeping these regionwide problems in mind, I shall focus most of my discussion on the nation of Indonesia. It has the largest population in Southeast Asia, and it includes within its borders the largest area of tropical humid forest in the region. How Indonesia uses its resources, including its human resources, will have a significant effect on the future of the Southeast Asian rain forest.

◁ In Indonesian tradition, a banyan tree is considered sacred and is never cut down. Although the observance of such traditional beliefs often wanes with modernization, they can play a role in modern conservation education.

Where soils and climate are favorable for agriculture, Southeast Asians have used every piece of land available. These terraced fields in central Java, Indonesia, support some of the world's highest human densities in rural areas.

Human Resources

The most important asset of any country is its human resources. However, this asset may turn into a burden if the number of people is excessive and their levels of education and training are low. The countries of Southeast Asia, together with the part of India that lies within the humid tropics, make up a mere 5 percent of the world's dry land. Yet not less than a quarter of the earth's total population inhabits this region. Even when India is excluded, 15 percent of the earth's total population lives in Southeast Asia.

Family-planning programs designed to control population growth are in operation all over Southeast Asia, and even though some results have been encouraging, the growth rate is still relatively high. Where the present rate of approximately 2 to 3 percent annual growth is not checked, in twenty years populations will increase by 60 percent or so. With such growth rates, Indonesia will in the year 2000 have a population of 210 million, Malaysia 21 million, the Philippines 76 million, Papua New Guinea 5 million, and Thailand 60 million, giving a regional total of 372 million. By contrast, in 1980 the total population of all these countries was 265 million.

The continuing growth of these populations is largely due to reduced infant and child mortality; unfortunately, reductions in the birthrate have not kept pace. The desire to have many children still prevails among Southeast Asian families, especially those with low incomes. The population of the region includes many young people, which gives great momentum to further growth. Thus family-planning programs still have a long way to go.

Not only the size but also the distribution of the population is important when considering conservation issues. In contrast to many other parts of the world, few Southeast Asians live in cities: roughly 80 percent are rural. While the majority of these people are agriculturists, this figure also includes members of traditional tribal groups who live at very low densities gathering, hunting, and fishing deep within forests.

The insular region of Southeast Asia has particularly skewed population distribution. Indonesia, for example, comprises 13,677 islands. Of the five major islands of Indonesia, Java is the smallest in size, yet 70 percent of the country's 170 million people are crowded onto this one island.

Problems and priorities arise not only from numbers of people, however, but also from their quality of life. Education has been given a high priority in such countries as Indonesia, but major problems still remain. The average level of education varies from country to country and also within each country. The problems of education are very complex, involving not only the need for schools and educational materials but also the difficulty of finding adequately trained instructors at all levels. Illiteracy is still a problem in every one of Southeast Asia's countries, although to differing degrees, and there continue to be great differences in literacy rates between rural and urban areas. In Indonesia, for instance, the literacy levels achieved are still far from the desired national goals.

The ultimate goal of national development is, of course, to raise the quality of life of the people. An Index of Quality of Life is sometimes used to measure just how far the living conditions fall short of a theoretical ideal in any country or region. This index is based on three measures: early death rate, life expectancy at the age of one, and the level of literacy. The highest possible score is 100 points, out of which the developed countries have reached an average of 90. Jakarta, Indonesia's capital city, scores 72 points, but in rural areas the quality of life is assessed at a much lower 53 points.

Although literacy is included in the quality of life index, it does not adequately indicate shortcomings in the general level of education. In today's world an understanding of science and technology is necessary, and this requires a certain level of education. Low educational levels also make it very difficult to convey the importance of environmental conservation to the general public.

Forest Resources

Most of the natural forests of Southeast Asia can be classified as tropical rain forests. There is, however, considerable variation in species composition, density, tree height, biomass, and other variables as one moves from the lowland to the subalpine forests. Many Southeast Asian rain forests are characterized by tall buttressed trees that form a closed canopy high above the shaded forest floor. The branches of these trees usually hold a great mass of woody lianas and epiphytic plants. The total area of this kind of forest in Indonesia is 90.6 million hectares (226.5 million acres), while Malaysia has 21 million hectares (57.5 million acres), and Thailand and the Philippines have 10 million hectares (25 million acres) each.

The rain forests of the Southeast Asian lowlands are especially diverse biologically. An inventory of a forest plot measuring 45 hectares (112.5 acres) in Brunei on the island of Borneo found a total of 760 plant species. And on only 1 hectare (2.5 acres) on the island of Sumatra, 60 plant species were found. In Peninsular Malaysia alone one can find no fewer than 75,000 species of seed plants (a category that excludes ferns, mushrooms, fungi and other plants), of which 4,100 are woody.

Many plants of Southeast Asian rain forests are particularly showy or unusual in appearance or habits. Lianas are among the most characteristic features of these forests; in Southeast Asia among the most in-

Among Southeast Asia's greatest natural treasures is the orangutan, a forest-dwelling great ape and one of man's closest relatives. Its continued existence in the wild is threatened by rapid deforestation.

teresting lianas are pitcher plants, strangler figs, and passionflowers. One gigantic liana belonging to the legume family grows up to 150 meters in length and has individual pods that measure a meter long.

Orchids grow both perched up in trees and on the ground. There are no fewer than five thousand species of them in insular Southeast Asia alone; in fact, the botanical family of orchids, Orchidaceae, includes more species than any other botanical family in the region. Many of them are of considerable economic importance, especially the *Dendrobiums* and *Vandas*.

Apart from orchids, Southeast Asia has more than its share of unusual flowers and inflorescences. The giant *Rafflesia,* which is found in the forests of Bengkulu, Sumatra, and Kalimantan, has the largest flower found anywhere in the world. The petals are very showy and grow to a meter in diameter. Attempts to cultivate this gigantic parasitic plant have, thus far, been unsuccessful. Another spectacular species, the giant arum (*Amophophallus titanum*) thrives in the forests of Sumatra as well. The single inflorescence of this unusual plant is up to a meter and a half long. Its distinctive smell reminiscent of rotting meat attracts the insects that pollinate it.

Rattans or canes are another special feature of Southeast Asian forests; in fact, this region is the only place where rattans grow naturally. There are many species of rattans varying in thickness from about three millimeters (one-eighth inch) to that of a human arm;

an individual plant may attain fifty meters in length. They have a multitude of uses: the sale of rattans is an important source of income for interior peoples of Kalimantan and elsewhere.

Birds are another interesting feature of the tropical forests. Southeast Asians appreciate birds not only as sources of food but also for their song, their beauty, and other more mysterious qualities. Several tribal groups of Kalimantan take their important omens for farming, traveling, and ceremonial observances from rain-forest birds. Some groups of Central Kalimantan will not dance without the feathers of the rhinoceros hornbill attached to their hands in a graceful fan. Hornbills are also killed for their large casques, which tribal people carve into precious ornaments. In Irian Jaya, many species of the spectacular bird of paradise are also the victims of their beauty.

Southeast Asia is of great interest to zoologists. Wallace's line, a zoogeographical boundary that passes to the east of the Philippines, between the islands of Kalimantan and Sulawesi, and ends between Bali and Lombok, separates a distinct western region with a very diverse fauna of clearly continental Asian ancestry from an eastern region where a reduced array of Asian animals is intermingled with wildlife species that originated in Australia. A number of important animals found on the west side of this dividing line are not found in the east and vice versa. Large rain-forest animals of the west side, such as the one-horned rhino and the banteng (a species related to the cow), are absent from the eastern region. The rain forest of the western region is also rich in anthropoid apes, namely the orangutan, gibbon, and siamang, which are not found east of the line. Sulawesi Island, which is on the eastern side of the line, is especially important because of its endemic small mammals, such as the anoa, a dwarf buffalo, and the *babirusa*, a kind of boar with enormous tusks.

The forests harbor other natural resources, including important mineral deposits. Among these are metal ores, precious stones, petroleum, and other fuel resources. The discovery of such riches, however, often bodes ill for the forests. When these deposits are found under the forests' cover, interest in exploiting them is usually very strong, and destruction of the forest is frequently the result.

The Use of Forest Resources

The large variety of plants and animals of southeast Asia's tropical rain forests have been used by the people who traditionally live in or near the forests. They gather tubers, fruits, shoots, and leaves for food; they hunt deer, pigs, monkeys, and birds. Many plant species and animal products are valued for their medicinal efficacy. Others are sought for tanning and dyeing; resins, oils, and turpentine are tapped from certain species of trees. The forest people produce handicrafts from rattan, bamboo, and other fiber-producing plants, as well as animal skins, feathers, and horns. They gather fuelwood for cooking; in the highlands people also burn wood for heat. The knowledge of these forest products and the uses to which they can be put have been passed down from generation to generation; formal science has contributed little to this large body of knowledge.

Southeast Asians have long known uses for a large number of naturally occurring forest plants, but they also began to domesticate plants many thousands of years ago, and systems of traditional agriculture exist throughout the region. Perhaps the most widespread type of agriculture, and certainly one that concerns conservationists, is shifting cultivation. Under this system farmers clear and crop forest land for a year or two, although they may also cultivate some secondary crops for a longer period. The domestication of many forest plants, especially fruit trees and medicinal species, has accompanied this type of agriculture. While it is an effective way of raising crops in forested areas with small human populations, shifting cultivation is generally characterized by the use of relatively simple tools and low labor input in tending the field.

In Indonesia and elsewhere, however, more intensive and commercially oriented forms of shifting cultivation also exist. Cultivators often use such non-traditional tools as chainsaws for clearing and select crops primarily for their market price and not because they satisfy subsistence needs. The great diversity of crops common in traditional shifting cultivation are frequently replaced by monocultures or a few commercially important crops.

Agriculture is not the only reason why forests in Indonesia and the rest of Southeast Asia are cut. Tropical rain forests in the region have been logged manually since before the Second World War. In the past twenty years, however, this exploitation intensified as the logging industry has been mechanized. The lowland rain forest has been the principal target of such logging. Foresters have developed several systems of harvesting timber in a diverse rain forest to ensure minimum damage to the original plant communities; however, none as yet is really satisfactory. Therefore, the disappearance by the end of this century of most lowland rain forest in Southeast Asia continues to be a serious possibility.

Some reforestation programs, often taking the form of plantation establishment, have been launched in Southeast Asia to cope with the deforestation caused by timber exploitation. Less than 10 percent of the fuelwood demand in the year 2000 will be filled by plantations, however, if the current rate of establishment continues. We have little hope of increasing the reforestation rate greatly in the near future, as much basic scientific research on reforesting humid tropical areas is yet to be done.

Conservation Issues

Is there any conservation program that can ensure the availability of forest resources for the coming generation? Conservation programs were developed in Southeast Asian countries long before large-scale forest exploitation began. Rules and regulations exist that tell the public what is allowed and what is not allowed in the forests. Understanding why such programs are not effective is crucial to any planning for the future.

Following a world trend, early conservation efforts focused on the protection of particular species, primarily animal wildlife, which is naturally more appealing to most people than plant species. The list of animals protected in Indonesia and neighboring countries includes such rare endemic species as the anoa, tapir, bird of paradise, and some primates. A shorter list of protected plant species also exists.

Physical uniqueness of an area was also considered an important element in the early conservation program. Among protected areas were such geologic formations as volcanic caldera, sand dunes, and limestone hills. In the 1960s conservationists began to include unique biota as well; particular endangered ecosystems included mangroves, peat swamp forests, and lowland forests of trees in the Dipterocarp family. This emphasis on whole ecosystems also followed changes in worldwide thinking on environmental issues.

Many people consider the conservation movement to be nothing but an expression of sentiment, be it for beauty, rareness, or uniqueness. Indeed, it is very often difficult to put a precise economic value on the conservation of rare plants, animals, landscapes, or ecosystems. For this reason in the early 1970s, an emphasis was placed on educating people about the economic importance of protecting the related wild species of widely cultivated crop plants. The maintenance of such wild species is often crucial for improving cultivated varieties, and thus the conservation of these plants and animals is in many instances imperative for the future existence of successful agriculture.

Because Southeast Asia is one of the centers of crop diversity, the countries of the region have followed the world movement in conserving their wealth of such genetic resources. Many crop varieties are preserved not through cultivation but by conserving their seeds in cold storage facilities known as gene banks. Thailand and the Philippines, for example, have established gene banks for such important crops as the winged bean, green bean, and others.

Many native plant species of Southeast Asia, however, produce seeds that cannot be stored in such facilities for a long period of time, including such economically important plants as durian, rambutan, some citrus fruits, and various timber species. Therefore, if these species are to be preserved in their genetic richness, it is best to conserve them in their natural habitat. When such conservation is not feasible, however, samples of the species are maintained in living collections. Arboreta, collection gardens, and botanic gardens are now playing an important role in the conservation of plant resources.

The rain forests of Southeast Asia are known to produce many wonderful tropical fruits, but there are a variety of still unappreciated species in these forests whose economic potential could be exploited. Many forest species have long been used locally, but their domestication and their broader diffusion is only beginning. Arenga palm (*Arenga pinnata*), for example, which is commonly found in the moist forests, is the main source of palm sugar. All parts of this palm are useful in village subsistence. The fruits are edible, the trunk produces starch, the leaves are good for roofing, and the leaf midribs are the raw material for basketry and brooms. A serious attempt to cultivate it, however, has never been made although its wild population has been drastically reduced by the cutting of rain forests.

Many people believe that the destruction of rain forests in Southeast Asia can be slowed only if there is a clear national policy on the forests' use and conservation. Each Southeast Asian country claims that it follows a sustained-yield policy in using its forest re-

sources; hence, they insist, conservation is a built-in process. While it is true that such policies are often included in national development plans, their actual implementation is often modified to suit particular situations.

The problems of national development in Southeast Asia are as complex as the rain forests themselves. Actions taken by governments to solve immediate, pressing problems often seem shortsighted. As long as many Southeast Asians wake up each morning wondering whether they will get enough to eat, however, it is understandable that conservation does not always get the highest government priority.

Because labor and funds to back conservation programs are scarce, the Southeast Asian countries have established cooperative ties within the region and with other regions. Collaboration is carried out under the auspices of regional agencies such as the Association of South East Asian Nations (ASEAN), South East Asian Ministers of Education Organization (SEAMEO), and Association for Scientific Cooperation in Asia (ASCA); they also cooperate through such international agencies as the Food and Agricultural Organization (FAO), the United Nations Environmental Programme (UNEP), and the United Nations Educational, Scientific and Cultural Organization (UNESCO). The establishment of International Biosphere Reserves, in which a core of natural habitat is conserved, is an example of international cooperation in Southeast Asia in conserving important areas, among them rain forests. National parks serve the same function within each country. With the establishment of national parks that include human groups within or near their borders, any previous activity of the local community in and around the protected area is considered an integral part of the conservation program.

The important role of nongovernment organizations in developing an awareness of the need for conservation within society cannot be overemphasized. The World Wildlife Fund (WWF), for example, has assisted Southeast Asian countries in protecting endangered native animal species. In Indonesia, the WWF together with the Department of Forestry has developed management plans for several national parks. Meanwhile, the International Union for Conservation of Nature (IUCN) is actively stimulating work on endangered plant species. The recently established International Board for Plant Genetic Resources (IBPGR) is also now aiding the conservation movement in Southeast Asia, particularly in the preservation of crop varieties and their wild relatives.

Nongovernment organizations on the national level dealing with the conservation of nature also have an important role in assisting the government, which certainly needs to be augmented. Many of those who join such organizations are young and full of enthu-

The rain forests of Southeast Asia produce many wonderful fruits. Durians are regional favorites. A vendor in Sumbawa, Indonesia, arranges the spiky fruits for sale.

siasm. If given proper guidance, a challenge, and a chance, they will become a powerful force spurring public participation.

Conservation Is Everybody's Business

It is imperative for Southeast Asian governments to decide what part of their natural endowment of resources will be tapped to advance national development and how that exploitation will take place. The decision of the Indonesian government to exploit timber from the rain forests is heavily criticized for having been executed with less than appropriate conservation safeguards. Insufficient planning and lack of trained labor for monitoring timber concessions allowed concessionaires to avoid complying with laws and regulations. The government of Indonesia, realizing the important consequences of such inadequate supervision, recently created a separate Department of Forestry. Within this department, the Directorate General for Forests and Nature Conservation handles the conservation program in Indonesia. The creation of this department demonstrates the commitment of the Indonesian government to the conservation movement.

There is no doubt that a formal system for dealing with forest conservation is needed in Indonesia. Without public participation, however, the implementation of any conservation program will not be effective. The Minister of State for Population and Environment has attempted to enhance the role of popular culture in promoting forest conservation, and examples of traditional philosophy, local practices, and religious teachings on natural resources and environment have been gathered and used in education.

In the Indonesian tradition, for example, the banyan tree is considered sacred. Springs are often found under mature banyan trees. Indonesians believe that holy spirits reside in the trees, which helps ensure the availability of clean water. A banyan tree is never cut down, no matter where it grows. The Javanese, who form 70 percent of the Indonesian population, also believe that sacred spirits dwell deep within forests. Shadow plays, based on the age-old Mahabharata and Ramayana traditions, are repositories of this knowledge. Such plays include *gunungan,* a figure that illustrates a forest ecosystem in which plants, animals, human beings, holy spirits, and devils live together. The play suggests that to develop inner strength, one should meditate in the undisturbed forest and live harmoniously with its inhabitants. With modernization, however, this kind of traditional teaching is fading in importance.

To spur public participation in conservation efforts, the government created an environmental award, KALPATARU, that is given annually to an individual or group that distinguishes itself in conservation activities in Indonesia. Recipients have included low-ranking officials of the Directorate General for Forest and Nature Conservation who performed more than their assigned responsibilities and groups in remote areas who were successful in preserving unique ecosystems or in making previously barren areas green with trees.

Indonesia educates the public in the conservation of rain forests in many ways. Posters of endangered or rare species of plants and animals native to Indonesia have been distributed by the Man and the Biosphere (Indonesia) Programme. In addition to individual species, posters also show examples of virgin forests and the effect of human activities on the rain forests. Television and radio programs featuring rain forests and their functions are scheduled regularly to inform the public and to invite their participation in conservation. Newspaper articles voicing concern for the future of rain forests appear from time to time and have attracted the attention of the government and general readers. Theoretically, then, public support for the conservation of rain forests should be developing in Indonesia.

What Is Wrong?

It has often been stated that education at all levels, both formal and informal, is necessary to ensure that conservation becomes a way of life. It is also well understood, however, that education is a long process. It is difficult or impossible to tailor educational programs to suit

Although exploitation of mineral resources need not result in extensive deforestation, access roads and the promise of jobs frequently bring with them many people who cut down the forest for agriculture. This oil field is in the rain forest of Sumatra, Indonesia.

CENTER: Although most Southeast Asians have probably never been in a rain forest, the region still includes many tribal groups whose daily existence depends on forest products. A Dayak tribesman of central Borneo dries wild boar meat for his family's future use.

BOTTOM: Sago palms, found in the forest, provide the starchy staple of the Penan diet. A man splits a sago trunk.

exactly the needs of each region or community in an area as diverse as Southeast Asia, where the Computer Age lives next door to the Stone Age.

Existing conservation education programs, including those channeled through schools or the mass media, do reach the target groups—politicians, policy makers, the public at large—who live in rural and urban areas. It is probable that the message to conserve rain forests has gotten through, but awareness alone is not enough to implement the suggested programs of action. Problems of national development are enormous and require the government to make tough decisions about its priorities. In Southeast Asia rapid population growth is the most pressing concern; associated with this are food, health, and education problems. Food needs alone create many difficulties, which in turn may lead to political and social instability. All of these overshadow the need for conservation.

Southeast Asian policy makers must face these dilemmas daily. While they are convinced that the rational use of natural resources is crucial, the need to cultivate more food crops and cash crops, coupled with the need for land to accommodate those who are resettled, also demands their attention. Policy makers also understand that rain forests can attract tourism, but natural beauty alone will attract only a small number of people. Mass tourism demands considerable infrastructure: developing the necessary facilities is a problem in itself.

The majority of the Southeast Asian public has never had the experience of being in a rain forest. What knowledge they have of rain forests and their endemic plant and animal life has been acquired through reading, listening, or watching television. They may feel proud of having such unique species within their countries, but they are rarely committed to do much because their lives are not directly affected by the forest. In contrast, those Southeast Asians who live in and around rain forests depend on them for their daily existence. Neither newspapers, radios, nor television are part of their lives. Often the message of the forests' widespread destruction and the need for conservation has not reached them. Day in and day out they have to think about where to get the forest resources they need for food and cash. To them forest conservation definitely has a different meaning, and conservation programs are sure to affect them differently. Sometimes their needs for forest clearing conflict with conservation agenda. Therefore, the inclusion of these groups in conservation programs is imperative. Programs that involve the participation of such communities in national parks or International Biosphere Reserves are still in their infancy. Although such programs may be difficult to implement successfully, they must be tried if rain forests are to survive.

The timber concessionaires must also be given special attention. No matter how ecologically sound the official conditions for harvesting timber are, if the concessionaires ignore them, forest destruction will result. Timber concessionaires are businesspeople, sometimes foreigners, and even if some of them do believe that forest resources should be conserved, business and the profit motive come first. Therefore, the national governments of Southeast Asia and international agencies must establish firm policies and safeguards to protect the rain forests from the abuses of some of the timber concessionaires.

The fear that the rain forests of Southeast Asia are disappearing is well grounded. Both scientific and practical solutions have been offered, but none resolves the problem. What hope there is lies in the commitment of everyone concerned. The conservation of rain-forest resources is not only the business of the government but also that of the people who own the forests and live in them. If the belief that rain forests are the common heritage of humanity still prevails, then the entire international community must commit itself to the effort to conserve those forests and not just to involve itself peripherally in some activities. Moreover, the commitment cannot just last until the end of some project period—any project—but far beyond any official term of agreement. Is not all education a long process?

I wish to thank Christine Padoch for encouraging me to write this text. I also wish to thank Peter Brosius and Lena Chan for their help and for sharing their knowledge about Penan society with me. Finally I wish to acknowledge my great debt to Matu Tugang for teaching me so much about his own society. I alone am responsible for any errors or misrepresentations. This article is the personal work of the author and is not a statement of policies or views of the government of Sarawak.

THE PENAN STRATEGY

JAYL LANGUB

The Malaysian state of Sarawak forms the northwest part of the large tropical island of Borneo; 82 percent of its one and one-half million people live in rural areas and depend on the forest for their daily domestic needs, as well as for materials used in local and national trade and even in international commerce. The Penan are traditionally a nomadic people, and they make more use of the forest than any other group in Sarawak. Even those who have now settled still derive a large part of their food and income from the forest.

The Penan occupy a vast area of tropical forest in the watersheds of the Baram and Rajang, the largest rivers in Sarawak. Penan country is an endless carpet of green rain forest interrupted only by small patches of swidden clearings and old fields owned by the Penan's settled neighbors. The Penan feel a profound affinity with the forest, which plays a central role in their lives. The forest provides their staple foods: the starchy pith of the sago palm (*Engeissona utilis*), *uvud* (young sago plants), *lekak* (an edible palm leaf bud), a variety of fruits, and the meat of the bearded pig (*Sus barbatus*). The forest also has for centuries provided them with necessary trade items such as camphor, jelutong (a wild rubber), dammar (a resin), *gaharu* (incense wood), bezoar stone (from the stomachs of certain ruminants, believed to have medicinal properties), and rattan (for making the mats and baskets that are in demand in coastal cities). From the forest the Penan get wood for building houses and boats and saplings for the construction of huts.

Matu Tugang is the thirty-year-old son of the community leader of the seminomadic Penan of Long Jaik. He sums up the importance of the forest to his community thus: "From the forest we get our life. Fruits are important, many different fruits. Uvud and lekak are necessary; these are our food. From the forest we also get other necessities. Rattans we use to make carrying baskets. And we hunt in the forest. We look for pigs, for deer. With blow pipes we hunt the gibbon and monkey. Just from this land we get all we need for our life."

The Penan consider themselves guardians of the forest. They use it for their own subsistence, and when they die they leave it for the next generation to look after, use, and manage. They have a sense of stewardship over the forest in which they live. Their strategy in harvesting forest products is based on a principle of sustainable use. For instance, sago palms grow in clumps of several trunks that rise from a mass of aerial roots. Penan always harvest sago by cutting only one or two of the trunks, leaving the palm to resprout; they never cut down the entire plant at the root clump, which would kill it. According to Matu Tugang, "If there are many trunks we will get one or two. We thin it out so it will thrive. If there is a lot of sago, we will harvest some, and we will leave some. We don't like to kill it all off, in case one day there is nothing for us to eat. This is really our way of life." Rattan, greens, fruits are all harvested in such a way that the plants will continue to produce in the future.

The Penan also have a custom, *molong,* by which they may claim a forest product but preserve it for future use. They will mark a tree as theirs, for instance, and use it later, often much later, to make a boat or a house.

Wildlife populations in the Penan country have not been seriously depleted as in many areas of Sarawak. Deer, gibbons, langurs, macaques, hornbills, bears, and otters are all hunted, but the most important animal for the Penan is the bearded pig. Traditionally Penan have hunted with dogs, spears, and blowpipes and have little threatened the stability of the animal populations. They do not wander indiscriminately in the forest but keep within the territory where they claim stewardship, moving from one area that has been harvested to another where resource replenishment has taken place.

Logging activities threaten these old patterns of stewardship and resource management; the lives of some Penan groups have been disrupted by them. Although loggers have not yet reached the Seping River where Matu Tugang and his small community of seventy-eight people live, they are worried about their impending encroachment. "We don't want the loggers to destroy our land. The sago will be gone. The rattan will be gone. Our uvud will be gone. Our *ketipe* [wild rubber] will be gone. All the materials of our life and work will be gone. There will be no pig here. They will run away. The *bangat* [langur], with all the rest of the forest animals, will leave. It will be difficult to fish if the rivers are muddy. This is the truth. There are other things on our land. Our fruit trees, all the fruits that we eat, all the fruit trees that are growing in the forest. These will be finished. Where will we get food? And if the loggers take away the trees that we molong, how will we make boats? Do you think we Penan have helicopters?"

The Penan are rational people. They realize that

timber extraction is important for state revenue but believe that logging should be organized so that the least damage is done to the land and forest. "We don't really prohibit them [the loggers] from coming in. We really don't prohibit them from making a road. But if a certain piece of land is the land that we ask them to preserve, we expect them not to touch it. If they are working on the right side of the Seping stream, they should preserve the left side. If they are working on the left side, preserve the right side. They should preserve the right side for rattan, for gaharu, for fruits, for uvud."

of their ancestors. They are also conscious of the fact that their descendants will someday want to walk in their footsteps. In their view, the only way that the state can help them develop in the way they want is by resolving their conflicts with the loggers. "If the [state] authority really wants to help us, keep them [the loggers] from cutting all our trees. That would be good. That is what is necessary for us to live. If they really want to help us, preserve our land for our uvud, for our rattan, for our pig, for our game. That would show that the authorities care about us. Because this is our only way of life."

15

THE NEW
GREAT AGE
OF CLEARANCE
AND BEYOND

HAROLD BROOKFIELD

Policy makers in the equatorial lands and the scientists who offer them advice know they must find ways to develop the forests that will offer improving and sustainable livelihood to the people of these countries. This long-term goal has an air of unreality in an era when much of the forest is being rapidly cleared, causing major disruptions in the life of the rain-forest dwellers, and when waves of timber harvesters and permanent or would-be permanent settlers are swelling the population. Most scholars—though few governments—now recognize that hunter-gatherers and shifting cultivators (in small numbers in the right environment) can use the rain forest without destroying its essential character, but it would be idle to hope that any large part of the tropical rain-forest lands can successfully be reserved for their use or that their livelihood systems can remain unchanged. Growing population and the imperatives of development demand that large areas of forest—indeed most of it—be put to use for the benefit of a much larger and more widely distributed population.

This statement will not please passionate and committed conservationists but not many such people reside in the rain-forest lands, and those conservationists whose numbers are growing in tropical countries mostly take a more pragmatic view. It is therefore necessary to review the transformations that are taking place before we are able to move toward what seems the best possible scenario for the future. To do this effectively demands a degree of regional concentration, and most of this chapter is concerned with island and peninsular Southeast Asia where the most rapid and far-reaching transformations are taking place on a scale that exceeds what is happening in the Amazon basin or in Africa.

Before we join those who decry the tragedy of our tropical rain forests, it is important to remember that some people see the productive development of these forests and the land they mask as a great modern achievement. Their complaint concerns the manner in which these changes are being brought about more than the fact of development itself. For the people of tropical lands, the rain forests themselves are a resource and so are the lands beneath them, and the development of these resources since the colonial period has contributed importantly, even basically in some countries, to improving national income and relieving poverty. These are important goals, even though some of the things that have happened to the forest and their people have been so hastily or greedily done that much of the potential achievement has been lost or imperiled.

At its simplest what is happening is a new great age of clearance, the successor to earlier periods of clearance in medieval Europe and more recently in North America, where the modern landscape of cities and farms would not exist if the forests that once mantled these lands had not been destroyed. A more continuous clearance, penetrating deep into the tropics, has created the agricultural landscapes of China and India. In the broad sweep of human history, what is now happening to the tropical rain forests is no more than the completion of this transformation. There is, however, a qualitative difference in the way in which it is being done, a qualitative difference in the problems of managing the soils cleared from tropical rain forest, and an important difference in the number of species threatened with extinction.

Identifying reasons why much of the tropical rain forest has so long been preserved is important in evaluating what is now taking place or discussing means by which greater stability might be attained. One reason is certainly the virulence of certain diseases and parasites deadly to people and animals that are or have become endemic in the tropical forest lands; they have defeated numerous attempts at colonization or have killed large numbers of people when they have spread into new areas. Malaria is of outstanding significance but is not alone. Another reason the rain forest has been preserved is the intractability, deep weathering, and low mineral fertility of soils on which rain forest can, through its recycling efficiency, survive and flourish once established. The fact that until recently adequate supplies of hardwood could be obtained from temperate forests has also protected tropical resources. Other reasons are more positive. Unlike the open-field pattern of farming in the temperate lands, some of the principal grain and root crops of tropical countries grow best in specialized environments, particularly wetland environments or on the limited areas of more fertile soils; only in modern times have more intensive uses been found for large areas of the tropical lands. Moreover, until lately the tropical crops in demand in world trade were few in number and rather specific in their environmental requirements.

An important part of world agriculture began in the tropics, usually in the tropical margins rather than in the hot, wet tropics themselves. Clearing the forest for agriculture took place as much as nine thousand years ago in New Guinea and only a little later in South and Central America, while a lighter interference in the forests, as indicated by pollen findings, may have taken place more than twenty thousand years ago in Sumatra and in southern India. There is substantial evidence of extensive wetland systems during the last three millennia in tropical South America, and pollen and archaeological evidence indicates that clearance for agriculture took place in every part of the tropics where such evidence has been researched. Yet some of these areas, particularly the wetland systems of South America, have subsequently been abandoned and recovered by forest; we do not know why this happened.

The Timeless Forests?

While the sustained attack on the remaining areas of tropical rain forest is a modern phenomenon, it would be wrong to suppose that these forests have been preserved from all serious human interference until our own times. Not only were quite large areas converted to agricultural land over a period of many centuries—some of them later to revert to forest—but it is also clear that people have lived in most parts of the tropical forest regions since the Pleistocene ice ages, and that over most of the last ten thousand years—during which the world climate has been broadly similar to that of the present time—most forest dwellers have practiced agriculture. The density of their occupation has varied from place to place and from time to time, so that some forest areas—that of Papua New Guinea, for example—consist mainly of continuously worked-over secondary forest and show every indication of having been so for a very long time. In others, at least at times, the impact has been lighter so that something resembling what is often called primary forest has become established.

Modern research has shown that the notion of primary or undisturbed forest is of dubious scientific value, as Hutterer and others show elsewhere in this book. Under the generally cooler conditions of the ice age, atmospheric circulation was reduced and rainfall in the tropics was less than it is today. During the several thousand years of the last glaciation, the tropical rain forest of Africa and South America was reduced to pockets of small remnants. The rest of these great regions seems to have been an open savanna, and the effect on the soils was not unlike that of forest clearance today: fertility declined, soil structure deteriorated, and likelihood of erosion greatly increased. Yet in the subsequent rainy period, which set in some ten millennia ago, forest trees were able to recolonize these grasslands, and by reclothing the landscape, trees checked erosion. Much of the timeless forest is no more than a few tree-generations old, and the notion of a primary forest is hard to sustain under these conditions.

In Southeast Asia, Pleistocene conditions remained more humid. Even though the sea withdrew from the continental shelves, open water remained within and on either side of the region. The rain forests of Southeast Asia are much richer in plant species than those of Africa and most of Latin America. The region comprising Sumatra, Peninsular Malaysia, Borneo, and western Java has a forest of particularly great richness, more diverse than any other tropical rain forest. The seas that helped preserve the Southeast Asian forests from the climatic shocks of the Pleistocene, however, have also facilitated invasion by humans, so that in this region alone we find large areas of intensive agriculture, extensive tracts of modern plantations, and great cities in a tropical rain forest region.

Some Natural Models of Human Interference

Even though the most long-lived rain-forest trees require from three hundred to seven hundred years to attain full height and girth, all die, and the forest is in a constant state of dynamic change. Climatic variations have a major impact on the directions of the change, and even the lesser fluctuations of the last few hundred years may have their effects on rates of growth and recolonization of the gaps that occur when trees die and fall. Exceptional periods of drought occur even deep within the equatorial tropics and permit forest fires to gain hold and persist in regions where average rainfall figures show heavy rain in each month of the year. This happened in eastern Borneo in 1983, but there are records of widespread, though probably smaller fires in the past, particularly during the drought of 1914. Exceptional rain can also wreak widespread damage by causing hillsides to break away in landslides, even under dense continuous forest. Such events can bring about very long-lived changes. In Malaysia, the so-called Kelantan *storm-forest* resulted from the destruction of a large area of trees by a freak storm in 1880, an event unusual in this region though common enough in cyclone-prone areas. A hundred years later early-colonizing species still dominate, and the floristic variety characteristic of the region has not been reestablished. In Sabah (formerly British North Borneo) a grassland plain that originated from fire in the drought of 1914 still exists today.

These natural or near-natural events provide a model for the effects of human interference. Depending on local conditions there may be a complete change to another ecosystem: for instance, grassland or a forest of different species composition may become established and only very slowly give place to something like the former forest. Given the dynamic nature of the forest and the extent and long duration of human interference in many areas, some of the variation found within the rain forests may reflect the combined effect of human impact and natural events as much as it reflects adaptation to a particular soil or site or the availability of colonizing species. In the Solomon Islands a pure stand of *Campnosperma* trees, exploited for a few years until high costs and economic depression brought the business to an end, seems to have become established in old fields after a former agricultural population was eliminated in about 1830. But much of the

modern damage will not so easily be stitched over by nature.

Human interference in the forests ranges from simple harvesting of readily renewable forest produce to totally eradicating and replacing the forest with a large city. Interference is not easy to classify: for instance, the tapping of gum copal from natural forests of *Agathis* or of jelutong (an ingredient of chewing gum) from the swamp-forest species *Dyera lowii* differs only in intensity and method from the tapping of rubber latex from *Hevea brasiliensis,* an introduced species. The replacement of forest by plantations is similar to the deliberate planting or encouragement of specific trees in natural regrowth after clearance. Swidden fallows planted to *Casuarina* at least three hundred years ago in the highlands of New Guinea/Irian are only a degree removed from modern forest plantations of Caribbean pine or eucalyptus species. Whether the forest has been cleared to make rice fields or to make a city, it has still been destroyed.

The three principal forms of interference in Southeast Asian forests at the present time are the extraction of timber using a variety of logging practices; conversion to tree-crop plantations and cropland; and swidden or shifting cultivation, to some the most controversial of the three practices.

The Extraction of Timber

While the agricultural use of forest resources is mainly responsible for the rapid decrease in the area occupied by tropical rain forests, the more extensive activity of timber extraction affects very large areas that still are indicated on maps as forests. Including losses due to timber extraction in estimates of the rate of forest destruction lifts these estimates to the very high levels often quoted. We shall not discuss these estimates because they vary enormously, are mostly based on guesswork, and, if they do rely on measurement from satellite or aerial photographs and other objective tools, are still dependent on highly subjective interpretation, and draw conclusions based on a few, scattered ground measurements. Moreover, *destruction* is a subjective term when applied to an activity that does fearsome damage but leaves a part of the resource intact and hence capable of ultimate recovery. What is certainly destroyed is the forest in the form it had before the loggers arrived, just as shifting cultivators similarly destroy the forest that they clear for crops. As we have already seen, however, millennia of natural events and human use of the forests have similarly destroyed large areas, and a substantial part of the present forest has been recovered from this destruction. What is really destroyed, what is damaged but will recover in however long a time, and what is in fact sustainable management or could readily become so, depends on the practices of the timber industry.

The large-scale conversion of rain forest to plantations of tree crops continues at a great rate, particularly in Southeast Asia. This large tract is in the Malaysian state of Sabah.

The Logging Boom in the Tropical Forests

Before the logging boom, which began at varying dates between the late 1950s and late 1960s in various parts of the region, extraction of timber was a limited activity carried out by nonmechanized methods. Few stems were removed at a felling, exempting younger specimens of a desired species. Trees felled by axe and sawn on the spot were brought down with minimal damage to adjacent trees. A sustained-yield system, based on low levels of demand, held good everywhere except close to main roads, railroads, and rivers, where greater pressure led to some degradation. These methods preserved the slower-growing shade-bearing trees and left the composition of the forest little changed.

Higher levels of demand, commercialization of a larger number of species, and especially the introduction of chain saws, bulldozers, log-hauling vehicles, and rough-built forestry roads changed all this very quickly. It became the practice to fell at once all merchantable trees in an area, creating larger openings, which in principle favored faster-growing light-tolerant species. Unwanted trees might be poisoned, so that a more uniform-aged forest would arise. But while this is the theory, practice can be very different.

The heavily mechanized new system of forestry requires a large outlay of capital, and the short life of expensive equipment and roads demands their heavy use. The concessions of state land (or shifting cultivators' land claimed by the state) are normally for twenty or thirty years, giving the concessionaire no interest in the next crop of trees and hence no incentive to conserve the forest. The concessionaires usually let the work out to contractors who move from concession to concession, obtaining the best timbers in the cheapest and quickest way before moving on. The concessionaires seek maximum profit within the period of the concession, and the contractors maximize their take to offset large costs. If one is to get rich, this must be done quickly. While the industry is now supposedly governed by sound forestry policies, both in Indonesia and Malaysia these policies are infrequently observed.

These practices suggest the fever of the boom. Only the higher-value timbers are cut, though the proportion varies with the quality of the stock and the economics of the operation. Large companies with good stands may take 40 percent of trees, but small contractors operating far inland can afford to take only the best, perhaps 5 percent of the whole stand. Unfortunately selectivity of the take alone does not save other trees from damage with the methods currently used. The tall timbers bring down many other trees, including many adolescent trees, to which they are linked by lianas. Seedlings are crushed as logs are skidded or hauled to the collection point. The logging roads are roughly constructed and often impede drain-

While agriculturists clear more forest, extensive timber extraction affects very large areas. Logs await processing and export in Sarawak, Malaysia.

CENTER: Commercial tree crops, like this oil palm plantation in Sumatra, Indonesia, have replaced forests over substantial parts of Southeast Asia.

BOTTOM: Given sufficient fallow time, land under shifting cultivation is capable of again bearing high forest. As Lun Dayeh women of interior East Kalimantan, Indonesia, harvest rice, healthy forest regrowth cloaks last year's swidden (back right).

age, causing further tree death. Selective logging of this kind may destroy, immediately or later, as much as 50 to 70 percent of the original forest. Only from the undamaged 30 to 50 percent can anything like a species-rich rain forest regenerate, and the loss of species is considerable.

As with any boom, however, some timber of value does remain. Behind the first rush sometimes come small-time operators who enter undamaged areas with chain saws, cut merchantable timber, saw it on the spot, and then transport it by simple means. Less physical damage is done, but the ability of the forest to recover is further reduced. National policies designed to increase income from forestry by setting up sawmills and plywood mills—of which there are 107 in the heavily worked-over province of East Kalimantan, Indonesian Borneo alone—provide incentive to such entrepreneurs working along the still-passable forestry roads.

Clear felling of large areas is so far mainly confined to areas cleared for resettlement schemes and plantation crops; wood-chipping of timber of all types for pulp and particle-board making is not much developed, though it is already used to harvest the less-valuable timbers of Papua New Guinea. In Southeast Asia contractors who clear the forest for conversion to agriculture remove and sell only the minority of merchantable trees that will repay the cost plus a profit; the rest is burned. Such wasteful use of the forest resource merely accelerates the depletion, speeding toward the day on which insufficient timber will be left even to meet domestic needs.

Such a day may not be far off. In 1977 it was estimated that all land in Peninsular Malaysia earmarked for conversion to permanent agriculture would have been cleared by 1990 and that the permanent forest would, under current, extravagant selective-logging practices, be unable to meet even domestic demand after 1991. These projections were realistic, and Peninsular Malaysia is now expected to become a net importer of timber by 1992. The end of abundant timber resources in Borneo is not much further off. The timber boom in Southeast Asia is almost at an end, and if there is to be new rush elsewhere, in New Guinea and Amazonia, it will have to exploit a range of timbers to which the market is as yet unaccustomed.

Those who warned of these trends in the 1970s sought the withdrawal of some of the land proposed for conversion to permanent agriculture so that these more fertile lowland areas could be developed instead for a sustained and much more careful forestry. In this they were unsuccessful although, at least in Indonesia, the rate of conversion has slowed down for economic rather than conservation reasons. Conversion to permanent agriculture, unlike selective forestry, means its replacement by a wholly different ecosystem and its

settlement by large numbers of people. These become people who replace the rain forest rather than people of the rain forest even in the sense that the itinerant timber contractors are people of the rain forest while they are there. Nonetheless, it is important that the role of agriculturists not be ignored in this discussion.

What Logging Does to the Environment

The impact of timber extraction is not limited to the forest itself. There are also important effects on the capability of the land for agriculture after conversion and on downstream areas. The most dramatic effect of logging is certainly erosion. The operations of the timber companies have created large bare patches within the forest over which runoff is greatly increased and water penetration is reduced. Erosion undermines tree roots and brings down yet more trees thus creating still more bare ground from which topsoil is lost. A large amount of eroded material flows into the rivers at all times, which has the effect of making them shallower so that they more readily cut into and overflow their banks. Floods become larger and more frequent, and in dry spells the flow so diminishes that irrigated areas downstream often lack water for their crops.

The turbidity of Southeast Asian rivers has certainly grown much worse in the last decade, although not all of it is due to the recent operations of the logging companies. The contrast with a remoter past is strikingly shown by Sir Frank Swettenham's description of the Perak River in Peninsular Malaysia during the last century. In his *British Malaya*, published in 1907, Swettenham wrote:

> The water ran clear as crystal over its sandy bed, and it was for the most part very shallow, with deep pools at unexpected places. Throughout the whole of this river-length were villages, large and small, usually divided from each other by several miles of heavy forest.

Streams as "clear as crystal" are still to be found in Southeast Asia, not only in the forest but also in agricultural areas; there are such streams only a few miles from Malaysia's capital city of Kuala Lumpur. But where forest clearance has been heavy, and especially where the timber companies have been at work, the "silver streaks" that Swettenham espied in the "limitless jungle" are now orange-brown swirls of silt-laden water that carry away huge quantities of soil eroded from the land. The Perak River is one of them.

The trash left behind by forestry can become a fire risk, so that in exceptional drought major fires can break out as they did in East Kalimantan and Sabah in 1983, creating smoke that darkened the sky as far away as Singapore and Kuala Lumpur. At least such events help generate awareness, and the still-young environmental movements in these countries have gained greater public support in consequence.

Conversion for Permanent Agricultural Use

Clearance of the forest for agriculture has from ancient times been the main consumer of primary forest, the main creator of extensive stands of secondary forest, and the main cause of the creation of grasslands in place of either forest or farming. It continues so today, notwithstanding the depredations produced by the timber industry.

Two forms of clearing have been practiced for many centuries; the third is essentially confined to the last 150 years and mainly to the last 80 years. The conversion of lowland forests to permanent agricultural fields has been in progress for most of the last two millennia in a few core areas. This clearance was offset by failures to create permanent settlements in some areas as ancient states declined and areas were depopulated, leaving the forest to reclaim the fields. Since 1500, however, and especially since 1800, there have been few retreats and an almost continuous advance of rice fields and dry-crop lands accompanied by the orchards of fruit trees—selected inhabitants of the original forests for the most part—that mask every village. Except in Java and a few other areas, these conversions have been confined mainly to the river valleys and their margins, leaving most of the higher land in forest to be used for shifting cultivation and for collecting wood and forest produce.

Other forest land has been cleared for plantation crops. Coffee, grown above the upland limit of food cultivation in Java in the mid-nineteenth century, was the first plantation crop, followed by tobacco, rubber, and oil palm. Some plantation crops have been grown by shifting-cultivation practices, but the large-scale conversion of forest to plantations of tree crops has proved to be durable and sustainable over a long period of time; it still continues at a great rate. Thus of the 5.9 million hectares (14.8 million acres) of forested land surveyed in Peninsular Malaysia in 1977, no fewer than 1.3 million hectares (3.2 million acres) were marked for agriculture; this land will all be farm land by 1995. To drive along the new road through central Peninsular Malaysia north into the state of Kelantan is a sobering experience. Where almost continuous forest stretched a decade ago, only a narrow band survives, and a striking landscape of limestone towers now arises from an extensive tract of recently cleared land and young oil palms, dotted with the raw new villages of the settlers. It is much the same in Pahang, where the last of the forest along the new highway has now gone and a rolling landscape mantled with oil palms, a little rubber and tea, one area of grassland for cattle, and scattered settlements and new towns stretches from horizon to horizon. This planned conversion of great tracts of forest into managed settlement areas growing tree crops for export is by anyone's standards a major achievement, and it contrasts favorably not only with the development of the Amazon but also with the less-well-financed transmigration in Indonesia, where much greater problems have been encountered.

The environmental effects of conversion of forest to tree crops are debatable. Initial clearance leads to some substantial erosion, although this is checked by contouring and on roadsides even by the application of a biodegradable latex emulsion that protects the soil until a ground cover is established. The ground under the tree crops must be kept reasonably clean, and rubber trees do not offer much protection from rain—certainly far less than the forest. Erosion under rubber trees is as much as sixteen times greater than that under rain forest. Oil palm offers better protection, but the less fertile, more hilly, and hence more erodable land is unsuitable for oil palm and is likely to remain under rubber.

The creation of a forest-replacement landscape of tree crops has now been accomplished over substantial parts of Southeast Asia. In many ways it is the tropical equivalent of the replacement of forest by open-field farming in Europe and North America, and similarly it creates a new ecosystem that, while more sensitive to damage than the forest ecosystem, nonetheless is largely sustainable. The problems of replacing rain forest with tree crops are not mainly ones of sustained productivity, provided that management principles now established continue to be applied. One problem is that tree crops still support only a relatively low population density compared with multicrop systems of rural production, and further conversion of tree-crop land to field crops would, on most of the soils that carry tree crops with success, raise new problems of management. The Indonesian transmigration program, which has emphasized food crops (especially rice) from the outset often to the exclusion of cash crops, has encountered severe problems. Research into improved management of tropical soils, particularly in the Amazon, has yielded some encouraging results, but the use of sophisticated agricultural techniques is expensive if synthetic fertilizers are used and labor-intensive if organic methods are employed. The early efforts of the new International Bureau for Soil Research and Management in collecting and disseminating information hold out hope that sustainable management systems for upland soils cleared from rain forests may become widely available and applicable within a few years.

The real problems of the tree-crop plantation areas are, however, economic. The price not only for rubber but for oil palm and most other tropical crops declined steeply after 1981. Some analysts regard this as symptomatic of a structural change in the world economy and consider that no sustained improvement in these prices is likely: world demand for raw materials has been checked by technological advances, and persistent

Several decades of research have shown that traditional shifting cultivation usually results in much less permanent degradation than previously alleged. Farmers set fire to a multifamily swidden in Sarawak, Malaysia.

BOTTOM: A group of Kenyah swiddens cut from secondary forest in Sarawak, with the most recently cleared in the background and a few in different stages of early fallow in the foreground. The swiddens are planted with upland rice and other crops. The frame of last season's temporary swidden hut can be seen in the lower left.

HAROLD C. BROOKFIELD

Greed and hastiness can lead not only to wanton forest destruction but to extreme land degradation. This severe erosion was caused by poor farming practices in the Solo River basin, Java, Indonesia.

overproduction has been created by the expansion of the past forty years. At the same time, however, the prices of manufactured goods and services imported by the raw material–producing countries have not suffered a similar depression. This situation not only affects the incomes of the farmers, it also reduces the disposable incomes of their governments, which have financed much of the agricultural research and management. Unless these trends are corrected, the new colonization areas may long retain their frontier aspect, able to support only farmers whose incomes are considerably below earlier expectation.

In Defense of the Shifting Cultivator

Until a few decades ago, critical views on shifting cultivation were almost universal among natural and social scientists. The view of the swidden system as inevitably destructive of the forest is still current in official circles and, since the rain forest timbers have become so valuable, are often expressed with redoubled force.

The argument usually states that shifting cultivators regularly work over much more land than they use in any one season. By burning forest, cultivators open the way to the invasion of grasses that are not shaded out by the recovering forest because new fires—often escaping from the fires lit intentionally to clear adjacent gardens—destroy the young trees before they can become established. Thus the shifting cultivators are, it is said, the principal destroyers of the forest in many regions, doing far more damage than the timber industry. Moreover, since only low population densities can be supported by shifting cultivation, fewer people can be supported and at a lower level of income than by selective forestry. The state loses revenues from the potentially merchantable timber that is felled or burned for the sake of a few, who do not pay for the trees they clear. Notwithstanding this wasteful consumption of valuable resources, shifting cultivators are able to support themselves only in dire poverty. From the earliest days of colonial government, the authorities have continually sought to restrict the depredations of these careless shifting cultivators, to resettle them, and to teach them better ways of farming, all with small success.

Among all this, only the complaint that shifting cultivation causes a loss of timber revenues to the state holds any merit; everything else is questionable. It probably is true that much of the present grassland occupying former forest areas in Southeast Asia—perhaps some 10 to 15 percent of the once-forested area—was created by fires, but even before colonial times fires were used to clear land for spice cultivation by settled farmers and not by tribal shifting cultivators. Moreover, there are large areas—and they include much of the island of New Guinea/Irian—in which shifting cultivation and the forest have coexisted for centuries.

The realization is emerging that large areas of present-day forest were more densely peopled in the precolonial period than they are now. Before the intensification of contact with outsiders that took place in the eighteenth and nineteenth centuries, the forest people had not acquired immunity to the diseases to which they were more frequently exposed. Strong evidence suggests that both in New Guinea and Borneo populations were larger and villages more numerous in a not-distant past. The recovery of a complex forest in these areas, despite continued but much lighter interference, is an important reminder that destruction need not be permanent and that the shifting cultivation system, lightly practiced, can coexist with a recovering and merchantable forest.

This reminder should not be necessary, for long ago it was demonstrated that a fallow period of eight to ten years is sufficient to control the growth of the aggressive grass, *Imperata cylindrica,* in Southeast Asia and central Africa, and that even shorter periods of fallow are sufficient to maintain sustainable systems in more favored areas. While sustainability is measured by the cropping capacity of the land, it is surely an error to describe as destructive a system that leaves the land—if rested for the minimum period necessary—capable of again bearing high forest. Most of the indigenous cultivation systems of the Southeast Asian forests are of this nature, and it is more commonly the newcomers and would-be permanent settlers, who seek to grow subsistence or cash crops without the indigenes' knowledge of the forest, who do the damage.

Moreover, shifting cultivation is adaptable, and shifting cultivators are neither without resources nor are they among the poorest rural people of the countries where they now live. The most erroneous myth concerning this system is that which describes it as a single, essentially unvarying, slash-and-burn and plant-and-fallow method offering only limited productivity. Many variants are incorporated and are still being adopted and adapted. Relay-cropping—planting the next crop in the shade of the first—is very common, and fast-growing trees are sometimes planted to assist recovery during the fallow. Tillage and technologies to control erosion on slopes and manage the flow of water are often utilized. In a wide-ranging study one writer found seven major and twenty minor elements necessary to any typology of shifting cultivation; within the western Pacific region alone I have used twenty-two diagnostic elements of cultivation, all more complex than simple slash-and-burn, to classify the farming of forty-four places. Cash cropping, especially of permanent tree crops, is now very widely adopted by shifting cultivators although their remoteness from markets makes it hard for them to obtain good prices for such products.

The Kenyah of Sarawak

Francis Jana Lian, a member of the Kenyah people of Sarawak, recently finished his PhD in Human Geography at the Australian National University. I have been his supervisor and visited him in the field in Sarawak in 1985. Lian's people live in a longhouse near the head of boat navigation on the Tinjar River; they practice shifting cultivation of rice and a range of minor crops in the surrounding hills; they have rubber gardens. Many of the Kenyah are employed in the timber industry, which exists up and down the Tinjar, with at least as many men—most of them outsiders—living in the timber camps as in the villages. The Kenyah have moved into this region from more remote areas in stages over the past century, moving first to gain better access to the down-river buyers of their forest produce, then to gain access to cash cropping and employment opportunities. Using boats to transport themselves and their produce, they make gardens only within walking distance of the river and its tributaries and mainly work secondary forest between seven and twenty years old. They can obtain good yields of rice, but these are highly variable; mistiming of the burn, planting, or weeding in relation to the weather or the natural cycle of pests can have drastic consequences for a household's production; only after a poor harvest, however, will a family enter primary forest farther from the river to make some of the next year's gardens.

Lian argues that his people have always sought to make the best use of their opportunities without giving up the core of their system, which is rice. They sold forest produce to gain wealth formerly counted in brass gongs, fine cloth, and other imports and now counted more often in outboard engines, new longhouses and furniture, electricity generators, and—down river where reception from the coast is possible—television sets. They live quite well and spend cash freely in the shops that have sprung up in every village. They eat imported food and unaccountably prefer beer and whisky to the traditional rice wine and brandy. They are unenthusiastic about the rubber they planted some years ago and seek money in the timber industry while it lasts.

This society is undergoing many changes. The aristocratic families have lost their former privilege as wealth has become more widely available. Very significant is a move to establish wet rice, by no means an unknown technology in the Borneo interior. With expectations of higher production and lighter work and the encouragement of the agricultural extension service, they started some *sawah* (wet-rice fields) in the 1960s, but the plots were sited close to the rivers where

they suffered from fast-flowing floods. Without modern tools, farmers found the labor needed to clear grass from the swamps back-breaking, and without introduction of suitable varieties of rice, the expected yields were not achieved. These schemes perished, but since 1978 there has been a new surge of interest. Better sites have been selected, leveling and irrigation better planned; hybrid rice has been used, and hoeing machines used to prepare land.

The reason for adopting sawahs springs from the changes introduced by employment in the timber camps. Though young men return home to prepare the swiddens, they spend most of the year in the camps, leaving the women to do more of the work than before, especially the hard task of weeding. This task has itself grown more onerous, for Kenyah now use fertilizers in their swiddens, and these encourage the weeds as well as the rice. The Kenyah hope the new sawahs will make their work easier.

At this stage the wet rice is expected only to supplement production from the swiddens, but the establishment of the new rice fields is already leading to the break-up of some longhouse groups into individual farm houses, thus accelerating social change. I have studied rural societies in several parts of the tropics and have never seen social and economic change as rapid as that now in progress in the interior of Sarawak. I am impressed by Lian's argument that the central changes are logical selections from the available choices, with sustained improvement in living standards the goal. It is perhaps fortunate for the Kenyah that the trend toward partial stabilization of their agriculture corresponds with the wishes of government to achieve this same result.

The Future of the Shifting Cultivators

The Kenyah use the forest, inconveniencing the timber industry, which has to work farther inland from the rivers along which the Kenyah live or pay handsomely to cut timber on Kenyah land. They are willing to make this payment for access to the river across Kenyah land and for goodwill. Had the Kenyah not been there the timber along the river would have been taken by now. But arguments such as this carry little weight in the corridors of power or in forest destruction statistics, which count each season's new swiddens as so much forest destroyed. It is the loss of forest resources, both real and supposed, that is important. We should not suppose that such views reflect only a bias toward business and commercial gain under capitalism. The Food and Agriculture Organization of the United Nations recently engaged an expert to report on the compelling need to end the destructive farming practices of minority peoples—shifting cultivators—in the mountains of Vietnam. He found that the real destroyers of the forests of northern Vietnam are the

Two traditional Asian farming technologies: a swidden field (left), a *sawah* or irrigated rice field (right). The latter, which some interior groups of Southeast Asia are utilizing more frequently, does not require large-scale forest clearance.

The cities of Southeast Asia are biting into the forest edge. This view of a new section of Kuala Lumpur, the capital of Malaysia, shows the massive works undertaken for urban development and the resulting erosion.

CENTER: Land preparation for new urban development moves into the forests of the main range behind Kuala Lumpur.

BOTTOM: This view of the Tinjar River in Sarawak shows patchy regrowth of secondary forest following shifting cultivation on the farther bank.

Timber camps are not beautiful. Logs can be rafted out of this small camp far upstream on the Tinjar River in Sarawak, Malaysia, only when the river level is high.

state-run timber enterprises; the shifting cultivators are simply blamed for using already destroyed forest. The same story can be recounted all over Southeast Asia, whatever the system of government. Forests are wanted for the money and construction material contained in their timbers and for conversion to permanent agriculture, whether under subsistence or cash crops; the shifting cultivators are in the way.

The pressures on shifting cultivators are very strong in all parts of the region except Papua New Guinea where they are in the majority and have more political clout than elsewhere. In the rest of Southeast Asia the state claims title to all primary forest and to much secondary forest, including land that the shifting cultivators regard as their own. There are regulations against clearing primary forest and using fire, except for permanent conversion to other forms of agriculture. These regulations may be defied but they constitute an oppressive environment. Where forest land is privately owned, as it is in certain areas, even access to the forest for collection of natural produce may be denied.

Some of the changes brought about by government policies also work against the farmers. Thus in the forests of Borneo the employment of men in the timber industry and other approved activities lead those remaining to make their swiddens closer to the villages so that their women can work them more readily and more safely. Fallow periods are inevitably shortened as less forest is used, and certain species have already disappeared from the secondary succession.

Shifting cultivators have already been dislodged from large areas all over Southeast Asia. In others they use a forest degraded by the timber industry and are blamed for its further destruction. In countries where shifting cultivators form only a small minority in the population, the further erosion of their habitat is inevitable. The end of the timber boom will not bring the pressures to an end because the establishment of numerous plywood factories and sawmills—jobs and businesses that are politically important to retain—will sustain the demand for timber and probably increase the market for a wider range of tree species. Some shifting cultivators have already joined in the business of cutting timber for profit, even illegally, to the detriment of their own farming and long-term resources.

In some areas the forestry roads have been linked to form a network opening up larger areas to timber cutting and to cash-crop farming. Where cash crops are grown by shifting cultivation methods the swiddens are often larger than those made for subsistence crops, and recovery of the forest becomes less probable. Shifting cultivators are again demonstrating their old adaptability to changed conditions, but some of the new practices are more damaging environmentally than their traditional methods. Adaptation is necessary, however, if they are to survive. The pressures in these developing countries with their burgeoning populations and need to use their resources more completely are too great to be resisted.

The pressures on the shifting cultivators need not be as brutal as seems inevitable had the use of forests over the last twenty years been less rapacious. It seems, however, untenable to suppose that large areas of forest can be retained in the future for the unfettered maintenance of an extensive system of agriculture. Moreover, even the conservationist pressures developing in response to the waste of resources will militate against their farming practices. Controls must come, and the tropical equivalent of the "sodbuster" and "swampbuster" penalties recently introduced in the United States will certainly strike severely at those who try to live and work in balance with secondary forests that are also wanted by many others. The shifting cultivators will survive and adapt, but shifting cultivation in its classic form will not.

The Future of People in the Rain Forest

The rain forests that survive into the twenty-first century will be much smaller than those of fifty years ago. Except where they have been reserved as national parks, biosphere reserves, or conservation forests or where inaccessibility, rugged terrain, and lack of population have exercised their own protection, the forests that survive will also offer a different and often much inferior environment. The remaining natural resource for quality timber production will be scattered and available only at much higher cost. Large areas of secondary forest will remain, including substantial areas that some fear are suffering destruction at the present time. Significant areas in which inroads for settlement are currently being made will have regrown to an impoverished form of forest and diminished by extensive conversion to grassland. Other areas, principally those where forest has been converted to tree-crop plantations, are still likely to be under their converted use.

Pressure on governments and developers for the adoption of sustainable management will grow as forests are diminished. The fact that far too little experimental effort has been put into generating systems of sustainable management during the past forty years will be appreciated and in all probability rectified. This means, however, that there are likely to be major efforts to renew the forest, not in its former diverse form but as an even-aged stand with a narrower range of species. Wood has special properties that none of its substitutes can match and will continue to be in demand; moreover, new industrial uses are likely to be found for wood. In these circumstances the squeeze on the present inhabitants of the rain forest is not likely to be relaxed, and these people will want to participate in the wider economy of forest use.

The definition of *people of the rain forest* will require a wider scope in the next century. I have used it to mean the indigenous inhabitants of the forest, the settlers who have come into converted areas, and the more temporary inhabitants who have come to harvest the timber. But there is another sense in which the forest is part of the national estate and in which the people of the rain forest include all the people of the countries in which forest areas survive. The people who live outside the forest and recently converted areas form the vast majority of this wider population; their direct experience of the forest is likely only to be through the wider development of parks. They will look for a system of management that will more securely and continuously contribute to revenue and employment. If we assume that large-scale conversion to agricultural use will have reached or at least closely approached its practical limits, the stable management will comprise two main elements: sustained forestry and more efficient use of the agricultural—and the agriculturally degraded—areas.

The Prospect for Managed Forestry and Agriculture

Plantations for forestry have never been very attractive in rain forest areas for two reasons. First, plantations do best on level, relatively fertile ground that is also suitable for agriculture. Second, such quick-growing species as conifers and eucalypts, which are most commercially attractive as planted trees, belong to more seasonal environments and seldom do well in rain-forest areas. Plantation forestry is perhaps best confined to the grasslands where no genetic pool of trees is available. Agricultural use of the grasslands is entirely possible with suitable technology, by using livestock to keep down the grass and to plough and manure the land, or with tree crops to shade out the grass.

For the rain forests, enrichment planting in logged-over areas and in larger gaps produced by cultivation with fast-growing secondary species that have good qualities as timber seems to be the best solution. There are many suitable species, some of which reach merchantable size in as few as twenty years, although others take considerably longer. Enrichment planting reduces but does not destroy the diversity of the forest. Some seedlings from nearby survivors of the more valuable hardwood species will flourish and with more careful logging methods could be treated as a long-term crop, growing more slowly to mature after the faster-growing secondary species have been harvested. But this requires careful maintenance and policing of the forests and the timber cutters. Any continuation of the timber boom methods of recent years could quickly destroy the prospects for such management.

If regional governments were to recognize the prior title of the forest-dwelling shifting cultivators to much larger areas of forest than is the normal practice today, it is surely possible that these people, with their substantial knowledge of the forests and more recent experience of the timber industry, might prove to be the best forest managers. They and the government, through taxation and royalties, would thus share the benefits of a more sustainable system of forestry. While the forest people are still regarded as the enemy of commercial timber production such a new approach is unlikely; but were such a new relationship established, it would provide the cultivators with an incentive to restrict cultivation in order to develop enrichment planting. This is essentially the old *taungya* system of Burma, under which teak seedlings were planted after swiddening in order to establish patches of teak forest.

Whether by cooperation or by enforcement, however, the shifting cultivators' lands seem almost certain to become favored sites for a new managed forestry; these forests are often on the best and most accessible land. If agriculture in the forests by the indigenous forest people is to survive, it will have to include both a long-cycle timber crop and other short-term tree crops for income when timber-camp employment becomes scarce. In this area modern research into effective management of tropical soils may become of prime importance. Whether the green revolution is based on plant breeding and chemicals or on the use of labor-intensive methods involving mulching and crop rotation, new methods *may* make it possible to develop a stable agriculture, more economical in its use of land, in the forest. If such methods are proven successful, and if the advantages to their adoption are clear, there is no reason to suppose that the present-day shifting cultivators of the Southeast Asian forests would resist their introduction.

What is needed first is a new realization of the value of the forest-dwelling people to the countries in which they are minority citizens. Sustained management of the forest requires the presence of forest-living people who know the forests and understand how to use their full range of resources. The application of research, hitherto devoted mainly to lowland rice farming, to the problems of upland farming in grassland and forest soils could yield considerable benefits. The development of a sustainable subsistence base and a broader economic base for these people corresponds not only to their own best interests but also to the national (and international) goal of stabilizing the future use of the tropical rain-forest resource.

This scenario is possible, but it cannot be predicted with certainty. Instead, rapacious destruction may continue, with shifting cultivators helping to complete the destruction, and what remains of much of the tropical rain forests will be a tangled secondary growth broken up by large patches of eroded grasslands, scarred by landslides on steep ground, contributing nothing to wealth but much to the devastation of agriculture in adjacent lowlands. Fortunately, there is some hope that wiser counsels will prevail and that a managed environment may come into being. This managed environment would contain substantial tracts of part-planted, part-natural forest, poorer in flora and fauna than the forest it replaced, but still a habitat of considerable diversity and a continuing source of wealth, employment, and even pleasure. Moreover, in national parks and conservation reserves (assuming that these survive the pressures to use them for production) there would remain tracts of the old forest large enough to survive; using the more accessible tracts for tourism might help protect them if the tourism also is well managed.

If large enough, the surviving protected areas would retain all the diversity of the present forest and a high proportion of its species. In this respect they would in some ways resemble the remnant forests that survived the Pleistocene dessication of Africa and Latin America. Just as those remnants were the genetic pool from which the growth of more extensive forests was supplied during the wetter period since the ice age ended, so the protected remnants in Southeast Asia would provide the material from which the wasted forests around them might be recolonized. Moreover, if in a future time the production of food and industrial crops becomes more intensive and requires less land than today, these protected remnants could also be the genetic pools from which areas now being converted to extensive agricultural use might be recovered by forest.

Despite extensive destruction during the present era, it is not too late for such a scenario to be achieved, and—sad though it may be to those who loved the limitless forests of yesteryear—this is perhaps the best scenario that can be envisaged in the fast-changing conditions of a crowded and developing world.

Thanks are due to my research assistant, Ms. Yvonne Byron, for her enthusiastic search for references.

SUGGESTED READINGS

Tropical Rain Forests and Deforestation

Bates, M. 1952. *Where Winter Never Comes*. New York: Scribner's.

Blaikie, P., and H. Brookfield. 1987. *Land Degradation and Society*. London/New York: Methuen.

Burley, F. W., and P. Hazlewood. 1986. "Tropical Forest Action Plan." *Journal 86*, The Annual Report of the World Resources Institute. Washington, D.C.: The World Resources Institute.

Caulfield, C., 1985. *In the Rainforest*. New York: Knopf. Reprint. 1986. Chicago: University of Chicago Press.

FAO. 1981. *Forest Resources of Tropical Asia*. Rome: FAO.

Flenley, J. R. 1979. *The Equatorial Rain Forest: A Geological History*. London/Boston: Butterworth.

Kartawinata, K., and A. P. Vayda. 1984. "Forest Conversion in East Kalimantan, Indonesia." In *Ecology in Practice*. F. DiCastri et al., eds. Dublin: Tycooly International Publishing.

Longman, K. A., and J. Jenik. 1987. *Tropical Forest and its Environment*. 2d ed. Longman Scientific and Technical.

Lanly, J. P. 1982. *Tropical Forest Resources*. Rome: FAO.

Myers, N. 1980. *Conversion of Tropical Moist Forests*. Washington, D.C.: National Academy of Sciences.

———. 1984. *The Primary Source: Tropical Forests and Our Future*. New York: Norton.

Prance, G. T., ed. 1982. *Biological Diversification in the Tropics*. New York: Columbia University Press.

Prance, G. T., and T. E. Lovejoy, eds. 1985. *Amazonia*. Oxford: Pergamon Press.

Richards, P. W. 1964. *The Tropical Rain Forest: An Ecological Study*. Cambridge: Cambridge University Press.

UNESCO/UNEP/FAO. 1978. *Tropical Forest Ecosystems: A State of Knowledge Report*. Paris: UNESCO.

Whitmore, T. C. 1984. *Tropical Rain Forests of the Far East*. 2d ed. Oxford: Clarendon Press.

Forest People of Latin America

Biocca, E., ed. 1970. *Yanoama: The Narrative of a White Girl Kidnapped by Amazonian Indians*. New York: E. P. Dutton.

Chagnon, N. A. 1968. *Yanomamo: The Fierce People*. New York: Holt, Rinehart & Winston.

Goldman, I. 1979. *The Cubeo: Indians of the Northwest Amazon*. 2d ed. Urbana: University of Illinois Press.

Hames, R. B., and W. T. Vickers, eds. 1983. *Adaptive Responses of Native Amazonians*. New York: Academic Press.

Hiraoka, M. 1985. "Mestizo Subsistence in Riparian Amazonia," *National Geographic Research* 1(2): 236–46.

———. 1986. "Zonation of Mestizo Riverine Farming Systems in Northeastern Peru." *National Geographic Research* 2(3): 354–71.

Meggers, B. J. 1971. *Amazonia: Man and Culture in a Counterfeit Paradise*. Chicago: Aldine Publishing Company.

Nations, J. D., and R. B. Nigh. 1980. "The Evolutionary Potential of Lacandon Maya Sustained-Yield Tropical Forest Agriculture." *Journal of Anthropological Research* 36(1): 1–30.

Parker, E. P. 1985. *The Amazon Caboclo: Historical and Contemporary Perspectives*. Studies in Third World Societies 32. Williamsburg, VA: College of William and Mary.

Perera, V., and R. D. Bruce. 1982. *The Last Lords of Palenque: The Lacandon Mayas of the Mexican Rain Forest*. Boston: Little, Brown and Co.

Shoumatoff, A. 1978. *The Rivers Amazon*. San Francisco: Sierra Club Books.

Siskind, J. 1973. *To Hunt in the Morning*. New York: Oxford University Press.

Wagley, C. 1976. *Amazon Town: A Study of Man in the Tropics*. 2d ed. London, New York: Oxford University Press.

Williams, D. 1985. "Petroglyphs in the Prehistory of the Northern Amazonia and the Antilles." *Advances in World Archeology* 4: 335–87.

Forest People of Southeast Asia

Bellwood, P. 1985. *Prehistory of the Indo-Malaysian Archipelago*. Orlando, FL: Academic Press.

Brosius, P. In Press. "River, Forest, and Mountain: The Penan Gang Landscape." *Sarawak Museum Journal*.

Cooper, R. 1984. *Resource Scarcity and the Hmong Response*. Singapore: Singapore University Press.

Dunn, F. L. 1975. *Rain-Forest Collectors and Traders: A Study of Resource Utilization in Modern and Ancient Malaya*. Kuala Lumpur: Monographs of the Malaysian Branch of the Royal Asiatic Society 5.

Geddes, W. R. 1976. *Migrants of the Mountains: The Cultural Ecology of the Blue Miao (Hmong Njua)*. Oxford: Oxford University Press.

Hutterer, K. L. 1983. "The Natural and Cultural History of Southeast Asian Agriculture." *Anthropos* 79: 169–212.

Kunstadter, P. 1978. "Ecological Modification and Adaptation: An Ethnobotanical View of Lua' Swiddeners in Northwestern Thailand." In *The Nature and Status of Ethnobotany*. R. I. Ford, ed. Ann Arbor: University of Michigan Museum of Anthropology, Anthropological Papers 67.

———. 1983. "Animism, Buddhism and Christianity: Religion in the Life of the Lua' People of Pa Pae, Northwestern Thailand." In *Highlanders of Thailand*. J. McKinnon and W. Bhruksasri, eds. Kuala Lumpur: Oxford University Press.

Kunstadter, P., E. C. Chapman, and S. Sabhasri. 1978. *Farmers in the Forest: Economic Development and Marginal Agriculture in Northern Thailand.* Honolulu: The University Press of Hawaii.

Lemoine, J. 1972. *Un Village Hmong Vert de Haut Laos.* Paris: Centre National de Recherche Scientifique.

Spencer, J. E. 1966. *Shifting Cultivation in Southeastern Asia.* Berkeley and Los Angeles: University of California Publications in Geography 19.

Tropical Forest People of Africa

Bailey, R. C., and N. R. Peacock. In Press. "Efe Pygmies of Northeastern Zaire: Subsistence Strategies in the Ituri Forest." In *Coping with Uncertainty in the Food Supply.* I. de Garine and G. A. Hariison, eds. Oxford: Oxford University Press.

Cavalli-Sforza, L. L., ed. 1986. *African Pygmies.* New York: Academic Press.

Duffy, K. 1984. *Children of the Forest.* New York: Dodd, Mead and Company.

Hart, T. B., and J. A. Hart. 1986. "The Ecological Basis of Hunter-Gatherer Subsistence in the African Rain Forest: The Mbuti of Eastern Zaire." *Human Ecology* 14(1): 29–55.

Hiernaux, J. 1975. *The People of Africa.* New York: Scribner's.

Murdock, G. P. 1959. *Africa: Its People and Their Cultural History.* New York: McGraw-Hill.

Turnbull, C. M. 1983. *Mbuti Pygmies: Change and Adaptation.* New York: Holt, Rinehart & Winston.

Economic and Commercial Development in the Rain Forest

Aiken, S. R., C. H. Leigh, T. R. Leinbach, and M. R. Moss. 1982. *Development and Environment in Peninsular Malaysia.* Singapore: McGraw-Hill.

Fearnside, P. M. 1986. "Agricultural Plans for Brazil's Grande Carajás Program." *World Development* 14(3): 385–409.

Fearnside, P. M., and J. M. Rankin. 1982. "The New Jari: Risks and Prospects of a Major Amazonian Development." *Interciencia* 7(7): 329–39.

Galey, J. 1979. "Industrialist in the Wilderness: Henry Ford's Amazon Venture." *Journal of Inter-American Studies and World Affairs* 21:264–83.

Hecht, S. B. 1985. "Environment, Development, and Politics: Capital Accumulation and the Livestock Sector in Eastern Amazonia." *World Development* 13(6): 663–84.

Kumar, R. 1986. *The Forest Resources of Malaysia: Their Economics and Development.* Singapore: Oxford University Press.

Repetto, R., and M. Gillis, eds. In Press. *Public Policies and the Misuse of Forest Resources.* Cambridge: Cambridge University Press.

Shane, D. R. 1986. *Hoofprints on the Forest: Cattle Ranching and the Destruction of Latin America's Tropical Forests.* Philadelphia: Institute for the Study of Human Issues.

Migration and Settlement in Tropical Forests

Hemming, J., ed. 1985. *The Frontier after a Decade of Colonization.* Vol. 2, *Change in the Amazon Basin.* Manchester: Manchester University Press.

Mahar, D. J. 1979. *Frontier Development Policy in Brazil: A Study of Amazonia.* New York: Praeger.

Moran, E. 1981. *Developing the Amazon.* Bloomington: Indiana University Press.

———, ed. 1983. *The Dilemma of Amazonian Development.* Boulder: Westview Press.

Schmink, M., and C. Wood, eds. 1984. *Frontier Expansion in Amazonia.* Gainesville: University of Florida Press.

Smith, N. 1982. *Rainforest Corridors.* Berkeley and Los Angeles: University of California Press.

Vayda, A. P. 1987. "Self-Managed Land Colonization in Indonesia." In *Community Management: Asian Experience and Perspectives.* D. C. Korten, ed. West Hartford, CT: Kumarian Press.

Vayda, A. P., and A. Sahur. 1985. "Forest Clearing and Pepper Farming by Bugis Migrants in East Kalimantan: Antecedents and Impact." *Indonesia* 39 (April 1985): 93–110.

Vayda, A. P., and T. C. Jessup. 1986. "Tropical Forest Migrations: Case Studies of Movements by Kenyah and Bugis People in Indonesia." *Wallaceana* 45 (September 1986): 3–5.

INDEX

Note: **Boldface** *numerals indicate illustrations.*

JACKET/COVER

Background: James P. Blair, National Geographic
Left to right, back to front: Edward Tronick; Peter Kunstadter;
Peter Brosius; Peter Brosius; Kent Redford; Steven Winn;
Michael K. Nichols, Magnum; Peter Kunstadter

FRONT MATTER

James P. Blair, National Geographic: p. 2–3
H. W. Silvester/Photo Researchers: p. 6–7
National Space Technology Laboratory of the National
Aeronautics and Space Administration (NASA): p. 11
Loren McIntyre: p. 14–15

CHAPTER 1

Francis E. Putz: p. 26
François Gohier, Photo Researchers: p. 27 top
Victor Englebert, Photo Researchers: p. 27 bottom right
Peter Kunstadter: p. 27 bottom left; 31
Georg Gerster, Photo Researchers: p. 30
H. H. Iltis: p. 34
Carol Gracie: p. 35

CHAPTER 2

Museum of Fine Arts, Seville: p. 38
Museum of Fine Arts, Boston: p. 39; 41
Metropolitan Museum of Art, New York: p. 42–43
Museum of Modern Art/Film Stills Archive: p. 44; 45; 48 left
Museum of Modern Art, New York: p. 46 top; 50
Bancroft Library, University of California: p. 46 bottom
National Gallery of Art, Washington, D.C.: p. 47
Library of Congress: p. 49

CHAPTER 3

George Holton, Photo Researchers: p. 54
Victor Englebert, Photo Researchers: p. 55; 58
Betty J. Meggers: p. 57; 59 top; 59 bottom; 60; 62
Denis Williams: p. 61

CHAPTER 4

Peter Brosius: p. 66; 67 top; 67 center; 67 bottom; 70
After P. I. Boriskovskii, 1966 Vietnam and Primeval Times,
    Moscow, Nauka Publisher: p. 69
Dean Conger, National Geographic: p. 71

CHAPTER 5

Robert L. Carneiro: p. 74–75, all photos
Steven King: p. 76
Stan Wayman, Photo Researchers: p. 80 left
Victor Englebert, Photo Researchers: p. 80 center; 80 right; 84
    top left
Kent Redford: p. 81
Claudia Andujar, Photo Researchers: p. 84 bottom left; 84 top
    right; 84 bottom right
Loren McIntyre: p. 85; 91 left; 91 right
J. J. Foxx/NYC: p. 88
Darrell Posey: p. 90

CHAPTER 6

All photographs by Peter Kunstadter

CHAPTER 7

David Wilkie: p. 112; 113; 117; 118 left; 118 right; 119; 125
Edward Tronick: p. 116; 124
Steven Winn: p. 120; 121

CHAPTER 8

Allen Rokach: p. 128; 129 bottom right; 140 top; 140 bottom
right
Michael Balick: p. 129 left
Christine Padoch: p. 129 top right; 133 top; 133 bottom; 136;
137
Mario Hiraoka: p. 132; 140 bottom left; 141
Library of Congress, Carpenter Collection: p. 135

CHAPTER 9

Gloria Davis: p. 144 left; 144 right; 148 top; 148 center; 152
  right
Hans Thias: p. 145; 148 bottom
Michael K. Nichols, Magnum: p. 149; 152 left

CHAPTER 10

Loren McIntyre: p. 156 bottom; 157; 160; 161 bottom
H. Silvester, Photo Researchers: p. 156 top
Douglas Daly: p. 161 top
Nigel Smith: p. 161 center

CHAPTER 11

Loren McIntyre: p. 164 top; 164 bottom left; 171
Douglas Daly: p. 164 bottom right
Paul Crum, Photo Researchers: p. 165 top right
H. Silvester, Photo Researchers: p. 165 left; 168 top
Gary Hartshorn: p. 165 bottom right
Collections of the Henry Ford Museum and Greenfield Village:
  p. 166
Marianne Schmink: p. 168 bottom
Juca Martins/f4: p. 170
Companhia Vale do Rio Doce: p. 175 top; 175 bottom

CHAPTER 12

John J. Ewel: p. 178; 179, all photos
Mark Leighton: p. 182; 183

CHAPTER 13

Alain Evard, Photo Researchers: p. 186
Forest Department, Malaysia: p. 189; 192
Peter Ashton: p. 190 left; 190 right
Doranne Jacobson: p. 191

CHAPTER 14

Roland Birke, Peter Arnold Inc.: p. 198
Georg Gerster, Photo Researchers: p. 199; 204
Edward Drews, Photo Researchers: p. 201
Paolo Koch, Photo Researchers: p. 205 top
Victor Englebert, Photo Researchers: p. 205 center
Peter Brosius: p. 205 bottom

CHAPTER 15

John J. Ewel: p. 212
Francis E. Putz: p. 213 top
Dieter Blum, Peter Arnold Inc.: p. 213 center
Christine Padoch: p. 213 bottom; 216 top; 220
United Nations: p. 217
Harold Brookfield: p. 216 bottom; 221, all photos; 222